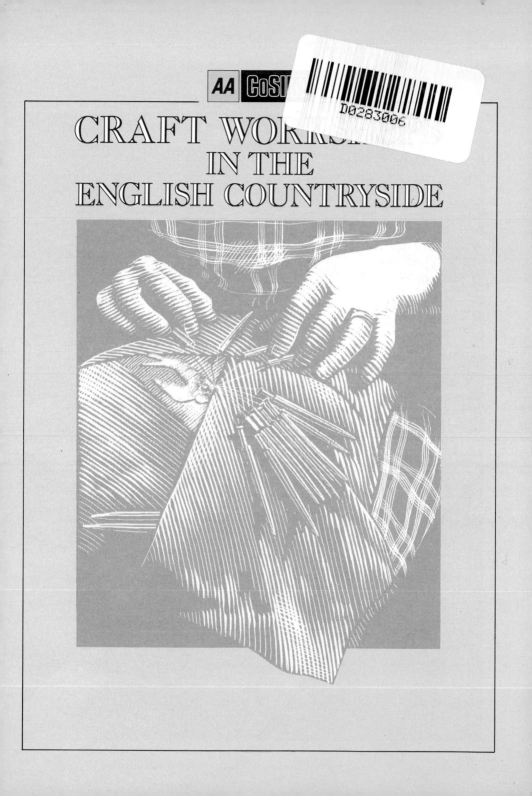

AA CoSI

CRAFT WORKSHOPS
IN THE
ENGLISH COUNTRYSIDE

CRAFT WORKSHOPS
IN THE
ENGLISH COUNTRYSIDE

Produced by the Publishing Division of the
Automobile Association in conjunction with
CoSIRA (the Council for Small Industries in
Rural Areas)

Editor   Barbara Littlewood

Art Editor   Peter Davies

Directory   Elizabeth Baldin

Directory compiled by Rebecca Snelling
Maps prepared by the Cartographic Services
Department of the Automobile Association
Photographs by David Walker, Graham
Sapsford and Paul Eastaugh of CoSIRA
Illustrations by KAG Design Ltd

Head of Advertisement Sales: Christopher
Heard ✆ (0256) 20123 ext 2020
Advertisement Production: Karen Weeks
✆ (0256) 20123 ext 3525
Advertisement Sales Representatives:
London, East Anglia, East Midlands, Central
Southern, South East England: Edward May
✆ (0256) 20123 ext 3524 or (0256) 467568

South West, West Midlands, Bryan Thompson:
✆ (0272) 393296
Wales, North of England, Scotland: Arthur
Williams ✆ (0222) 620267

Filmset by Tradespools Ltd, Frome, Somerset
Printed and bound in Great Britain by
Purnell and Sons (Book Production) Ltd,
Paulton, Bristol

ISBN 0 86145 314 X

Published by the Automobile Association,
Fanum House, Basingstoke, Hampshire RG21
2EA

AA Ref 59129

CONTENTS

Several old farm buildings belonging to the Duchy of Cornwall have been converted for use as craft workshops. His Royal Highness the Prince of Wales talks to some of the craftspeople at North Street Farm Workshops, Stoke sub Hamdon, near Yeovil in Somerset, which he opened in October 1985

HRH The Prince of Wales, Duke of Cornwall

More and more people today seem to want at least a few things in their houses which are made by craftsmen rather than mass produced; perhaps in contrast to the uniformity of so much modern household equipment. The pleasure of ownership is increased if one has met the craftsman and seen him at work. I know that I get great pleasure from seeing craftsmen at work in some of the Duchy of Cornwall workshops.

The AA and CoSIRA, both well known national institutions, have got together to produce this Guide which will help people touring the countryside to find the working places of a large number of rural craftsmen. The Guide will, I feel sure, give purpose and incentive to many journeys of exploration into the English countryside. It will also help to solve the difficult problem of tracking down specialists who can restore or repair a treasured family possession such as a well loved clock, or a piece of porcelain.

There have always been able craftsmen in England, but it is my impression that even in today's "jet propelled" world, with all its mass production, there are more competent craftsmen working to a generally higher standard than we have seen for many years. A great deal of credit for this improvement must go to organisations like the Crafts Council and CoSIRA, whose job it is to revitalise the rural areas of England, and with whom the Duchy of Cornwall has an important scheme for creating new workshops from old farm buildings.

More and more craftsmen are seeking satisfaction by having their workshops in the countryside. As a landowner, I very much welcome this development which brings new jobs to the villages and new life to old buildings. It also helps to revive and revitalise some of the traditional elements of village life.

I hope this Guide will help craftsmen to find new business and prosper and help the public to discover and delight in their work.

Charles

HOW CoSIRA WORKS

The Council for Small Industries in Rural Areas, CoSIRA, exists to help businesses of all sorts to start up, survive, and prosper in villages and small towns in England. CoSIRA is financed by the Development Commission from the Development Fund created in 1909 by Lloyd George. It shares with the Development Commission the long-term objective of creating balanced and prosperous rural communities where people of all ages can both live and work.

Happily there are signs that such communities are on the increase, despite the decline of jobs on the land. These are the villages which can sustain schools, village shops, bus and medical services, as well as swimming pools, cricket teams, WI's and drama groups. The key is that young people and particularly young married couples should be able to find houses and jobs in or near their own village rather than being forced to move away or commute daily to large towns. Jobs of all sorts in villages and small towns is what CoSIRA is about.

It is people with ideas, skill and drive who create jobs, but CoSIRA can help the enterprising man or woman make the big decision whether to start up or not. After that CoSIRA can help at every stage from finding a workshop and working capital to producing the goods or service efficiently, costing and pricing, and finally, selling. There is no shortage of enterprise in the English countryside. CoSIRA, through its thirty-two county offices, is in touch with 19,000 small businesses – a fifty per cent increase in four years. Only a few CoSIRA clients make a fortune but most achieve job satisfaction and a reasonable income, and the failure rate, even in the first year, is small.

There are CoSIRA Small Industries Organisers in every rural English county backed up by local Voluntary Committees. They look after the interests of small businesses at all levels and the Organiser usually makes the first contact

Rural conversion: Atlow Mill, Derbyshire

with rural businesses or with those who are planning to start up. The Organiser may have spent half his working life with small firms in his county and is a shrewd judge of what businesses will and will not make a profit. He can suggest where a workshop might be found or created and which bank manager might be most sympathetic to a new starter. He can advise on the intricacies of Planning Permission and VAT and suggest local sources of raw materials. Perhaps most important of all the CoSIRA Organiser is someone who the boss of a small business can turn to when a problem arises, whether it is a bad debt or an exciting export order.

The Organisers are CoSIRA's general practitioners and they are backed up by some eighty specialists who travel all over England to advise small businesses. Their mix of professional, technical and training skills has been worked out in practice over the years – management accountants, marketing men, publicity consultants, building and woodworking advisers, engineers of all sorts and specialists in crafts such as wrought iron work, upholstery, saddlery, ceramics, furniture restoration, welding, plastics

The first CoSIRA-sponsored thatching course (right) at Knuston Hall near Northampton

and thatching. CoSIRA also has its own loan fund which makes some 300 loans each year, usually to help a business buy or build a small factory or workshop and usually in partnership with one of the banks or other sources of finance.

A large part of CoSIRA's and the Development Commission's work is the creation of premises for small business. In thousands of English villages, there are no workshops or small factory buildings either for sale or to let and starting a business or following a trade without proper premises is at best very difficult. Fortunately, fewer people today retain a chocolate-box image of village life and recognise the need of local jobs. Planning permission is, therefore, easier to obtain for well designed new industrial buildings or for the conversion of a redundant barn or outbuilding.

In remoter areas of the English countryside which have been designated Rural Development Areas, the Development Commission has built over a thousand small factories to be leased to businesses, and CoSIRA administers 25% grants to encourage the conversion of redundant buildings to new job-creating uses. Elsewhere, CoSIRA buildings advisers can give expert advice on the design or conversion of workshops and CoSIRA encourages the creation of craft centres, often in farmyards no longer required by farmers.

The majority of wheelwrights were over sixty when this lad started a two year course arranged by CoSIRA in 1983.

Many of CoSIRA's clients are traditional craftsmen. CoSIRA instructors have helped in recent years to ensure that thatchers are as skilled as at any time in our history and last year (1985) the first four apprentices for twenty years completed a formal course in wheelwrighting arranged by CoSIRA. However, CoSIRA is happy to help any enterprise which will create job opportunities in the countryside. Repair of farm machinery, though noisier, is as traditional as thatching but a precision engineering shop can also fit unobtrusively into a village, as can an antique restorer or a small textile firm.

An exciting development in recent years has been the growth of high technology in the countryside. A steady stream of computer, microfilm, silicon chip and micro-biology businesses are moving into villages attracted by the lower costs and the easier pace of life. Such firms provide part-time and full-time jobs of a sort not previously available.

At the other end of the scale, CoSIRA provides advice and brief training courses for small retail businesses and village shopkeepers. A good village shop provides a job or two, an important service and, usually, the village's communications centre.

CoSIRA does not claim to have expertise in every trade but every business needs finance, premises, accounting skills and markets. Anyone with a rural business or anyone planning to start up could hardly do better than consult the local CoSIRA office when, or preferably before, a problem arises.

AA CoSIRA CRAFT CENTRE OF THE YEAR AWARD

Furniture-making at Hatton Craft Centre

R **ecent arrivals** in the countryside, few craft centres are more than 15 years old and most have been opened during the last 10 years, as enthusiasm for traditional craftsmanship has revived. They are, however, becoming increasingly popular and there are now at least 50 of them in England, with more being opened all the time.

What is a craft centre? The essential factor is a group of some half dozen or more workshops, where different trades are practised, producing hand-made goods of decent quality, and where the public is welcome. Beyond this basic requirement, facilities may vary, but there will be good parking, and usually a shop and a restaurant or tea room. Craft centres offer customers the advantages of choice, convenience, the interest of seeing skilled people at work, and the opportunity to commission, say, a piece of furniture or an item of jewellery. Since most centres are housed in converted farm buildings, old mills, former breweries, even, in one case, in a redundant fort,

there is the added attraction of an interesting environment in which to browse and shop.

The well-run craft centre keeps the emphasis on the workshops and the goods produced there; it is neither a shopping arcade, selling 'gifts' and 'souvenirs' made anywhere but in this country, nor a tourist trap, with the craft workshops merely existing as one of a number of commercial sideshows on the fringes of a gift shop. Of all the many craft centres, from North Yorkshire to Devon, that were considered for the Craft Centre of the Year Award, the one that seemed best to fulfil our criteria was the Hatton Craft Centre near Warwick, which had the greatest variety of interesting crafts and employs about 50 people in its beautifully converted old farm buildings. Of the others, Golden Hill Fort, Wroxham Barns, the Dean Heritage Trust, the Jinney Ring Centre and the Cross Tree Centre all deserve special mention.

Saddler Mr May is one of the many craftsmen who work at Hatton

HATTON CRAFT CENTRE – Winner of the AA/CoSIRA Craft Centre of The Year Award

(for address and opening times, see page 145)

A busy community of talented craftspeople work in the imaginatively converted 19th-century buildings of Georges Farm, a few miles from Warwick, which forms part of an estate belonging to a descendant of Richard Arkwright, inventor of the water-frame that played such a significant part in the development of the textile industry during the Industrial Revolution. Georges Farm takes its name from that of the cowman who in the 1920s had charge of a prize herd of red-poll cattle that were bred here. The last of the cattle went in the 1960s, and it was not until the 1980s that the conversion to craft centre took place. In 1985, Hatton Craft Centre won the CoSIRA/CLA Rural Employment Award.

Most of the workshops are housed in two cobbled 'lanes' of buildings which have something of the atmosphere of a village street. Here you may find two furniture makers, a printer, candlemaker, specialists in needlecrafts, patchwork, ceramics, batik printing, horticrylics, mirrors and many others besides. In the main buildings are a wood-turner, specialising in a range of English woods, especially fruitwoods, cane- and rush-seated furniture restorers, a saddler, a sculptor and an armourer who makes reproduction swords and complete suits of armour. As yet there is no central shop, but refreshments are available and, if the weather is fine, there is a pleasant walk across the fields to Hatton Locks, the longest flight of canal locks in England.

GOLDEN HILL FORT

(for address see page 73)

Opened in May 1985, this craft centre in the west of the Isle of Wight is part of a larger complex based on the conversion of a hexagonal Victorian fort, originally built in the 1860s to defend the approaches to Portsmouth against possible attack by the French. The fort continued in military use through both world wars until the army sold it in 1964, after which it was used as an industrial estate until restoration began in 1984. Renovation is still in progress, but there are already plenty of craft workshops occupied. These are housed in the main barracks and are on two levels, with a balcony connecting the first-floor rooms. Crafts range from wood-turning, leathercraft and jewellery to more unusual skills such as guitar-making. There are also different kinds of craft shops and a book-binder. Some courses are also run here.

In addition to the crafts, the fort also houses some small industrial workshops, for example a lawn-mower repairer and a precision engineer. Other attractions are a military museum, telling the history of the fort, a charming museum of dolls, and a photographic museum. There is already a tea room, and future plans include a pub.

JINNEY RING CRAFT CENTRE

(for address and opening times, see page 79)

This small crafts centre near Bromsgrove in Hereford and Worcester is unusual in that it has been built up by one of the craftsmen, Richard Greatwood, a wood-turner. Starting with two derelict old timbered barns, he has transformed them into an exceptionally attractive centre which has already won two awards – one for the conversion work, the 1983 Henley Award, and one for Outstanding New Tourist Enterprise in the 1981 'Come to Britain' trophy.

At present there are five workshops in operation, and crafts include stained-glass-making, pottery, leatherwork, wood-carving and wood-turning. There is also living accommodation for some of the craftsmen, a flourishing gallery and shop, and a restaurant serving lunches as well as teas. More workshops and a new restaurant are planned for the future.

DEAN HERITAGE TRUST
(for address and opening times, see page 133)
The setting of this combined museum and craft centre in the Forest of Dean is delightful: an old stone building standing beside a peaceful mill pond at the foot of a wooded hill. The building itself was originally a foundry, and was later converted to a mill. The museum contains fascinating displays interpreting the history of the Forest and its people, and traditional forest crafts, such as charcoal-burning, are regularly demonstrated.

The restoration was completed only in 1985, and not all the workshops are occupied as yet, but the combination of museum and craft centre makes a visit here well worthwhile.

WROXHAM BARNS
(for address and opening times, see page 151)
The barns form an attractive group of buildings at Hoveton in the heart of the Norfolk Broads. As one might expect in an area devoted to sailing and cruising, boat-building is one of the crafts to be seen here. Others include cabinet-making, wood-turning, glass-engraving, spinning and patchwork. The craftware is on sale in the centre's excellent gallery, and there is also a produce shop selling locally-made wines, for which Norfolk is becoming well known, ciders, mustards, preserves, fruit and vegetables. There is a tea room, space for picnics, and an adventure playground as well, and the centre is ideally placed to attract holiday-makers.

Hand-painted rainbow mobiles are among the artefacts made by this young craftswoman at The Dean Heritage Trust Museum

Golden Hill Craft Centre (top), the converted Victorian coastal fort built in the west of the Isle of Wight, houses several workshops, among them (left) this toymaker. Wroxham Barns (above) is an attractive conversion on the Norfolk Broads, and Jinney Ring Craft Centre (right) belongs to one of the craftsmen, who converted the old buildings himself. Dean Heritage Trust (top right) is a combined museum and craft centre

CROSS TREE CENTRE
(for address and opening times, see page 71)

A stone tithe barn and associated out-buildings in the tiny Cotswold village of Filkins form the nucleus of this well established rural enterprise. The Cotswolds were historically one of the great wool-producing areas of England, and it seems fitting therefore that the main activity carried on here is weaving. The woollen mill produces lengths of cloth, rugs, shawls, scarves, ties, hats, sweaters, jackets and so forth in many colours and

A weaver at Cotswold Woollen Mills, Filkins

styles, and these are on sale in the adjoining shop.

In the adjacent buildings there is a stonemason's works, a restorer of antique furniture and a specialist in rush and cane seating. There is also a picture gallery displaying many original and local paintings and artists' prints, and some very attractive items of locally-made pottery. There is also a very pleasant little tea room serving home-made produce.

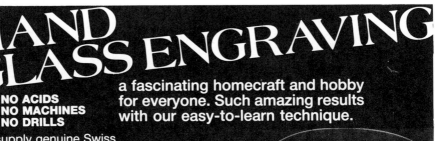

LAPIDARY

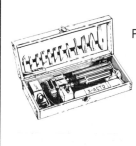

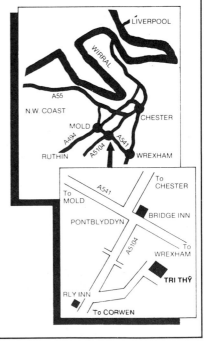

HOW TO USE THIS BOOK

The **Automobile Association** has worked with CoSIRA (the Council for Small Industries in Rural Areas) to produce this guide to craft workshops. It covers only the English counties where CoSIRA operates and there are therefore no entries for Scotland and Wales. Because CoSIRA is concerned mainly with the rural areas of England, most industrial cities and large towns are not included in the directory.

Finding your way
The directory is arranged alphabetically by place. As many of the workshops are in small country villages, they have often asked to be listed under the nearest place of any reasonable size, with directions where necessary. Although we have tried to give clear directions, it is not always possible to be explicit in a limited space, and it may therefore be advisable to telephone the workshop before setting out.

Where are the nearest workshops?
If you want to find out if there are any craft workshops in your area, or in a particular county, you can consult the location atlas (see below) where all the places listed in the directory are plotted.

How to find a particular craft
There is a subject index preceding the atlas section which lists the establishments by the type of craft work undertaken. If the workshop carries out repairs or restoration, the entry in the index is followed by the letter (R). Craft centres and shops and other places which practise a variety of crafts are listed separately.

Opening times
Most of the workshops listed welcome individual visitors without an appointment, although it should be remembered that craftsmen and women have a living to earn and are not there to provide free entertainment. If it is necessary to make

Arundel wheelwright Abel Pierce (aged 90)

an appointment, this is usually stated in the details given in the directory. However, many of the workshops are run by one person, and if that person has to go out, the casual visitor may find the workshop closed other than at stated times. If you are making a special journey, it is always advisable to telephone first. Where groups are concerned, it is always preferable to make an appointment.

Craft Centres
Information about the crafts that can be seen at craft centres or similar establishments has been compiled from details supplied to us, but individuals may have moved, or may move during the currency of this book. Opening times given apply to the craft centre as a whole, and not all the individual workshops will be open for the entire period. Again, it is advisable to telephone if you wish to see a particular person.

Admission charges
Most of the establishments we list make no admission charges, but a few of the commercially-run craft centres may do so. If in doubt it is advisable to telephone beforehand.

Carved bargeboards at Compton Winyates

Atlas and National Grid

Each place in the directory is referred to the location atlas by a map-page number, followed by a two-figure National Grid reference. This system of map reference is common to most modern atlases, of whatever scale, so it is possible to find any place on any atlas by use of the National Grid number. Each reference is preceded by two letters – for example – SX, SY, NU, TQ, TM. These identify the grid squares

marked on the atlas. Each of these large squares is subdivided into tenths, numbered 0–9 around the edges of the maps. To find any particular place, turn to the appropriate page of the atlas, find the square containing the correct reference letters, then look along the bottom edge of the map for the first of the two numbers, and along the side edge for the second number. If you draw imaginary lines vertically and horizontally from these two numbers, their point of intersection marks the bottom left-hand corner of the square in which the place will be found.

Symbols and abbreviations

The following symbols and abbreviations have been used in the directory:

✆	*telephone number*
🚍	*coaches welcome*
by appt.	*by appointment*
🚍	*no coaches*
C	*commissions undertaken*
R	*repairs/restoration undertaken*
W	*wholesale orders accepted*
E	*export orders accepted*
D	*sales direct to public*

Credit cards

- ⓐ *Access*
- ⓥ *Barclaycard/Visa*
- ⓧ *American Express*
- ⓓ *Diners' Club*

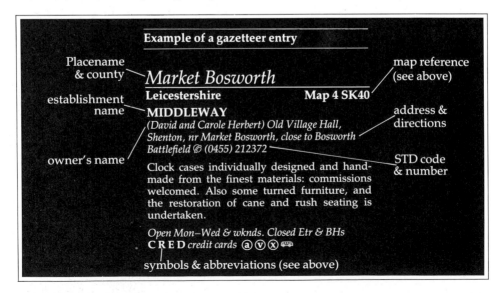

Example of a gazetteer entry

Placename & county → *Market Bosworth*

map reference (see above)

Leicestershire   **Map 4 SK40**

establishment name → **MIDDLEWAY**

owner's name → *(David and Carole Herbert) Old Village Hall, Shenton, nr Market Bosworth, close to Bosworth Battlefield* ✆ (0455) 212372

address & directions

STD code & number

Clock cases individually designed and hand-made from the finest materials: commissions welcomed. Also some turned furniture, and the restoration of cane and rush seating is undertaken.

Open Mon–Wed & wknds. Closed Etr & BHs
C R E D *credit cards* ⓐ ⓥ ⓧ 🚍

symbols & abbreviations (see above)

DIRECTORY OF CRAFT WORKSHOPS

Abbotsbury

Dorset Map 3 SY58

DANSEL GALLERY & DESIGN WORKSHOP
(Selwyn and Danielle Holmes) Rodden Row
✆ *(0305) 871515*

High-quality original items, including bowls, boxes, book-ends, clocks, mirrors, toys and furniture, all hand-made in a wide variety of woods. Also jewellery and prints.

Open Mon–Fri 9–5, wknds 10–5. Closed Jan & Feb
C W E D *credit cards* ⓐ ⓥ 🚗

Alconbury Weston

Cambridgeshire Map 4 TL17

DOUGLAS JAMES DAWSON
1 Safefield Farm Cottage, Alconbury Hill, nr Huntingdon ✆ *(04873) 376*

Furniture restoration, wood-turning, picture-framing and French-polishing undertaken, as well as specialist repairs in cane and rush seating. One-day courses in cane seating.

Open Mon–Fri after 6 pm & wknds 10–8 by appt.
C R D 🚗

Aldermaston

Berkshire Map 4 SU56

ALDERMASTON POTTERY
(Alan Caiger-Smith and Edgar Campden) ✆ *(0734) 713359*

Most kinds of domestic pottery and ovenware, including jugs, pitchers, goblets, dishes, bowls, mugs, plates and tiles. The earthenware is tin-glazed – which produces a white, opaque background – and painted with subtle colours in distinctive designs.

Open Mon–Sat 8–5 (advisable to telephone). Closed Xmas & Etr **C E D** 🚗

Alford

Lincolnshire Map 9 TF47

HEATHER & MICHEL DUCOS, POTTERS
The Pottery, Commercial Rd ✆ *(05212) 3342*

Domestic and decorative stoneware pottery specialising in oven-to-table ware, dinner services, tea-sets and pierced work, e.g. pomanders, lanterns and plant pots. Commemorative pieces undertaken.

Open Mon–Fri 9–5. Closed for lunch, and at Xmas
C W E D 🚗 *by appt.*

Alfriston

East Sussex Map 5 TQ50

J C J POTTERY AT DRUSILLAS
(Jonathan Chiswell Jones) Drusillas, off A27
✆ *(0323) 870234*

A wide range of hand-thrown stoneware and porcelain. Among the regular lines (about 50) are teapots, casseroles, door knobs, house numbers and name plates, as well as some high-quality brush-decorated porcelain pieces.

Open Mon–Fri 9–5.30, Sat 12.30–5.30. Closed Xmas **D** *credit cards*
ⓐ ⓥ 🚗

Alkborough

S Humberside Map 8 SE82

CARANDA CRAFTS
(D J Cox) Cross La ✆ *(0724) 720614*

Wood-turned items made on the premises include thimbles, lamps, stair-spindles, clocks, barometers, lace bobbins, boxes, wall plaques. There are also other locally-made crafts for sale such as decorated eggs, pressed-flower work and pyrography. Woodturners' supplies in stock, e.g. stains, polishes, clock movements.

Open Tue–Sat 10–5, Sun 12.30–5.30. Closed Xmas **C W D** 🚗 *by appt.*

Allenheads

Northumberland Map 11 NY84

SPRING COTTAGE STUDIO
(Robert Maddison) Dovespool, ½m N of Allenheads off B6295 ✆ *(043485) 274*

Robert Maddison's work illustrates the Northumbrian and Cumbrian landscape: his media are egg tempera, water-colour, pastel, scraperboard and photography. Hand-coloured prints and stationery can also be bought at the studio.

Open Wed–Sun 10–5. Mon & Tue appt. only. Closed Xmas **C W E D** *credit cards* ⓐ ⓥ 🚗

Aller

Somerset Map 3 ST42

ALLER POTTERY
(Bryan and Julia Newman) The Pottery, nr Langport on A372 ✆ *(0458) 250244*

Stoneware domestic pottery, decorative plates and ceramic sculpture depicting boats, buildings, housescapes and bridges. Visitors are welcome to watch the potters working.

Open Mon–Sat 9–6. Sun open by appt.
C W E D 🚗

Alnwick

Northumberland   **Map 11 NU11**

BREAMISH VALLEY POTTERY
(Alastair Hardie) Branton West Side, Powburn (9m NE of Alnwick), 1m W of village off A697
🕾 *(066578) 263*

The pottery, housed in an old stable block, produces a wide range of hand-thrown kitchen and domestic stoneware, fired with wood.

Open Mon–Sat 9.30–6, but advisable to telephone. Closed for lunch, & Xmas **C W D** ♿

ROCK SOUTH STUDIO & GALLERY
(John and Janice Cartmel-Crossley) Gull Ha', Rock South, 3½m N of Alnwick on A1 🕾 *(066579) 275*

Water-colour paintings, etchings and limited-edition prints by John Cartmel-Crossley and mixed-media paintings by Janice Cartmel-Crossley. Tuition can be arranged.

Open daily 10–6. Closed Xmas **C D** ♿ *by appt.*

JOHN SMITH OF ALNWICK LTD
(Peter J Smith) West Cawledge Park 🕾 *(0665) 604363* **(See also p 49)**

Antique furniture restored, and fine furniture designed and made by a small team of crafts-men. An extensive range of furniture and some other craftware is for sale in the gallery.

Open daily 10–6 **C R D** *credit cards* Ⓥ ♿

THE TEXTILE WORKSHOP
(Margaret Blackett Hunter) Pinewood, Chathill, 11m N of Alnwick 🕾 *(066589) 218*

This is a teaching workshop, running courses in spinning, weaving and dyeing. Shop sells table linens, simple garments, soft furnishings, scarves and spinning and weaving supplies.

Open daily 10–5. Closed for lunch, Xmas & during Feb & Oct **C D** ♿

Alston

Cumbria   **Map 11 NY74**

GOSSIPGATE GASLIGHT GALLERY
(P and S Kempsey) The Butts 🕾 *(0498) 81806*

The gallery displays the work of 40 or more artists and craftspeople from Cumbria, Durham and Northumberland and has a regular programme of exhibitions. Crafts include pottery, textiles, leatherwork, marquetry, wood-work, furniture, glassware, jewellery and metalwork, plus paintings, prints and litho-graphs. Local foodstuffs – cheese, smoked meats, game and mustards also on sale.

Open Apr–Dec daily 10–5 (Jan–Mar closed Tue). Closed 25 Dec **C R W E D** *credit cards* Ⓐ ♿ *preferably by appt.*

Alstonefield

Staffordshire   **Map 7 SK15**

M K GRIFFIN
Wesleyan House, 7m NW of Ashbourne 🕾 *(033527) 249*

Oak furniture of modern and traditional design hand-made to customer's specifications. Also all kinds of gates, made-to-measure from oak, and garden furniture. Other English hard-woods available for special commissions.

Open Mon–Fri 8–9, wknds 9–7 by appt. Closed Xmas **C D** ♿

Alvescot

Oxfordshire   **Map 4 SP20**

ROBERT H LEWIN
Furniture Designer & Cabinet Maker, Overgreen 🕾 *(0993) 842435*

Furniture designed and hand-made from all types of English and foreign hardwoods. Items range from small boxes and bowls to fitted kitchens, with coffee-tables a speciality. →

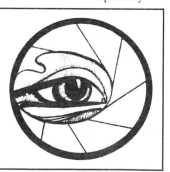

Unusual and individual commissions are also undertaken.

Open Mon–Fri 9–5, wknds by appt. Closed Xmas **C W D** 🚗

Amberley

West Sussex **Map 4 TQ01**

CHALK PITS FORGE

(Andrew Breese) Houghton Bridge, within the Chalk Pits Museum ✆ *(079881) 370*

Blacksmith producing high-quality traditional and contemporary forged ironwork to individual requirements. A selection of small items in stock.

Open Mon–Fri 8.30–5.30, wknds during summer only. Closed Xmas **C R D** 🚗

Ambleside

Cumbria **Map 7 NY30**

ADRIAN SANKEY GLASS

Rothay Rd, ✆ *(0966) 33039*

Functional and decorative lead-crystal glass made traditionally and hand-finished. Beautifully-coloured birds, candlesticks, bowls, vases, lamps and feathered and cased paperweights. The craftsmen can be seen at work. Member of the Guild of Lakeland Craftsmen.

Open daily 9–5.30. Closed 25 Dec–5 Feb **C W E D** *credit cards* ⓐ ⓥ ⓧ 🚗 *by appt.*

THE CHAIR LADY

(Jennifer S Borer) The Fabric Workshop, Old Stamp House Yard, off Lake Rd ✆ *(0966) 32641*

Chair-caning, rush-seating, traditional re-upholstery and tapestry-blocking. Curtains and soft furnishings made-to-measure from a range of fabrics, and a design service is available.

Open Mon–Fri 9.30–4.30, wknds by appt. Closed Xmas & Etr **C R D** 🚗

ZEFFIRELLI'S ARCADE

Compston Rd, arcade is part of complex with cinema ✆ *(0966) 33979 (Ripping Yarns); (0966) 32973 (Artisan)*

There are three craft shops within the arcade. *Artisan (Ian Fishwick):* silver, gold and semi-precious stone designer-jewellery. *Ripping Yarns (Cindy Thomson):* original, brightly-coloured knitwear in pure wool. *Spiral Pottery (Mike Labrum):* table, oven and decorative stoneware. All the craftsmen work on the premises.

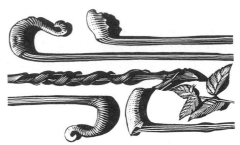

Hand-carved walking sticks

Open Mon–Sat 10–5. Closed for lunch **C W E D** *credit cards* ⓐ ⓥ ⓧ ⓓ 🚗

Ampleforth

North Yorkshire **Map 8 SE57**

AMPLEFORTH WEAVING & POTTERY WORKSHOPS

(James A and Mary Raynar) Central House ✆ *(04393) 503*

Handwoven, individually designed rugs and cushions, and earthenware and stoneware – mainly reduction-fired – for domestic use.

Open Tue–Fri 10–5, wknds 11–5 but advisable to telephone. Closed wknds Oct–Mar, except by appt., & Xmas **C W D** 🚗 *by appt.*

Ampthill

Bedfordshire **Map 4 TL03**

SYLVIE PENDRY

4A Woburn St ✆ *(0525) 402174*

Ceramics, specialising in Raku bowls and wall plaques. Also silk batik scarves and framed batik pictures.

Open by appt. only **C W E D** 🚗

Angmering

West Sussex **Map 4 TQ00**

PETER F BOCKH

Cottrell, High St ✆ *(0903) 786199*

Hand-made furniture for sale, as well as wood-turned items, walking-sticks and pictures.

Open Mon–Fri 9.30–5, Sat 9.30–12.30. Closed for lunch & Wed, Sun, Xmas & Etr **C R D** *credit cards* ⓐ ⓥ 🚗

Appleby-in-Westmorland

Cumbria **Map 11 NY62**

BURTREE CRAFTS

(Jeff and Pauline Bolton) Little Asby ✆ *(05873) 342*

Numerous items, all hand-made locally, include candles, pottery, knitwear, slate products, soft toys, glassware, sweets, jams and jellies. Pyrography (poker work), and herbal body preparations are produced on site and work can be seen in progress. Refreshments available.

Open daily 10–8. Closed Xmas & during Jan & Feb **C W E D** 🚌 *by appt.*

Ardington
Oxfordshire   **Map 4 SU48**

ARDINGTON POTTERY
(Les Owens) The Old Dairy, Home Farm (2m E of Wantage off A417) ✆ (0235) 833302

High-fired stoneware and semi-porcelain kitchen and table ware. Also gifts, including lamps, plant pots, an extensive range of vases, and commemorative plates and tankards.

Open Mon–Sat 10–5, Sun 2–5. Closed Xmas **C W E D** 🚌

THE OLD SCHOOL JEWELLERY WORKSHOP
(Jill Smith) The Old School, East Lockinge ✆ (0235) 833550

Jewellery and silversmithing workshop and gallery. Courses in jewellery-making run throughout the year.

Open Mon–Fri 11–4, wknds 12–6 by appt. Closed Xmas **C W E D** *credit cards* ⓐ ⓥ 🚌 *by appt.*

Armathwaite
Cumbria   **Map 11 NY54**

GLENLIVET WEAVERS
(Stephen Wilson) Eden Valley Woollen Mill, Ainstable, nr Carlisle ✆ (076886) 406

Woven and knitted textiles in wool, cotton, mohair and other natural fibres made into rugs, floor and scatter cushions, scarves, ties and garments. Knitting wools also for sale and commissions undertaken for soft furnishings.

Open daily 10–6. Closed Xmas **C W E D** 🚌

Arreton
Isle of Wight   **Map 4 SZ58**

ARRETON COUNTRY CRAFTS VILLAGE
(C and J Howard) Arreton Manor Farm, nr Newport ✆ (0983) 528353 →

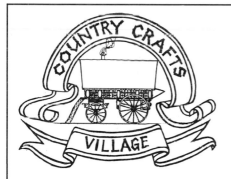

A most imaginative restoration of old farm buildings has created a craft village complex where more than a dozen local craftsmen have their studio/workshops.

This is a working craft centre where many different crafts are practised under one roof.
An excellent reputation has been maintained since its opening in 1978. Beautiful goods at reasonable prices direct from the makers. Lots to see and learn from professionals who are happy to offer advice. Licensed lunch bar and Bakery/Coffee Shop on the premises. There is an entrance charge during the summer season which is inclusive of all the facilities of the craft village, access to workshops, museum, gardens and picnic area, toilets and car/coach park.

Times of opening: WEEKDAYS 9.30 a.m. to 5.00 p.m. SUNDAYS 2.00 p.m. to 5.00 p.m. Bank Holidays only SATURDAYS & SUNDAYS 9.30 a.m. to 5.00 p.m.

Look for the Gypsy Wagon on the A3056 Sandown/Newport road at Arreton, 100 yards from the White Lion Pub. Bus routes 7 & 7A to the door and 27,28,29 to Arreton Cross.

Over a dozen craftsmen display their work here which includes knitwear, pottery, rocking horses, clocks, dried flowers, metalwork, macramé, swords, butterfly brooches, ceramic castware, leatherwork, photography and screen printing.

Open Mon–Sat 9.30–5, Sun 2–5. Closed Xmas. **C R W E D** *credit cards* ⓐ ⓥ 🚻 *(appt. preferred)*

Arundel

West Sussex   **Map 4 TQ00**

ARUNDEL DIALS SERVICE
(Rob Gillies) 38 Maltravers St ✆ (0903) 882574

Clocks repainted, re-silvered and antique dials rewritten. New dials also designed, and large (2ft–4ft diameter), outdoor clocks made in blue, black and green with gold-leaf numbers.

Open Mon–Fri 9–5. Telephone at wknds. Closed Xmas **C R E D** 🚻

DUFF HOUSE & GALLERY
(Derek Davis) 13 Maltravers St ✆ (0903) 882600

A wide range of decorative and functional ceramic, porcelain and stoneware pottery.

Open daily 10–7 by appt. Closed for lunch, & Xmas & Etr **C W E D** 🚻

GILLIBOB DESIGNS
(Jocelyne and Clive Newman) Pindars, Lyminster ✆ (0903) 882628

Individually designed dresses, jackets, skirts, bags and small children's clothes (up to 7 years) – all appliquéd or quilted in fine fabrics.

Open by appt. only **C E D** *credit cards* ⓐ ⓥ 🚻

Making traditional wooden rakes was a typical village craft

Ashby-de-la-Zouch

Leicestershire   **Map 8 SK31**

CLIVE JONES
The Stables, South St ✆ (0530) 414246

Picture-framer offering a complete framing service for oil paintings, water-colour paintings, embroideries, tapestries, mirrors and prints. All shapes of mount available. There is also a small gallery.

Open Tue–Sat 9.30–5.30 by appt. Closed for lunch & Xmas & Etr **C R D E** 🚻

Ashford

Kent   **Map 5 TR04**

TIM HUCKSTEPP POTTERY 'CLAYCLOCKS'
The Pottery, Barrow Hill, Sellindge, 6m SE of Ashford ✆ (030381) 2204

Functional stoneware pottery, e.g. mugs, cheese dishes, labelled storage-jars and salt pots, plus an exclusive range of pottery clocks decorated with a brown oatmeal or blue glaze, all individually boxed.

Open Mon–Fri 9–5, wknds by appt. Closed Xmas **C W E D** *credit cards* ⓐ ⓥ ⓧ 🚻 *by appt.*

Ashreigney

Devon   **Map 2 Sa61**

NORTHCOTT POTTERY
(Roger Cockram) Higher Northcott Farmhouse, 3m W of village, N of junction between B3217 & B3220 ✆ (07693) 242

Housed in the farm outbuildings, the pottery produces high-fired stoneware kitchen items as well as several individual pieces, particularly large crocks and bottle-forms in stoneware and porcelain.

Open Mon–Sat 9–6. Closed Xmas **C W E D** 🚻 *by appt.*

Ashwell

Hertfordshire   **Map 4 TL23**

CERDAN LTD
(Geoff Godschalk and Ann Walsh) Dixies Barns, High St ✆ (046274) 2837

A hand-weaver and furniture designer/maker share a converted barn as their workshop and display area, although most of their high-quality work is commissioned. Rugs, wall hangings, laminating and fruit-woods are their specialities. Visitors welcome to view work in progress.

Open Fri 10–6, other wkdys by appt. & wknds 10–6. Closed for lunch; Xmas & Etr appt. only **C (limited E) D** ♿ *by appt.*

LITTLE GARTH POTTERY
(Susan Morris) Little Garth, Mill St, nr Baldock ✆ *(046274) 2547*

Thrown and hand-built oxidised stoneware pots for domestic use. Also individual pieces.

Open wknds 11–5.30, but confirm by telephone. Closed Xmas **C D** ♿

SEVEN SPRINGS GALLERY
(Marie Whitby and Jeremy Chapman) 9–11 Mill St ✆ *(046274) 2564*

A variety of ceramic work, particularly figure groups, animals and buildings.

Open Mon, Tue, Fri 10–5, wknds 10–6. Closed for lunch **C W D** ♿ *by appt.*

Askrigg
North Yorkshire   **Map 7 SD99**

ASKRIGG POTTERY & STONE TROUGHS
(Paula and Andrew Hague) Old School House, West End, nr Leyburn ✆ *(0969) 50548*

Hand-carved sandstone garden troughs with relief decoration. Also functional stoneware items, and some brush-decorated porcelain.

Open occasionally. Telephone for details **C W D** ♿

Atch Lench
Hereford & Worcester   **Map 4 SP05**

LENCHCRAFT
(Graham Whitehouse) Springfield House, nr Evesham ✆ *(0386) 870734*

Woodworkers producing various turned items, including plant stands and small tables. Repairs and restoration work undertaken.

Open daily 9–6 by appt. Closed Xmas **C R D** ♿

Axminster
Devon   **Map 3 SY29**

DOLPHIN CANDLES
(J B and J M Nickolls) Myrtle Cottage, Greendown, Membury ✆ *(040488) 459*

Small showroom with large selection of decorative candles, small animal figurines, half-scale collectors' dolls' houses, miniature furniture and wooden toys.

Open daily 9–6 **C R W E D** ♿

Aylesbeare
Devon   **Map 3 SY09**

NEIL BOLLEN
The Works, Shutebridge Cottage, between village & Exeter airport ✆ *(0395) 32961*

Designer, manufacturer and restorer of all sorts of silver, including objets d'art and other decorative metalwork.

Open Mon–Fri 9–5.30 by appt. Closed Xmas & Etr **C R E D** ♿

Aylesbury
Buckinghamshire   **Map 4 SP81**

COLIN J URCH
Windacre, Chilton Rd, Long Crendon, nr Aylesbury ✆ *(0844) 208204*

Cabinet-maker, wood-carver and furniture-restorer working to commission. Cane- and rush-seating undertaken.

Open by appt. only **C R D** ♿

Aylsham
Norfolk   **Map 9 TG12**

CHARLES MATTS FURNITURE
Alby Crafts, Erpingham ✆ *(0263) 768060/761422/713088*

Individually and traditionally designed furniture from stock or to order. All hand-made from local woods. Solid craftsmanship includes kitchen, dining room, living room, bedroom and boardroom furniture. Refreshments available. See also entry for Alby Crafts under Erpingham, Norfolk.

Open daily 10–5. Closed at Xmas **C D** *credit cards* ⓐ ⓥ ⓧ ♿

Aysgarth
North Yorkshire   **Map 7 SE08**

AYSGARTH POTTERY
(Charles Boyce and Lucy Craven) Main St, nr Leyburn ✆ *(09693) 503*

Numerous stoneware and terracotta items displayed in the hayloft of a converted barn. These include herb pots, strawberry pots, bulb bowls, casseroles, salt-pigs, jam pots, colanders, goblets, vases and teapots. Other craftwork available includes wooden toys, soft toys and pine cupboards.

Open daily 9.30–5.30 Mar–Oct. By appt. other times. Closed Xmas **C W E D** ♿

Bagendon

Gloucestershire   **Map 4 SP00**

STONES POTTERY

(Arthur Hargreaves) nr Cirencester ✆ (028583) 370

Terrace pots of all shapes and sizes, ranging from bonsai containers to Ali Baba-style pots, bird feeders and baths. All made of Cotswold-stone-coloured pottery.

Open Mon–Sat **C W D** ♿

Bainbridge

North Yorkshire   **Map 7 SD99**

LONGBARN ENTERPRISES

(Dr Christopher Cole) Low Mill, Leyburn, nr Hawes ✆ (0969) 50416

18th-century working watermill housing fully decorated and furnished dolls' houses. Stock lines (also available as kits) include Georgian and modern styles, unpainted or painted. Any houses made to customer's requirements. Working model watermills, castles, and many other interesting craft items and a range of pot plants also available.

Open Wed & Fri 2–5 from Jun–mid Sep. Other times by appt. **C R D** ♿ *by appt.*

Bampton

Oxfordshire   **Map 4 SP30**

ALPINE EAGLE

(Roy Partridge and John Hodson) The Mill, Mill La, Little Clanfield, Clanfield ✆ (036781) 401

Full restoration of vintage and post-vintage motor cars undertaken. Includes bodywork repairs, painting, interior renovation and mechanical work. Specialists in Rolls-Royce, Bentley and many other great makes of historic automobiles.

Open by appt. only ♿

COLLEGE FARMHOUSE POTTERY

(Anthony Wakeham) Bridge St ✆ (0993) 850225

Large terracotta garden and terrace pots. Also unusual self-contained wall-hanging fountains (suitable for interior or exterior), fountain heads and wall plaques. Some glazed sculptural pots and slip-decorated domestic ware.

Visitors welcome anytime but advisable to telephone **C W E D** ♿

Banbury

Oxfordshire   **Map 4 SP44**

GOLDFORD FURNISHINGS

(Stuart M Golding and David S Langford) Hudson St, Deddington, 6 m S of Banbury on A423 ✆ (0869) 38165

Hand-made upholstered furniture of individual design.

Open Mon, Wed, Thu, Fri 9.30–5, Sat 10–1. Closed for lunch, & Xmas & Etr **C R W E D** *credit cards* ⓐ Ⓥ ♿

HOOK NORTON POTTERY

(Russell Collins) East End Farm House, Hook Norton ✆ (0608) 737414

Studio pottery with large showroom displaying domestic stoneware and porcelain, as well as various other crafts. Changing exhibitions. Tea and coffee available.

Open Mon–Sat 9.30–5.30 **C W E D** *credit cards* ⓐ Ⓥ ♿ *by appt.*

MICHAEL THOMAS COUNTRY FURNITURE

(Michael and Hilary Thomas) Manor Fields, Hook Norton ✆ (0608) 730015

Country furniture – hand-made from period designs – including refectory tables, dressers and corner cupboards. Church work also

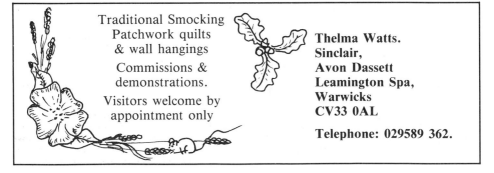

Stonemasons are skilled carvers

undertaken. All work made to order from a variety of English woods.

Open by appt. only **C R D** 🖝

TRADITIONAL COTTAGE CRAFTS
*(Thelma Watts) Sinclair, Avon Dassett,
Leamington Spa (Warwicks) 8 m NW of Banbury on
A41* ✆ *(029589) 362*

Specialist in traditional smocking, patchwork quilts, cushions and wall hangings. Sampler and needlepoint kits available. Demonstrations given in local tourist centres.

Open by appt. only **C R D** 🖝

Barnoldswick

Lancashire   **Map 7 SD84**

DOUG MOORE (BOATBUILDERS) LTD
*(Doug and Marie Moore) Lower Park Marina,
Kelbrook Rd, next to Craven High School* ✆ *(0282)
815883*

Situated beside the canal, the shop sells traditionally-painted canal ware, chandlery and brassware, together with a wide selection of unusual gifts – including garments – produced by local craftsmen.

*Open Mon–Fri 9–5.30 all year, wknds 10–3 May–
Sep only. Closed for lunch, & Xmas.*
C D 🚌 *by appt.*

Barnstaple

Devon   **Map 2 SS53**

NEWPORT POTTERY
*(Denis and Wendy Fowler) 72 Newport Rd, on
A361 300metres from junction with A377* ✆ *(0271)
72103*

Glazed earthenware specialising in house-name and number plates, lamp bases (with shades), bowls, goblets, tankards, candle holders, vases and commemorative pieces for all occasions.

Open Mon–Sat 10–8 by appt. Closed Xmas
C W E D 🖝

Barton-Under-Needwood

Staffordshire   **Map 7 SK11**

MAGGIE B KNITWEAR
*(Mrs M Bywater) 56 Oak Rd, nr Burton-upon-
Trent* ✆ *(028371) 2703*

Men's and women's machine-knitted garments – all hand-finished to a high standard. All sizes catered for, and items made-to-measure. Knitwear parties can be booked.

Open Mon–Fri 10–5, wknds 10–2. Closed Xmas
E D 🖝

Basingstoke

Hampshire   **Map 4 SU65**

LASHAM FURNITURE WORKSHOP
*(Hugo Egleston) Manor Farm Buildings, Lasham,
nr Alton, 6m S of Basingstoke* ✆ *(025683) 368*

Exceptionally high-quality furniture. All the pieces are commissioned and each is unique. Fine timbers such as walnut, oak, yew and cherry are used for these individually designed items.

*Open Mon–Fri 8.30–6 (advisable to telephone)
wknds by appt. only. Closed Xmas & Etr* **C D** 🖝

VIABLES CRAFT CENTRE
Harrow Way, off A30 southern ring road ✆ *(0256)
473634*

Several craftsmen share these converted farm buildings: *Basingstoke & District Model Engineering Society:* caters for those interested in making working models of railway locos, marine engines, clocks etc. *Tolivar Crafts:* big soft toys, →

especially woodland animals. *E W & A A Cooper Ltd:* hand-made clocks to order, repairs and restorations. *The Spinners Web:* traditional handcrafted garments and textiles. *Petra-Goldsmith:* jewellery manufacturer; repairs and alterations. *Floral Designs:* silk flowers and related accessories. *Phoenix Art Foundry:* bronze works – abstract and classical. *Carol Moreton:* patchwork items and co-ordinated soft furnishings. *Mike Burrows:* glass-engraving for every occasion. Many items in stock. *Jeanette Moore:* metal engraving – crests, portraits etc, also customising motor cycles undertaken. *Bowden Woodcraft:* woodturning, carpentry and joinery work, also antique restoration. *Roger Squires:* silver and gold jewellery, boxwork and hollowware; jewellery repairs. *Cairncraft Pottery:* decorative and sculptural stone and earthenware, fretwork lamps and anniversary plates; commissions undertaken.

Open Tue–Fri 1–4, wknds 2–5 **C R D** 🚗 *by appt.*

Bath

Avon   **Map 3 ST76**

GOLD & SILVER STUDIO
(Mr & Mrs John Middleton) 11a Queen St
📞 *(0225) 62300*

Designers, makers and repairers of jewellery in all precious metals and stones. Matching wedding and engagement rings, and remodelling old pieces of jewellery their specialities. Personal service assured.

Open Tue–Sat 9–5 by appt. Also open Mon in Nov & Dec. Closed after Xmas, Etr & for annual holiday **C R E D** *credit cards* ⓐ ⓥ ⓧ ⓓ 🚗

Battle

East Sussex   **Map 5 TQ71**

AUDREY C JARRETT
Pound Cottage, Woods Corner, Dallington, nr Heathfield, between Heathfield and Battle on B2096
📞 *(0424) 88233*

A selection of unusual figures and groups sculpted from hessian and wire. Audrey Jarrett also designs and makes traditional dolls ranging from peg dolls to floppy dolls (made from Sussex Puffs). Member of the Guild of Sussex Craftsmen; the Hawkhurst Guild of Arts and Crafts; the East Sussex Guild of Craftworkers.

Open daily 9–6, by appt. Closed Xmas **C** *(some* **W**) **E D** 🚗

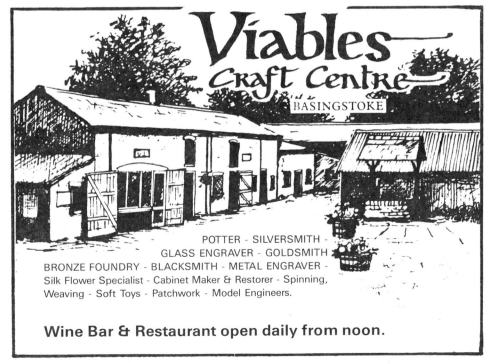

BLACKMAN, PAVIE AND LADDEN LTD
Marley La ✆ (0424) 87333. Telex 957597

Lumpwood charcoal manufacturers, packers, distributors and importers. Established 1888.

Open Mon–Fri 7–5 by appt. Closed Xmas & Etr **W E D** ♿

Beaford
Devon   **Map 2 SS51**
BEAFORD POTTERY
(Bernard Jones) Old Parsonage, ¼m N of village on B3220. Turn r at sign on tree ✆ (08053) 306

Hand-thrown stoneware pottery. All sorts of domestic pots and kitchen ware glazed in a range of semi-matt finishes and decorated with brushwork.

Open Mon–Fri 9–5.30, Sat 9–1. Closed for lunch, & Xmas. Advisable to telephone during winter **C W D** ♿

Bedale
North Yorkshire   **Map 8 SE28**
NORTH OF ENGLAND SADDLERY CO
(Lee Broadway) 1a Emgate ✆ (0677) 22213

Soft leather and hide in every colour used to make handbags, belts, ties, purses, and clothes to order. English leather saddles made to commission and all tack repaired.

Open Mon–Fri 9–5.30, wknds 10–2. Closed for lunch, & Xmas & Etr **C R W D** ♿

Bedford
Bedfordshire   **Map 4 TL04**
LAURA DUNN CERAMICS
Willow Cottage, Keeley La, Wootton ✆ (0234) 852750

Ceramic painted figures all about 7 inches tall and Victorian or Edwardian in character. The pieces, each one hand-made, include a lady seated at her mirror, a gardener with wheelbarrow and tools, and a seated pianist with cat.

Visitors welcome, by appt. only **C W D** *credit cards* Ⓥ ♿

THOMAS HUDSON
The Barn, 117 High St, Odell ✆ (0234) 721133

Established furniture maker offering high quality craftsmanship. Work includes commissioned hand-made furniture, restoration of antique pieces, panelling, relief carving and incised lettering.

Open Mon–Fri 8–6, Sat 8–12, by appt. Closed Xmas & Etr **C R E D** ♿

Belford
Northumberland   **Map 11 NU13**
THE BRENT GALLERY
(Molly and David Binns N.D.D., S.W.L.A.) Fenham-le-Moor ✆ (06683) 533

Water-colour paintings, hand-coloured lithographs, etchings, linocuts, ceramics and pottery on display. The work of David Binns and his son, Stephen, depicts wildlife, farmlife and the Northumbrian landscape.

Open daily 10–7. Jan–Mar by appt. **C W E D** *credit cards* Ⓥ ♿ *by appt. Jan–Mar.*

HAZON MILL KNITWEAR
(Christine Moffat) No Six, High St ✆ (06683) 808

A variety of hand framed knitwear items offered on a made-to-measure basis, together with a range of tweed skirts designed to complement the sweaters. There is a small stock of ready-to-wear garments.

Open Mon–Wed, Fri & Sat 10–4. Closed 25 Dec–mid Jan **C W E D** *credit cards* ⓐ Ⓥ ♿ *by appt.*

NORSELANDS GALLERY & STUDIO TWO WORKSHOP
(Barrie and Veronica Rawlinson) The Old School, Warenford ✆ (06683) 465

An assortment of crafts by some of Britain's leading craftsmen, including a large display by resident ceramic artists. Their work, in matt cream and brown glazed stoneware, includes fairies, witches, fantasy castles, dragons etc.

Open daily 9–5 (9–9 in summer). Closed Mon (except BH) & Xmas **C W E D** *credit cards* ⓐ Ⓥ ♿
See advertisement on p. 42

Bere Regis
Dorset   **Map 3 SY89**
PAWS JEWELLERY
(David Watts) Southbrook Workshop, Southbrook ✆ (0929) 471808

Jewellery manufacturers and diamond merchants encompassing setting, enamelling, polishing, plating, lost-wax and sand-casting. All kinds of fine metalwork also undertaken. →

Open Mon–Fri 9.30 am–mdnt, Sat 10.30 am–mdnt, Sun 2.30–mdnt, by appt. Closed for lunch & 5–6.30 pm, & Xmas **C R W E D** *credit cards* ⓐ ⓥ ⓧ ⓓ 🚐 *by appt.*

QUEEN POST WORKSHOP
(Kevin J Pope, Cabinet Maker) Briantspuddle, 3 m outside Bere Regis off A35 ✆ *(0929) 471153*

Work is mostly commissioned and includes four-poster beds, Welsh dressers, tables, small and large boxes. Kevin Pope works in both modern and traditional styles and uses all kinds of timbers: his range includes walnut, oak, sweet chestnut, sycamore, yew, cherry, mahogany, rosewood.

Open Mon–Fri 8.30–5.30, Sat 9–12.30. Closed Xmas **C R D E** 🚐

Berkeley

Gloucestershire   **Map 3 ST69**

BERKELEY SADDLERY
(Peter L Stiling) 12 High St ✆ *(0453) 811821*

New bridle-work and general leather goods, including shoulder bags, cartridge belts, purses, wallets and belts, hand-made on the premises. Also bridle, saddle and all leather repairs.

Open Mon–Sat 9–6. Closed for lunch, Xmas, New Year & Etr Mon **C R W D** *credit cards* ⓐ 🚐

CIDER MILL GALLERY
(Sally Roberts) Blanchworth Farm, nr Dursley, on North Nibley road from Berkeley, SP Blanchworth off A38 ✆ *(0453) 2352*

Restored horse-drawn cider mill and press, still occasionally in use. The art gallery and shop sell contemporary paintings, wood-turned items, patchwork and jewellery, and there is a fine Victorian dolls' house on display (not for sale).

Open Tue–Sun 11–5 Jun–Aug, Tue–Sat 11–5 Apr, May and Sep–Dec. Otherwise by appt. **D** *credit cards* ⓐ ⓥ 🚐 *by appt.*

ENGLANDS MILLS
(Richard England) Sea Mills ✆ *(0453) 811150*

Traditional millers of stoneground wholemeal flours. Visitors are welcome to look round the mill and buy a range of whole-foods, e.g. bran, wheatgerm, muesli, etc. which are offered for sale at wholesale prices.

Open Mon–Fri 8.30–5, Sat 8.30–12. Closed
Xmas, Etr & BH. **C W E D** 🖚 by appt.

Bethersden
Kent **Map 5 TQ94**
STEVENSON BROTHERS
(M A and A P Stevenson and D J Kiss) The
Workshop, Ashford Rd ✆ (023382) 363

Beautiful, hand-carved, wooden rocking
horses with bow rockers or safety stands – all
with flowing manes and tails, and leather tack.
Also carousel horses, horse sculptures and
fairground animals. Georgian and Victorian
horses restored. Member of the Guild of Master
Craftsmen.

Open Mon–Fri 8.30–5.30, Sat 8.30–12.30. Closed
Xmas & Etr **C R W E D** 🖚 by appt.

Beverley
North Humberside **Map 8 TA03**
**CHRISTINE MOORE ORNATE
CASTINGS**
(C and M E Moore) West St, Grovehill Rd ✆ (0482)
865634

Decorative plaster mouldings supplied, as well
as a comprehensive fitting service if required.
Work includes cornices, ceiling centres, fire
surrounds, marble hearths, niches, corbels and
panel strips. Gas fires also supplied.

Open Mon–Sat 9–5. Closed Xmas **C R W D** credit
cards ⓐ ⓥ 🖚

Bicester
Oxfordshire **Map 4 SP52**
HAYWARD, CAREY & VINDEN
The Stables, Garth Park, Launton Rd ✆ (0869)
249654

Commissioned cabinet work, woodturning and
architectural joinery, including staircases and
traditional sliding sash windows.

Open Mon–Fri 9–6, Sat 9–1, by appt. Closed
Xmas & Etr **C E D** 🖚

Bickleigh
Devon **Map 3 SS90**
**BICKLEIGH MILL CRAFT CENTRE &
FARMS**
(W V Shields) nr Tiverton ✆ (08845) 419

The craftsmen at Bickleigh change from time to
time, but many different skills are demon-

strated in the self-contained log-cabin workshops located in and around the old watermill.
A large shop displays all the craftwork produced here, e.g. pottery, jewellery, corn dollies, leatherwork, paintings, silk-flower arrangements, woven and spun goods, plus a
wide selection of other work – much of which is
made in the West Country. Admission charge.

Open daily 10–6. Closed Xmas **C W E D** credit
cards ⓐ ⓥ ⓧ 🖚

Billingshurst
West Sussex **Map 4 TQ02**
BARFLIES
(Roger E Smith) Broadford Bridge, between
Billingshurst & West Chiltington ✆ (07983) 3695

Contemporary and period furniture made from
hardwoods – particularly English oak, mahogany and rosewood – using traditional techniques. Work is individually designed. Small
production runs also undertaken.

Open daily, but advisable to telephone **C E D** 🖚

Bishop Auckland
Co Durham **Map 8 NZ22**
SPINSTERCRAFT
(Derek and Margaret Milton) Dans Castle, Tow
Law ✆ (0388) 730016

A selection of products from several local craftworkers, particularly soft toys and knitwear.

Open Mon–Fri 9–5.30 all year, & wknds Apr–Sep.
Closed for lunch, & Xmas **C W E D** 🖚

*Fitting a shoe to
a horse's hoof*

Bladon

Oxfordshire   Map 4 SP41

BLADON POTTERY
*(Graham and Corri Piggott) 2 Manor Rd, end of
Church St, 200 yds from graveyard ℰ (0993)
811489*

Specialists in fantasy and figurative stoneware
sculpture, such as dragons, wizards and Alice
in Wonderland characters. Also studies of children and animals, water-colour paintings and
unusual pottery. Everything is hand-made on
the premises.

*Open daily 10–6 (often later during summer). By
appt. other times. Closed Xmas*
C D *(E negotiable)* ⇔

Blandford Forum

Dorset   Map 3 ST80

BELCHALWELL POTTERY
*(Carol Lodder) Brooks Cottage, Belchalwell, 7m
NW of Blandford off A357, turn l at Okeford
Fitzpaine ℰ (0258) 860222*

Hand-thrown traditional English pottery
miniatures for dolls' houses and collectors.
Made to a one-twelfth scale in styles ranging
from Staffordshire slipware to modern stoneware, items include gin bottles, baby-feeders,
cider jars etc. Also a range of colourful, practical tableware.

Open daily 9–7 but advisable to telephone **C W E D**
⇔ *by appt.*

FOXDALE POTTERY
*(Keith and Carol Burbidge) The Old Bakery, Child
Okeford 6m NW of Blandford ℰ (0258) 860039*

Stoneware mugs, jugs, bowls, vases, cheese
dishes and butter dishes, as well as terracotta
garden and patio items – all the pottery on
display is hand-made.

Open daily 10–6. Closed Xmas **C W D** ⇔ *by appt.*

Blisland

Cornwall   Map 2 SX07

MOSS STUDIO
*(Ray Hunt) Bradford, Blisland, nr Bodmin
ℰ (0208) 850766*

Original landscapes of Bodmin Moor and the
surrounding area, Cornish seascapes and wild
flowers. All executed in acrylic, oil and water-
colour paints, as well as in pen, pencil and
charcoal.

Open daily 9–6 **C W E D** ⇔

Blyth

Nottinghamshire   Map 8 SK68

NORNAY ORIGINALS
*(Reg Pritchard) Bawtry Rd, nr Worksop, on A614
N of A1/(M) roundabout ℰ (090976) 205*

Stained-glass work using both lead came and
copperfoil techniques. Also glass-painting
using kiln-fired glass enamels. Products include windows, door panels, terrariums,
planters, light-catchers, window hangings and
original Art-Deco and Tiffany-style lamps.
Customers' designs can be made up as special
commissions.

Open daily 9–8. Advisable to telephone
C R W D ⇔

Boot

Cumbria   Map 7 NY10

*(Pam Stanley BA), Dalegarth Hall, Boot, 6m E of
Holmrook ℰ (09403) 237*

Hand-weaving, spinning and dyeing. English
wools and a variety of other yarns made into
rugs, hangings and cushion covers. Fabrics can
be dyed to match any colour. Also on sale is a
range of beautifully coloured, hand-painted
silks, including blouses, scarves and greetings
cards.

Open by appt. only **C W D** ⇔

Boscastle

Cornwall   Map 2 SX09

THE LEATHER SHOP
(Rob and Teresa Lloyd) The Old Mill ℰ (08405) 515

Every kind of leather object imaginable, all
hand-made on the premises. Rob and Teresa
Lloyd specialise in the unusual, e.g. clocks,
barometers and flowers. Replicas of 11th-cen-
tury tankards and water bottles as well as
leather 'cuir bouilli' armoury and shields can
be made to order.

Open daily 10–9 in summer, 10–6 in winter
C R W E D *credit cards* ⓐ ⓥ ⇔

STEVEN THOR JOHANNESON
(Steven Thor Johanneson) 8 Dunn St

Original landscapes and seascapes, predomi-
nantly of the North Cornish coast, with the sea
in all its moods as the main subject. The artist's
media are oil, water-colour, pastel and some
egg tempera, and he will undertake special
commissions.

Open by appt. only **C D** ⇔

Bourton-on-the-Water

Gloucestershire   **Map 4 SP12**

CHESTNUT GALLERY
(Peter and Mary O'Connor) High St ✆ *(0451) 20017*

Selected by the Crafts Council for the high quality of its merchandise and the standard of display, the gallery sells a wide variety of British-made crafts. Work includes pottery, glass, woodprints etc.

Open Mon–Sat 10–5.30, Suns & BHs 11–5.30. Nov–Jun closed Mon & Wed **D** *credit cards* Ⓐ Ⓥ Ⓧ Ⓓ 🚼

Bovey Tracey

Devon   **Map 3 SX87**

LOWERDOWN POTTERY
(David Leach) 1 m from village on Haytor–Widecombe road ✆ *(0626) 833408*

David Leach, son of Bernard Leach, and his son Simon produce hand-thrown domestic stoneware for oven, kitchen and table, as well as more expensive individual pieces in porcelain and larger pots in stoneware. Visitors are welcome to watch the potters at work.

Open Mon–Fri 9–5.30. Open Sat by appt. Closed for lunch & Xmas & Etr **C W E D** 🚼

Bowness-on-Windermere

Cumbria   **Map 7 SD49**

CRAFTSMEN OF CUMBRIA
(Roy and June Hargreaves) Fallbarrow Rd, next to Rayrigg Rd car park ✆ *(09662) 2959*

Several craftsmen exhibit their work here which includes ceramic sculpture, leatherwork, glass-engraving, woodcraft, jewellery, lapidary, wrought-iron, soft toys, enamelled coins, macramé and confectionery. There is also a studio for 'do-it-yourself' poker work,

spiral art and copper pictures. Coffee shop open in summer.

Open daily Apr–Sep 9.30–6 (also evngs at peak times); Oct–Mar Mon–Sat 9–5.30 **C R D** *(some W)* 🚎 *by appt.*

Brailsford

Derbyshire   **Map 8 SK24**

CANNON CRAFT
(Mr and Mrs J Platt) Sundial Farm ✆ *(0335) 60480*

High-quality engineering work. Products include models of 19th-century cannons and field guns made from brass and oak, brass sundials and armillary spheres, and rolling ball clocks. Also engraving of most metals and plastics.

Open Mon–Sat 9–5, Sun 2–5. Advisable to telephone. Closed for lunch & Xmas & holidays **C R E D** 🚼

Brampton

Cumbria   **Map 11 NY56**

ANDRU KNITWEAR
(Andru Chapman) Low Cross St ✆ *(06977) 3927*

Original sweaters and co-ordinates knitted in natural fibres; many yarns exclusive to Andru Knitwear. Knit Kits are also available, offering an average knitter the opportunity to make unusual and luxurious items. Various other craft goods are on display in the shop.

Open Mon–Fri 9.30–5.30 (closed Thu pm), wknds 10–4. Closed Xmas **C W E D** *credit cards* Ⓐ Ⓥ 🚼

BIRKHURST POTTERY
(Richard and Barbara Wright) High Birkhurst, Low Row ✆ *(06977) 397*

Hand-thrown, stoneware pottery for domestic use, e.g. dinner services, casseroles, mugs and jugs; decorative cut pots; wall plates, and →

earthenware biscuit stamps. Also commemorative pots.

Open Mon–Fri 9–6, Sat 9–5, Sun 2–5. Advisable to telephone Oct–Etr. Closed Xmas & Etr **C W D** 🚐 *by appt.*

Brandsby

North Yorkshire   **Map 8 SE57**

ACORN INDUSTRIES

(G J Grainger and Son) Westfield, nr York ✆ *(03475) 217*

Specialists in all types of traditional furniture made from solid timbers. Each order is designed individually, and customers may submit their own designs. Various woodcarvings and sculptures are for sale as well.

Open Mon–Fri 8.15–5.15, wknds 8.30–12.15. Closed Xmas, Etr, & BHs **C R** 🚐 *by appt.*

Bridgwater

Somerset   **Map 3 ST33**

RAMBLER STUDIO

(Oenone Cave) Holford ✆ *(027874) 315*

Embroidery specialist. Work includes individually designed lampshades, unusual complete lamps, miniature handwoven items and batik dyeing. Designs and materials available, and tuition can be arranged. Also paintings and glass engraving by Sylvia Cave.

Open during summer, other times by appt. only **C D** 🚐

Bridlington

North Humberside   **Map 8 TA16**

BESSINGBY POTTERY

(Michael and Sandra Wheeler) Bessingby Pottery, Bessingby, 2 m outside Bridlington, off A166 ✆ *(0262) 671198*

The pottery specialises in all types and sizes of red clay pots for garden use, including strawberry, herb, patio and wall pots, long Toms, alpine and cacti pans. There is also a range of stoneware pots for bonsai.

Open Tue–Sun. Closed Xmas **C D** 🚐

CARNABY COURT LEISURE CENTRE

(R H S and M A Sedman) Carnaby Court, Carnaby, off the Hull rd ✆ *(0262) 674039*

The work of several craftsmen here includes artistic glass-blowing, machine knitting, hand-decorated pottery and cast ware. Antiques and old books also for sale.

Open daily 10–5 🚐

COUNTRY WOODWORK

(Timothy and Lorraine Johnson) Eastfield Park, Lissett, 5m S of Bridlington on A165 ✆ *(026286) 487*

Designers and makers of all kinds of fitted furniture for the home, particularly kitchens and bedrooms. A range of reproduction furniture and some occasional pieces available.

Open Mon–Fri 9–5, wknds 10–4. Closed Xmas **C** *(some* **R***)* **W D** 🚐 *by appt.*

LONG LANE WORKSHOPS

(Peter Norton) 18 Long La ✆ *(0262) 671327*

Furniture-maker and woodworker specialising in fitted pine furniture, blanket boxes, Welsh dressers and tables. Also small hardwood items including some turned pieces.

Open Mon–Fri 9–5, & wknds, by appt. Closed Xmas **C R W D** 🚐

PARK ROSE POTTERY

Carnaby, off A165 ✆ *(0262) 602823*

The pottery's team of 35 craftsmen produce an extensive range of semi-porcelain gift and table

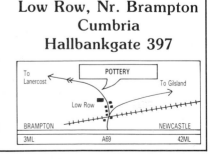

ware, including the unusual 'vase of light' – a shadeless ceramic table-lamp. Visitors can walk round the factory, and there is a factory shop, selling a wide range of ceramics, as well as a bar, restaurant and café.

Open daily 10–5. Closed Xmas **W E D**
credit cards ⓐ 🚱

Bridport
Dorset **Map 3 SY49**
AQUARIUS POTTERY
(David and Devi James) Yew Tree Cottage,
Uploders, 1 m off A35, E of Uploders at Matravers
Ⓒ *(030885) 426*

Small, country workshop with showroom displaying hand-thrown high-fired earthenware pottery. Domestic and ornamental items in a range of colours, including the studio's own 'Aquarius Blue' glaze.

Open daily 10–5.30. Closed for lunch **C W D**
(some **E***)* 🚱

SKITTLE PRINTS
(Roy and Sheila Sanford R.I., A.R., M.S.)
Sheepwash Cottage, Uploders, nr Aquarius Pottery,
above Ⓒ *(030885) 571*

Full-colour reproductions (framed or unframed) of Sheila Sanford's water-colour landscapes – mostly of Dorset but other areas and subjects too. Some original paintings are available, as well as miniature prints, all sorts of greetings cards and dolls'-house paintings for collectors.

Open daily, advisable to telephone. Closed Xmas &
Etr **C W E D** 🚱

Brighton
East Sussex **Map 4 TQ30**
RECOLLECT STUDIOS
(Carol and Jeff Jackman) Old Village School,
London Rd, Sayers Common. Village is situated
10 m inland from Brighton on A23 Ⓒ *Brighton*
office (0273) 681862

A varied selection of porcelain dolls, both original and reproduction, plus dolls'-house miniatures in porcelain, glass and copper. Many accessories for doll-makers also available and teaching courses are held regularly for porcelain doll-making and antique doll restoration.

Open Tue–Sat. Wknds by appt. Closed for lunch, &
Xmas & Etr **C R W E D** *credit cards* ⓐ ⓥ
🚱 *by appt.*

Decorative wooden butter mould

Brill
Buckinghamshire **Map 4 SP61**
HEATHER HARMS
(Heather Harms D.A. (Sculpture) Aberdeen,
Certificate of Royal Academy Schools, silver &
bronze medals) 12 The Square Ⓒ *(0844) 237869*

Decorative carving and lettering on stone and wood using traditional methods. Memorials, commemorative plaques etc, designed to order, and small-scale restoration work undertaken. Heather Harms also sculpts ceramic portrait heads, and does drawings and paintings. Special commissions undertaken.

Open any reasonable time, preferably by appt.
C R D 🚱

Brimscombe
Gloucestershire **Map 3 SO80**
DENNIS FRENCH WOODWARE
(Dennis and Désirée French) The Craft Shop,
Brimscombe Hill, r off Stroud/Cirencester road –
A419 Ⓒ *(0453) 883054*

Specialist in domestic woodware using mostly English woods. Products include bread boards, cheese boards, salad bowls, table lamps, ring boxes, platters etc and there is always a wide range of items in stock. Member of the Guild of Gloucestershire Craftsmen.

Shop open Tue–Sat 9–5. Workshop open by appt.
only **W D** 🚱

Brinklow
Warwickshire **Map 4 SP47**

OLD POST OFFICE POTTERY & GALLERY
(George and Diane Lindsay) 11 The Crescent, opp. Brinklow church ✆ (0788) 832210

Stoneware, earthenware and ceramics by the proprietors and local potters. Mostly functional items, but also individual pieces and a range of fantasy castles and dragons. Other high-quality craftwork of all kinds is also on sale.

Open evngs & wknds 9–6, all year. Also Mon–Fri 9–6 Jul–Sep. Closed Xmas. Other times open by appt. **C D** *credit cards* ⓐ ⓥ 🚃 *by appt.*

Bristol
Avon **Map 3 ST57**

A R DESIGNS
(Alan Ross, Nat.Dip. in Design) Hilltop, 66 Providence La, Long Ashton ✆ (0272) 392440

Furniture maker and woodworker offerng a design service to customers commissioning work. High-quality stools and lamps in English hardwoods kept in stock: other items to order, many designs available.

Open Wed 9–9, Sat 9–12, Sun all day. Other times by appt. **C W E D** *credit cards* ⓐ ⓥ ⓧ ⓓ 🚃

ALAN MILSOM, SADDLER
23 Barracks La, Shirehampton, nr Bristol, ½m from M5, junction 18 ✆ (0272) 822117

Master saddler specialising in all equestrian leatherwork, such as saddles, bridles etc. Belts, bags, sporrans and accessories for dogs for sale. Everything is hand-crafted and hand-sewn. Special items can be made to commission, and repairs are also undertaken.

Open Mon–Fri 9–5, Sat 9–1, by appt. Closed Xmas & Etr **C R D** 🚃

Brixworth
Northamptonshire **Map 4 SP77**

BRIXWORTH POTTERY
(Roda Watkins, Dorothy Watkins, Evelyn Campbell) Beech Hill, Church St ✆ (0604) 880758

Hand-made decorated ceramics ranging from teapots to terracotta planters. Specialities include commemorative plates, models of Brixworth Church, and various cats, dogs and rabbits.

Open Tue–Sat 1–6 **C R W E D** 🚃

Brize Norton
Oxfordshire **Map 4 SP20**

R GRIFFITHS WOODWEAR LTD
(Ray and Ann Griffiths and Clive Austin) Poplars Barn, Manor Rd ✆ (0993) 841289

Designers and manufacturers offering a wide range of hand-turned wooden giftware – bookends, shoe-horns, paper-knives etc – as well as any form of household fitting. This includes staircases and architectural joinery.

Open by appt. only **C W E D** 🚃

Broadway
Somerset **Map 3 ST31**

TOM KEALY
Boundary Barn, Hare La, Buckland St Mary, 1½ m along Hare La from Broadway ✆ (046034) 272

Designer and maker of high-quality furniture using English woods. Most pieces are designed and hand-made to meet individual requirements, but some standard products, such as chairs and chests, are also available.

Open Mon–Fri 9–5, by appt. Closed for lunch & Xmas & Etr **C D E** 🚃

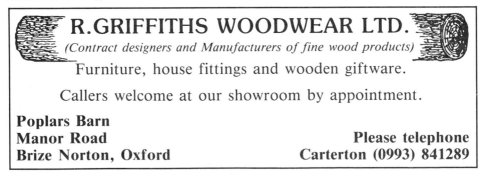

SETTING UP A WORKSHOP

This is the history of John Smith of Alnwick Ltd, a small company based in the north-east, but supplying customers all over the country, and how it grew in about a dozen years from a one-man business into a concern employing 10 people.

When taking the decision to set up an enterprise of one's own, there are a host of business problems to contend with, quite apart from the making of the product itself. Finance, book-keeping, marketing, staff-management and training, the finding of suitable premises, are all aspects of business in which the individual starting out has to acquire professional skills. CoSIRA can and does offer a wide range of practical help, both on the business side and in the courses it offers in craft training.

In the early 1970s John Smith, a young surveyor working for a large firm of builders, decided to leave the construc-

The old farm made ideal workshops

tion industry to set up business as a cabinet-maker and restorer of antiques.

He created his first workshop in an old farmhouse near Alnwick, which he converted himself, and by 1975–6 had established himself sufficiently to think of taking on an apprentice. At this stage he first got in touch with CoSIRA and found their accountancy advisory service a great help. In connection with his taking on an apprentice, he received advice from CoSIRA on the requirements of the Health and Safety at Work Act, and courses in Abrasive Wheel instruction and Woodturning and Polishing. By 1977 John Smith had taken on a second apprentice, and by the following year he had a staff of four, including his first NETS (New Entrant Training Scheme) apprentice. With CoSIRA's help, the staff were sent on courses of training in various aspects of

Furniture-making goes hand in hand with restoration at the West Cawledge Park workshops. John Smith, the owner of the firm (above), with a partly finished bureau and (left) one of his staff in the workshop. The finished products, and a selection of quality local crafts are displayed in the showrooms (top right), and commissions range from single pieces to complete sets like the dining table and chairs (right)

woodworking, and John himself received training in book-keeping and management accountancy.

By 1981 the firm of John Smith of Alnwick had begun to outgrow its original premises and had to move to somewhere larger, with the potential for further development as the business continued to grow. An abandoned 18th-century farmhouse and outbuildings, south of Alnwick and just off the A1, seemed an ideal location, and here again CoSIRA helped with the drawing up of plans and the obtaining of planning consent for the conversion. The work itself was done by John Smith and his staff, and they had to plan to close down for three months to transform the nearly derelict stone buildings into efficient workshops and showrooms. They found that the old cow byres still had their original wooden stalls and hayracks, and these were cleaned and restored to form a sequence of attractive display areas for furniture, wood-turned items and a selection of other local crafts.

The first stage of the conversion had to be financed without any grant aid as the scheme was not then in operation, but in 1984 a second stage of conversion began, for which a Development Commission grant was made. John Smith now has a staff of 10, most of whom came to him straight from school and have grown with the business. His first two employees have since left, but the second two are still with him. In 1983 he won a CoSIRA/Country Landowners Association award for rural employment in Northumberland. The firm now makes and restores furniture for clients all over the country – being so close to the A1 is an advantage here – and some of his products have gone to clients in Europe (for example, a set of banqueting table and chairs for a private customer in Hamburg), the United States and Australia. Local commissions have included the interior design and fitting-out of a mews house in Alnwick, the fitments for three all-mahogany bathrooms for a private house near Alnwick, and the restoration and erection of a traditional old chemist's shop as a showpiece for Winthrop Laboratories. When not engaged in making and restoring, John Smith and his staff run courses in furniture restoration which have proved very popular.

An extra showroom, in addition to the four already in use, is now being built, as well as a coffee room, serving light refreshments, which will also act as an exhibition gallery for some of the firm's own products and a range of other high-quality local craftwork.

The farmyard is now an attractive courtyard

Broadwindsor

Dorset   **Map 3 ST40**

DORSET PINE CRAFT
(Ivor and Rosa Downton) The Old Chapel, West St
✆ *(0308) 68814*

Traditional furniture hand-made in kiln-dried pine and hardwoods; customers' designs executed where possible. Sycamore boxes, stools, trays and spoons etched and painted with choice of name and nursery rhyme or design.

Open Mon–Fri 9–5, Sat 9.30–12.30. Closed Xmas
C R D ♿

Brockley

Greater London   **Map 5 TQ37**

LETTERING & STONECARVING
(Alec and Fiona Peever) 31 Vulcan Terr, London SE4 1DA ✆ *01-692-9213*

Lettering in stone, wood, brick, slate etc, for commemorative tablets, foundation stones, gravestones, churchwork, shop facias and so on. Specialists in sign-painting, glass engraving and calligraphy; heraldry in stone, wood and fibreglass also undertaken. All work individually designed and hand-crafted.

Open by appt. only **C D** ♿

Bromsgrove

Hereford & Worcester   **Map 7 SO97**

DAUB & WATTLE (CERAMICS) LTD
(Mr R P Cook) Windsor St, rear of 50 High St
✆ *(0527) 79979*

Lots of original ceramic gifts, such as clocks, mirrors, lamps, vases and bowls, with a distinctive hand-made quality.

Open Mon–Sat 9.30–5.30. Closed BHs **C D** *credit cards* ⓐ ⓥ ♿ *by appt.*

Bromyard

Hereford & Worcester   **Map 3 SO65**

THE COATES
(Timothy Ross-Bain) Linley Green, nr Whitbourne
✆ *(08864) 603*

Furniture maker and antique furniture restorer specialising in the design and construction of four-poster beds, from 17th century to Hi-Tec in style, including fabric and curtain designs. All furniture is hand-made using techniques appropriate to the period of the piece.

Open Mon–Fri 9–5, Sat 9–1. Other times by appt.
C R E D ♿

Brough

Cumbria   **Map 11 NY81**

CLIFFORD HOUSE CRAFTS & A J DESIGNS
(Jane Chantler and Ailsa McKenzie) Clifford House, Main St ✆ *(09304) 296*

Gold and silver jewellery designed and made on the premises. The craft shop (a restored barn) displays many local and other crafts, including glass, ceramics, designer jumpers, turned wood, pewter, prints, soft toys, etc. Coffee shop with home baking also on premises.

Open Mon–Sun 9–6, but closed Sun Nov–Etr
C R W E D *credit cards* ⓐ ⓥ ♿ *by appt.*

Broughton-in-Furness

Cumbria   **Map 7 SD28**

COUNTRY MATTERS
(A E Candy, Traditional Herbalist) The Old Bull Pen, Hallthwaites, nr Millom ✆ *(0657) 2068*

A comprehensive range of exclusive herbal products – including sleep pillows and pot pourris – are hand-blended on the premises. Herbal remedies also for sale after consultation, and all forms of traditional herbalism practised, including natural healing processes.

Open Mon–Fri 10.30–5, except Tue, appt. preferred. Telephone advisable wknds **C R D** ♿ *by appt.*

Bruton

Somerset   **Map 3 ST63**

BRUTON POTTERY
(John and Bruce Crisp) Patwell La, opp. the church ✆ *(0749) 813328*

A wide range of hand-thrown stoneware, both functional and ornamental, in several colours and designs. Pots can be decorated to order with names, inscriptions or animal pictures of customer's choice. Potters can often be seen at work.

Open Mon–Sat 9–5.30. Closed for lunch, & Xmas
C W D ♿

Bubwith

North Humberside   **Map 8 SE73**

CHAPEL HOUSE POTTERY
(Glynis and Phil Savage) 26 Church St, 6m NE of Selby ✆ *(075785) 393*

Hand-thrown, high-fired earthenware made and demonstrated on the premises. Each →

piece is hand-decorated by painting or sgraffito. Commissions taken for house plaques, commemorative plates etc.

Open daily 10–5, except Tue & Wed
C D 🚌 *by appt.*

Buckden
Cambridgeshire
See under St Ives for L'Bidi Studio

Budleigh Salterton
Devon   **Map 3 SY08**

OTTERTON MILL
(Desna Greenhow), nr Budleigh Salterton, off A376
✆ *(0395) 68521/68031*

Four workshops at the Mill produce fine modern furniture (Peter Kuh); stoneware distinguished by a greeney-grey glaze (Keith Smith); woodcarvings and woodland crafts (Stan Herbert), and individual quilted items (Clare Horry). There is also a craft shop, called Mill Hands, where several different local craftsmen display their work. This includes ceramic jewellery (Anna Gray); sculptures (Grace Critchley); fabric printing (Sylvia Brace, Jane Price); woollen products (Colin Jones); pressed-flower work (Maureen Crook); toys (Robin Stammers) and water-colour paintings of flowers (Denny Silverthorne). Bakery food made from flour milled here is available.

Open 10.30–5.30 but telephone call advisable.
Entrance fee **C R D** *credit cards* ⓐ 🚌

Bugbrooke
Northamptonshire   **Map 4 SP65**

THE OLD WHARF FARM STUDIO
(Linda Sgoluppi) on B4525, ¼ m after village, turn l to Cornhill, then immediately l again. Studio is above The Old Wharf Inn ✆ *(0604) 831893*

Hand-made raw-wool felt hangings and woven tapestries of images taken from nature. A highly imaginative use of colour with the felts reflects blurred environmental conditions, whereas the tapestries are more defined.

Work can be seen at The Old Wharf Inn during normal licensing hours; open by appt. at other times
C R D 🚲

Bungay
Suffolk   **Map 5 TM38**

NURSEY & SON LTD
The Sheepskin Clothing Specialists, Upper Olland St ✆ *(0986) 2821*

Manufacturers of all lamb and sheepskin products. Pioneers of the sheepskin coat, they also make hats, gloves, slippers, rugs, gifts etc.

Factory Shop open Mon–Fri 9–5. Closed for lunch, Xmas, Etr & 2 wks Jul/Aug. **R** *(on own products)*
W E D *credit cards* ⓐ ⓥ 🚌

Burnham Market
Norfolk   **Map 9 TF84**

MANOR FARM POTTERY
(Glynis Clack and Leslie Rayner) North St ✆ *(0328) 738570*

Earthenware casting works producing mainly creamware decorated with onglaze enamels, lustres and liquid metals. Unusual range includes vases of tulips, coffee pots, floral and other imaginative shapes of teapots.

Open Mon–Sat 9.30–5, and most Suns
C W E D 🚌

Burnham-on-Sea
Somerset   **Map 3 ST34**

HAVEN POTTERY & CRAFT CENTRE
(David and Sylvia Lemon) West Huntspill, nr Highbridge ✆ *(0278) 783173*

Individual craftsmen may change from time to time but there is always a good range of goods being produced. Crafts include pottery, David Lemon; leatherwork, Brian Wiles; hand-spun clothes, Madge Sutton; picture-framing, Lionel and Nikk Elstob; wrought-iron work, John Smith. Other crafts also on display. Play area

Raising a pot on the wheel

and refreshments are also available.

Open Mon–Sat 10–5, Sun 2–5. Closed for lunch
C W E D *credit cards* ⓐ ⓥ ⓧ 🚗

Burnopfield
Co Durham   **Map 11 NZ15**
PICKERING NOOK CRAFT CENTRE
(Jean and Steve Strathearn) Pickering Nook, A692
Gateshead–Consett rd, 4 m N of Sunniside
🕿 (0207) 71682

Over 100 artists and craftsmen display their
work here. The range covers woodcarving/
turning, pyrography, spinning and weaving,
screen printing, designer dress-making, brass-
rubbing, picture-framing and trout and salmon
fly-tying. Refreshments available.

Open daily 10–5. Closed at Xmas **C R W E D**
credit cards ⓥ 🚗 *by appt.*

Burton Bradstock
Dorset   **Map 3 SY48**
WOODTURNERY
(Cyril Standley) Bredy Farm, Bredy La, between
Burton Bradstock & Litton Cheney 🕿 *(0308)*
897141 (home)

Wood-turned products using locally-grown
woods. Stock ranges from egg cups to large
salad and fruit bowls, kitchen and foot stools
etc. Private woodworking courses offered by
the hour or by the day.

Open Mon–Fri 9.30–5, Sat 9–1. Evngs by appt.
Closed for lunch, & Xmas & Etr **C R E D** 🚗

Burton-upon-Trent
Staffordshire   **Map 8 SK22**
RICHARDS OF BURTON
(C E Lowe) Woodhouse Clockworks, Swadlincote
Rd, Woodville 6m SE of Burton 🕿 (0283) 219155

Clockmakers and repairers. Complete restoration of antique clocks undertaken, also skele-
ton clocks, clock parts and dials manufactured
– including gear-cutting.

Open Mon–Fri 9–5.30 and wknds, by appt. Closed
for lunch, & Xmas & Etr **R W E D** 🚗

Bury St Edmunds
Suffolk   **Map 5 TL86**
BARROW POTTERY
(Chris Southall and Issa Cochran) 27 The Green,
Barrow, 6m W of Bury 🕿 (0284) 810961

Hand-made domestic stoneware pots always in
stock. Orders taken for anything – house-name
plates to dinner services – and named pots for
children a speciality. Also cards and small
paintings on silk of East Anglian landscape.

Open daily 9–6 but advisable to telephone. Closed
for lunch, & Xmas **C R D** *credit cards* ⓥ 🚗

CLARE CRAFT POTTERY
(Bernard and Isobel Pearson) Windy Ridge, Broom
Hill La, Woolpit, 8m E of Bury 🕿 (0359) 41277

Fantastic, hand-built ceramic figures taken
from myths, legends and fairytales, including
castles, dragons and wizards. Also architectural and garden sculpture, hand-thrown pots,
moulded wall plaques and tile reliefs depicting
villages, towns and historical features.

Open daily 10–4 **C W E D** *credit cards* ⓐ ⓥ 🚗
See advertisement on p 88

CRAFT AT THE SUFFOLK BARN
(Margaret Ellis) Fornham Rd, Gt Barton
🕿 *(028487) 317*

A wide range of East Anglian crafts for sale, as
well as numerous plants and herbs.

Open mid Mar–Dec Mon–Sat 10–6, Sun 12–6
D 🚗 *by appt.*

DAN'S PATCHWORK
(Marian Lacy Scott) The Old Angel, 44 College St
🕿 *(0284) 67781*

Patchwork floor and scatter cushions, table
cloths, bedspreads and placemats in traditional
and contemporary designs, using both cotton
and silk. Cushions in F.A. Club colours a
speciality. Also rag dolls.

Open by appt. only **C W E D** 🚗

JOHN TRUSSELL
The Hollies, Fornham St Martin, 1¾ m from Bury
on A134 Thetford rd 🕿 (0284) 4932

Hand-made furniture designed to customer's
specification in walnut, oak or mahogany. A
limited selection of articles in stock.

Open daily 9–5, & wknds, by appt. Closed Xmas &
for annual holidays **C R D** 🚗

KOHL & SON
(K W Kohl) 2 Finchley Ave, Industrial Estate,
Mildenhall, 11m NW of Bury 🕿 (0638) 712069

All kinds of high-quality leather goods such as
handbags, purses, light luggage and gift items.→

Open Mon–Fri 10–4, telephone advisable. Wknds by appt. Closed Xmas & Etr **C R W E D** ♿

Camberley
Surrey   **Map 4 SU86**
ERSKINE COLLECTION
(Mrs Sheila Erskine) 13 Wishmoor Rd (turning opp. Cambridge Hotel on A30) ✆ *(0276) 62577*

Traditional Aran knitwear hand-made in pure wool. Garments, made-to-measure and in stock, include jackets, sweaters, hats, shawls, berets and waistcoats. All in natural colours such as oatmeal and caramel.

Visitors welcome, by appt. only **C E D** *& Mail Order. Credit cards* ⓐ Ⓥ ♿

Cambridge
Cambridgeshire   **Map 5 TL45**
BRIGNELL BOOKBINDERS LTD
(Barry Brignell) 2 Cobble Yard, Napier St, nr Grafton Centre ✆ *(0223) 321280*

Specialists in fine bindings and the restoration of old books and manuscripts. Work includes boxes, gold lettering, writing boxes, leather table-tops and binding of magazines, journals etc, all carried out in cloths or leather.

Open Mon–Fri 8.30–5, Sat 8.45–1, by appt. Closed for lunch, & Xmas & Etr **C R D E** ♿

KEITH BAILEY'S STUDIO
63 Eden St ✆ *(0223) 311870*

Memorial tablets, headstones and all kinds of architectural carving and lettering undertaken. Also heraldry and sculpture.

Open any time by appt. **C R D** ♿

MOMO THE COBBLER
(Aid Mohamad Iraninejad) Unit 8, Craft Centre, Cobble Yard, Napier St ✆ *(0223) 358209)*

All styles of surgical, fashion and work shoes made-to-measure, and shoes altered to fit. Also a full repair service available while you wait.

Open Mon–Sat 9–6 **C R D** 🚲

SCOTTS BINDERY
(James Cassels and Lucy Wolfendale) 53 Panton St, nr Botanical Gdns ✆ *(0223) 64862*

Specialists in the conservation, restoration and binding of antiquarian books. New and fine binding, including visitors' books, game books, photograph albums and box-making also undertaken. Notebooks, address books and miniature books always available.

Open Mon–Sat, advisable to telephone **C R D E** ♿

Mark Bury's Workshop, see Oakington

Canon Pyon
Hereford & Worcester   **Map 3 SO44**
BAOBAB
(Nick Sherwood – Grad. John Makepeace School) The Cots, Westhope, nr Canon Pyon on A4110 ✆ *(043271) 204*

The workshop produces high-quality furniture and other woodwork, including tables, chairs, garden furniture, bowls, architectural joinery etc. Work is hand-crafted and finished. Small-batch production undertaken, and timber-drying facilities available.

Open most times, by appt. only **C W D** ♿

Cark-in-Cartmel
Cumbria   **Map 7 SD37**
CANDLEMAKERS CO LTD
(William and Annie Lamb) Hill Foot, nr Grange-over-Sands ✆ *(044853) 252*

Numerous hand-sculpted candles, each made by building up several layers of hot wax onto wax 'blanks' then carving them into intricate shapes. Some can be burnt but last for years, and all are washable.

Open Mon–Sat 10–5. Also Sun 1–5 May–Sep. Closed Jan & Feb **C W D** *credit cards* ⓐ ⓥ 🖮

Carlisle
Cumbria   **Map 11 NY35**
HEDGEROW BASKETS
(S J and S P Fuller) Daffiestown Rigg, Longtown, take 3rd turning l off A7 after crossing river at Longtown ✆ *(0228) 791187*

Strong English willow baskets of all sorts: log, shopping, cat, dog, bicycle, linen, washing and baby cribs. Also a selection of imported willow, cane, bamboo and rush work. Some repair work undertaken.

Open Mon–Fri 10–8, wknds by appt. **R W D** 🖮

Castle Hedingham
Essex   **Map 5 TL73**
CASTLE HEDINGHAM POTTERY
(John and Margaret West) The Pottery, 37 St James' St, nr Halstead ✆ *(0787) 60036*

John and Margaret West, who produce hand-made domestic stoneware and garden pots, also give talks and demonstrations at the pottery to adult and school parties. One-day courses (no experience needed) are also available. Please contact the pottery for more information.

Open Tue–Sat 9–9, Sun 10–5 & BHs **C R W E D** 🖮 *by appt.*

Cauldon Lowe
Staffordshire   **Map 7 SK04**
STAFFORDSHIRE PEAK ARTS CENTRE
(Adrian and Lindy Hindle) The Old School, nr Waterhouses ✆ *(05386) 431*

The many types of quality craftwork (both traditional and modern) on display reflect the skills of workers in clay, wood, textiles, precious metals, glass and other materials. There is also a whole-food, licensed restaurant on the premises. Commissions can be accepted. Please contact the centre.

Open Apr–Oct daily 10.30–5.30; Nov–Mar Fri–Mon 10.30–5.00. Closed Xmas **C D** *credit cards* ⓐ ⓥ ⓧ ⓓ 🖮 *by appt.*

Cerne Abbas
Dorset   **Map 3 ST60**
CERNE VALLEY FORGE
(Stephen and Nancy Frank) Mill La, nr Dorchester ✆ *(03003) 298*

Ornamental, hand-forged metalwork including fire-baskets, fire-irons, fire-screens, gates, railings, garden furniture and various gift items.

Open Mon–Fri 9–4.30, Sat 10–4. Closed for lunch **C R W D** 🖮 *by appt.*

Chalgrove
Oxfordshire   **Map 4 SU69**
CANZIANI CERAMICS
(Len and Linda Canziani) 48 Brinkinfield Rd ✆ *(0865) 890117*

Unusual sculpture and mould work in bone china. The artists' speciality is a range of originally-styled thatched cottages, each numbered and signed. Also a bizarre line in hedgehogs, e.g. between a sandwich, plus various castles. All processes of the work demonstrated on request. Member of British China and Porcelain Artist Association.

Open daily 8–7, advisable to telephone. Closed Xmas **C W E D** *credit cards* ⓐ ⓥ ⓧ ⓓ 🖮

Chapel-en-le-Frith
Cheshire   **Map 7 SK08**
CAMERON PEARSON
(John Chaloner Ltd) Sheffield Rd, nr Stockport, nr junction of A6 & Sheffield Rd ✆ *(0298) 2740*

Specialist in the manufacture of cast aluminium, brass and bronze signs and plaques – in particular decorated aluminium house-name signs with relief motifs.

Open Mon–Thu 8–5.15, Fri 8–4.15. Other times by appt. Closed for lunch & Xmas & Etr **C E D**

Charlestown
Cornwall   **Map 2 SX05**
RASHLEIGH POTTERY
(David Carew) Quay Rd, nr St Austell ✆ *(0726) 64014*

Utilitarian hand-thrown stoneware pottery finished in a transparent glaze with freehand brushwork decoration. Also some work with a reduced magnesium glaze and sgraffito decoration; plus various terracotta garden pots.

Open daily 9–6. Closed Xmas **C W E D** 🖮

Charmouth

Dorset   **Map 3 SY39**

CHARMOUTH POTTERY
(Michael and Susan Hendrick) ✆ *(0297) 60594*

Stoneware and earthenware domestic pottery
and a range of earthenware for the garden.

Open Mon–Fri 9–5, wknds 9–1 **W E D** ⚒

Cheddar

Somerset   **Map 3 ST45**

CHEDDAR POTTERY
*(John and Valerie Joyce Bayly) Cheddar Gorge,
below Lion Rock* ✆ *(0934) 743860*

Commemorative royal figures, hand-painted
vases, sprigged mugs and jugs and various
cottage-style ornaments in traditional slipware
and thrown earthenware and stoneware.

Open daily 10.30–6 Etr–Nov. Closed for lunch
D ⚒

MENDIP LEATHERCRAFT
(David and Doreen Treasure) Sidcot La, Winscombe
✆ *(093484) 2783*

Fashion handbags, purses, belts, gift items and
small leather goods available in a choice of over
250 different fine leathers. Basic designs can be
varied to suit customers' requirements.

*Open Mon–Sat, closed Wed & Sat pm. Closed for
lunch & Xmas & Etr* **C R W E D** ⚒

Cheddington

Buckinghamshire   **Map 4 SP91**

MENTMORE SMITHY
*(Roger Mildred) Stag Hill, Mentmore, nr Leighton
Buzzard* ✆ *(0296) 661760*

Architectural ironwork, e.g. large gates, decorative ironwork – fire-grates, canopies etc – and

restoration of ornamental ironwork all undertaken. Also general and agricultural repairs.
All work commissioned.

*Open Mon–Fri 8.30–6, Sat 8.30–1, by appt.
Closed for lunch & Xmas, Etr & BHs* **C R W E D** ⚒

Chedington

Dorset   **Map 3 ST40**

CHEDINGTON POTTERY
*(Beresford Pealing) Manor Farm House, nr
Beaminster, turn off A356 at Winyards Gap Inn*
✆ *(093589) 482*

Good, functional kitchen and tableware hand-
thrown in stoneware, as well as more unusual
ceramic objects such as a range of Dorset clocks
– complete with precision quartz movements.

Open most daylight hours **C W E D** 🚌 *by appt.*

Chepstow

Gwent   **Map 3 ST59**

MALTHOUSE POTTERY
(Peter Naylor) Brockweir, nr Chepstow on A449
✆ *(02918) 291*

Stoneware items, ranging from spotlights to
casseroles, decorated in greens, browns and
blues by using local river mud. Some sgraffito
decoration. Also a small quantity of porcelain
work.

*Open Mon–Sat 9.30–5.30, Sun 11–5.30. Closed
Xmas* **C R D** 🚌 *by appt.*

Chesham

Buckinghamshire   **Map 4 SP90**

MICHAEL WALLIS
*Norfolk Cottage, Hanridge Common, off
Berkhamsted rd, turn r at Nashleigh grge*
✆ *(024029) 8172*

Restoration work of all kinds, covering woodwork, glassware, brass locks, boule work (inlaid brasswork), piano actions and polishing, metal polishing, cane and rush work. Challenging jobs welcomed.

Open Mon–Fri 8–6, wknds 9–6, by appt.
C R D ✍

Chester

Cheshire   **Map 7 SJ46**
CHESHIRE CANDLE WORKSHOPS LTD
Burwardsley, 9m SE of Chester off A41
☎ *(0829) 70401*

Hand-carved candles, wax figurines and plaques, gifts in wood and glassware all made on the premises. There are also many other gifts on display in the shop. Restaurant in old granary and coach house.

Open daily 10–5. Closed Xmas **C W E D** *credit cards* ⓐ ⓥ ✍ *by appt.*

CHESHIRE WOOD CRAFTS
(Nicholas Gordon Pedley) 5B Barrowmore Estate, Gt Barrow, 3 m E of Chester ☎ *(0829) 40554*

Top-quality, hand-made furniture from solid hardwoods such as oak, chestnut, cherry and yew. The work, in traditional and contemporary designs, is mostly made to order but there is a small display at the workshop. Fitted cabinet work also undertaken.

Open Mon–Fri 9–5.30. Sat am by appt. Closed Xmas & Etr **C D** ✍

DEREK RAYMENT ANTIQUES
Orchard House, Barton Rd, Barton, nr Farndon ☎ *(0829) 270429*

Specialist dealers and restorers of antique mercury and aneroid barometers and associated instruments. Cabinet work also undertaken.

Open any time by appt. **C R W E D** ✍

Chesterton

Oxfordshire   **Map 4 SP52**
CHESTERTON POTTERY
(Tony Smythe) nr Bicester ☎ *(0869) 241455*

Small country workshop and showroom in an old village barn producing hand-made earthenware with traditional slip decoration. High-fired for domestic use, items include mugs, tankards, bowls, plates, plant pots, goblets and 'crazy' mugs.

Open Mon–Fri 9–5. Also most wknds, but advisable to telephone. Closed Xmas **C W E D** ✍ *by appt.*

Chiddingly

East Sussex   **Map 5 TQ51**
LONGBARN FURNITURE WORKSHOP
(Rod Wales and John Wyndham) Muddles Green, ¾ m from Golden Cross on A22 ☎ *(0825) 872764*

Domestic, office, executive, reception and boardroom furniture designed and made to commission. Some batch products are occasionally available from stock.

Open Mon–Fri 9–6, Sat 9–4 (usually), by appt. **C W E D** ✍

Chillington

Devon   **Map 3 SX74**
CUTLANDS POTTERY
(Paul H Metcalfe) nr Kingsbridge on A379 ☎ *(0548) 580390*

Hand-thrown stoneware pottery – domestic ware, vases etc – decorated with a unique, →

Thatcher carrying reed to the roof

attractive fuchsia design. Also a range of cast, hand-finished models of birds and wildlife, plus a selection of other crafts and gifts. Paul Metcalfe can usually be seen working.

Open Mon–Fri 9–5.45. Also Sat am during peak season. Closed for lunch & Xmas **C W E D** ⊞

Chipping Campden
Gloucestershire   **Map 4 SP13**
CAMPDEN WEAVERS
(E A and J E Green) 16 Lower High St ✆ *(0386) 840864*

Numerous hand-woven and knitted items, such as gloves, hats, scarves and sweaters: many in natural colours. Also children's jumpers with large motifs on the front. Other sundry items for sale include notelets, toy sheep and badges.

Open Mon–Sat 9–5.30, closed Thu pm. Closed for lunch & Xmas **E D** *credit cards* @ ⓥ ⊞

Chipping Norton
Oxfordshire   **Map 4 SP32**
IN STYLE
(Gloria Williams and Josie Cran) Whitehills Farm, Sibford Rd, Hook Norton ✆ *(0608) 737234/737706*

High-quality designer knitwear made to the customer's specification. Garments based on customer's own designs can also be made up if required.

Open Mon–Fri 10–3 by appt. Closed Xmas & Etr **C D** ⊞

PAUL FISCHER (LUTHIER)
West End Studio, West End ✆ *(0608) 2792*

Paul Fischer, maker of musical instruments, specialises in the classical guitar from the 16th century to the present day. All his instruments are made by hand from the finest exotic tonewoods.

Open Mon–Fri 10–5 & Sat, by appt. Closed for lunch, Xmas, Etr & 2 wks annual holiday **C R E D** ⊞

JOHN HULME
11A High St ✆ *(0608) 41692*

Specialist in the restoration and conservation of antique furniture, including clock-cases, boxes, treen, marquetry, boule and carving. Also brass and iron locks, keys, handles and fittings.

Open Mon–Fri 8.30–6. Wknds by appt. Closed Xmas & Etr **C R W E D** ⊞

LUCY COLTMAN TEXTILE DESIGNS
Netting Cottage, Netting St, Hook Norton, nr Banbury ✆ *(0608) 730011*

An assortment of garments, scarves, ties and stoles, plus a range of soft furnishings – cushions, curtains etc – all made from individual hand-woven fabrics and ikat-dyed silk.

Open by appt. only **C E D** ⊞

Cholmondeley
Cheshire   **Map 7 SJ55**
WITCHCRAFT LUXURY KNITWEAR
(Mrs S M O Foden) Park House, nr Malpas; Park House is in Cholmondeley Park. Follow signs for Cholmondeley Castle Gdns from A49 or A41 ✆ *(082922) 484*

A cottage industry producing luxury, hand-knitted garments in mohair, alpaca, pure English wool etc. Each autumn and spring Witchcraft assembles a collection of 30–40 designs, all of which are for sale and can be ordered in different colours and sizes.

Open by appt. only. Closed Xmas **C** *(some***W***)* **E D** ⊞ *by appt.*

Chorley
Lancashire **Map 7 SD51**
SLATER KITCHEN
(James Slater and Peter Kitchen) Natural Stone Centre, Abbey Mill, Bolton Rd, Abbey Village, off A675 ✆ (0254) 831606

All requirements for cut or dressed stone catered for. This includes the design and manufacture of fireplaces, feature stonewalls, heads, sills etc, using stone, slate and other materials.

Showroom open Mon–Fri 8.30–5.00, Sat 9.30–12, by appt. Closed Xmas & Etr **C R W D** 🚲

Chudleigh
Devon **Map 3 SX87**
BIG JUG CRAFT STUDIO
(Ian and Barbara Steele) 31 Fore St ✆ (0626) 852191

A wide range of domestic, hand-thrown stoneware, designer knitwear, and handloomwoven garments and cushion covers, all made on the premises. Individual orders taken. Send S.A.E. for brochures.

Open Mon–Sat 9–5.30. Other times by appt. Closed Xmas & Etr **C W E D** 🚲 *by appt.*

WHEEL CRAFT WORKSHOPS & RESTAURANT
Town Mills, Clifford St ✆ (0626) 852698

The co-operatively-run workshops are housed in the town's historic mill buildings. Craftsmen at present in residence are: Norman Rose, blacksmith; Charles Anketell-Jones, furniture-maker (see below); Anne Smullen and Liz Lambert, potters; Bruce Chivers, porcelain; Dik Garood, toymaker; Colin George, ceramic artist; Sally Clayden, mobiles; Louise Yale, print and textile designer; Sarah Vivian, weaver; Kim Bartlett, silversmith; Deborah Flack, hand-printed dress designer; Sue and Iain Gunn, leatherworkers; Roselle Sentito, shoemaker; Alan Taylor, stained-glass artist. Also whole-food, a gift shop and a licensed restaurant.

Workshops open daily 10–5.30. **C R W E D** *credit cards* ⓐ ⓥ ⓧ ⓓ *(each business varies)* 🚲 *by appt.*

CHARLES ANKETELL-JONES (WHEEL CRAFT WORKSHOP)
Town Mills, Clifford St (see above) ✆ (0626) 852698

Fine, distinctive contemporary furniture handmade to order. Restoration of furniture and upholstery also undertaken.

Open daily 10–5 **C R E D**

Cirencester
Gloucestershire **Map 4 SP00**
CIRENCESTER WORKSHOPS
Brewery Court ✆ (0285) 61566

A number of independent workshops occupy the old brewery buildings, and there is a gallery where the craftsmen's work, together with articles made elsewhere, is displayed and sold. The resident craftsmen are: Richard Overs, blacksmith; Tara McKee, potter; Philip Windsor Stevens, jewellery-maker and designer; Ann Sharman, knitwear designer; Mike Smith, willow-basket maker; Hilary Genillard, bag maker; Athene English, saddler; Jonathan Beach, antique-clock restorer; Tristan Salazar, antique restorer and cabinet maker; Penelope Smith, designer in leather; Sarah Beadsmoore, weaver; Ester Barrett, embroidered textiles; Pamela Richmond, bookbinding and restoration; Rosanna Mahony, etcher and print maker; Wendy Harding, clock-dial painter and restorer; Jennie Sedgwick, contemporary jeweller; Martin Bland and Shirley Harris, brewers. There is also a coffee shop with whole-food bakery.

Open Mon–Sat 10–5.30. The workshops are open at varying times **C R D** *credit cards* ⓐ ⓥ 🚲

Clevedon
Avon **Map 3 ST47**
CLEVEDON CRAFT CENTRE
(D A and P Huxtable) Newhouse Farm, Moor La, turning opp. Clevedon Court (NT) on B3130, then 1st r beyond the motorway ✆ (0272) 872867

Several workshops (see also individual entries below) occupy the outbuildings of this 17th-century farm which was once part of the Clevedon Court Estate. The crafts here are silversmithing and jewellery; porcelain pottery; wood-turning and furniture-making; signwriting; tiled tables and diamond-cut tableware; cabinet making; weaving; leatherwork; glass blowing and engraving; cold casting and brass rubbing. There is also a tea room.

Open Mon–Sat 9.15–5, Sun 2.15–5. Closed for lunch & Etr. Some workshops close Mon **C R W E D** *credit cards* ⓐ ⓥ ⓧ *(each business varies)* 🚲

W H DAVIES
(William Davies) Studio 9, Clevedon Craft Centre (see above) ✆ (0272) 871696 (day) 871627 (evngs) →

Cabinet-making, wood-turning, antique and modern furniture repair and upholstery. Work ranges from bowls, lamps, candlesticks etc, to all types of chairs and tables (including rocking chairs), stair bannisters and newel-posts. Specialist in colonial and Shaker furniture. Complete rooms designed and made. Member of the Guild of Master Craftsmen.

Open daily 9–6 (closed Thu). Closed for lunch
C R W E D

A C A SMITH LEATHERCRAFT
(Arnold Smith) Studio 6, Clevedon Craft Centre (see above) ✆ *(0272) 836102*

Various high-quality leather goods all hand-carved or stamped and hand-stitched or thonged. Items include belts, bags, cheque book covers, wildlife pictures, portraits and presentation plaques. Leathermaking books, tools and accessories also available.

Open daily 10–5 (closed Mon). Closed for lunch
C R D

STEAR & BRIGHT
(David Stear and Jeffrey Bright) Studio 1, Clevedon Craft Centre (see above) ✆ *(0272) 872149*

Designers and makers of gold and silver jewellery, silverware, trophies, chains of office, promotional jewellery, church silver etc.

Open Mon–Sat 9.15–5, Sun 2.15–5. Closed for lunch & Xmas **C D** *credit cards* ⓐ ⓥ ⓧ

Cley-next-the-Sea
Norfolk   **Map 9 TG04**

MADE IN CLEY
(B Widdup, G Espelage, W Altman, K B Vollmar, Q Proctor-Gorssen) High St ✆ *(0263) 740143*

Jewellery and pottery are made here. Pottery includes a full range of domestic stoneware, including ovenware, and some porcelain and sculptural pieces. Jewellery is mainly silverware, with precious and semi-precious stones, but some other materials are also used. Work is also done to commission.

Open Mon–Sun 10–6. Closed Wed Oct–Jun.
C W E D 🚐

Clovelly
Devon   **Map 2 SS32**

HARTLAND WORKSHOPS
(situated in the village of Hartland, nr Bideford; for addresses and opening times, see below)
C R W E D 🚐

HARTLAND POTTERY
(Clive C Pearson) The Forge, North St ✆ *(02374) 693*

Small pottery mainly producing stoneware – including functional oil lamps.

Open Mon–Sat 9.30–6

DAVID CHARLESWORTH
Harton Manor ✆ *(02374) 288*

Fine furniture made to commission only.

Open by appt.

MILLTHORNE CHAIRS
(Bob and Sue Seymour) 10 Fore St ✆ *(02374) 590*

Traditional children's and full-size Windsor chairs in beech, ash and elm.

SPRINGFIELD POTTERY
(Philip and Frannie Leach) Springfield ✆ *(02374) 506*

Hand-made earthenware pottery for the table, kitchen and garden.

Open daily

FORD HILL FORGE
(RH Conibear) ✆ *(02374) 208*

One of the oldest established forges in Devon. Wrought-ironwork, horseshoes etc. *See separate entry under Hartland.*

Clun
Shropshire   **Map 7 SO38**

RIVERSDALE STUDIO
(Peggy and Antony Lewis) Buffalo La, by bridge at junction of A488 & B4368 ✆ *(05884) 521*

Hand-printed original designs and 'personalised' designs on table mats, napkins, handkerchiefs, bags, tea towels and head squares.

Open Mon–Sat 9.30–5.30, also some Suns, but advisable to telephone **C W E D** 🚐

Coggeshall
Essex   **Map 5 TL82**

COGGESHALL POTTERY
(Peter Turner) 49 West St ✆ *(0376) 61217*

A wide range of reasonably-priced hand-made pottery. Most of the work is functional, but some castles and animals are produced too. Terracotta garden pots available in various shapes and sizes.

Open Wed–Sun 10–5. **W D** 🚐

Coniston

Cumbria **Map 7 SD39**

FELLWARE STUDIO POTTERY & CRAFTS
(Lilian N and Roy Cooksey) Brocklebank Ground, Torver, 3 m from Coniston on A593 ✆ *(0966) 41449*

A varied selection of hand-thrown stoneware items including coffee, tea and wine sets, plates, plaques and small model animals. Celtic decoration a speciality.

Open Mar–Nov. No set times so advisable to telephone **C W D** ♿

Constantine

Cornwall **Map 2 SW72**

BOW WINDOW CRAFT CO-OPERATIVE
(Deborah Carne, Secretary) 48 Fore St ✆ *(0326) 40703*

Ten local craftsmen display their work here and take it in turns to man the shop. Their crafts are: pottery, leatherwork, hand-painted silks, wood-turning, machine knitting in Shetland wool; hand-made mohair knitwear, weaving, wooden and soft toys, enamel work, patchwork and pressed-flower work.

Open Mon–Fri 10–5, Sat 10–1 **C W E D** *credit cards* Ⓥ ♿

Corbridge

Northumberland **Map 11 NY96**

ARC DESIGN
(Peter Brooks) Station Yard, S of Corbridge on A68 past station then sharp l turn on LH bend ✆ *(043471) 2239*

Fine furniture hand-made to order in English or exotic hardwoods. Woods and photographs of completed commissions on display.

Open by appt. only **C D** ♿

Corby

Northamptonshire **Map 4 SP88**

EAST CARLTON CRAFT WORKSHOPS
Old Coach House, East Carlton Countryside Park, 3m W of Corby off A427 ✆ *(0536) 770977 (warden)*

Several craftsmen work and sell their products in the coach house, which is shared with the Industrial Heritage Centre. The craft work includes glass models, oil and water-colours, Victorian photography, pine furniture, gal-

leons in horn, lace accessories, sign-writing, knitting and spinning.

Open: summer, daily 9–6; winter, daily 9–4. Closed 25 Dec–1 Jan **C R D** ♿

Cowbeech

East Sussex **Map 5 TQ61**

READING & LEAHY FURNITURE
(R J Reading and J G Leahy) Westwood, Trolilloes La, nr Hailsham, opp. Merry Harriers PH ✆ *(0435) 830249*

Quality furniture, using solid hardwoods and specialising in nursery and children's furniture. Also desks, tables and cabinets, both to original designs and reproductions. Small range of work kept in stock.

Open Mon–Fri 8–5.30 & some Sats, by appt. Closed Xmas **C W E D** ♿

Coxwold

North Yorkshire **Map 8 SE57**

COXWOLD POTTERY
(Peter and Jill Dick) nr York ✆ *(03476) 344*

A good range of practical stoneware and earthenware, most of which is slip-decorated and wood-fired. Kitchen and tableware, plant pots and so on, as well as more expensive individual work.

Open Mon–Fri 10–5.30 & some wknds. Advisable to telephone. Closed for lunch & Xmas. **C W D** ♿ *by appt.*

Cranleigh

Surrey **Map 4 TQ03**

SMITHBROOK KILNS
2 m N of Cranleigh on A281 ✆ *(0483) 276455*

About 20 different craftsmen and artists occupy these premises and can be seen at work. Their skills include furniture-making; brass-restoring; perfume-making; picture-framing; photography; knitting and piano-restoring. There is also an art gallery, a plant display and a restaurant.

Open Tue–Sat 9–6 **C R W E D** *(each business varies)* ♿ *by appt.*

STUDIO WORKSHOP
(Sean Fitzgerald) Smithbrook Kilns (see above) ✆ *(0483) 275900*

'Fine furniture in the English tradition'. Limited batch production of contemporary designs in various hardwoods. Restoration of antique furniture also undertaken and there are some antique items for sale.

Open Tue–Sat 9–6. Closed Xmas & Etr **R W E D**

SMITHBROOK PICTURE FRAMING
(David Snell) 25/26 Smithbrook Kilns (see above)
℘ *(0483) 275450*

All aspects of picture-framing undertaken, including hand-cut mounts and wash and line application: full range of mouldings, mirrors and swept frames available. There is also an art gallery containing original oil and water-colour paintings, etchings and hand-coloured engravings etc.

Open Tue–Sat 9–6. Closed for lunch & Xmas & Etr
C R D

Crediton
Devon　　　　　　　　　　**Map 3 SS80**

STONESHILL POTTERY
(John Maltby) Stoneshill, 1 m from Sandford on the Kennerleigh rd ℘ *(03632) 2753*

Various unusual and highly original adult toys; most of them are wooden and many have a nautical flavour. Also a range of ceramics, usually stoneware (both oxidised and reduced) and decorated with enamels.

Open Mon–Sat any reasonable time. Advisable to telephone **C W E D** ⊕

Carving a Tudor moulding in a piece of oak

Crewkerne
Somerset　　　　　　　　　　**Map 3 ST40**

ABBEY STREET POTTERY
(Rory Morgan McLeod) 14 Abbey St, 50 yds W from The Square ℘ *(0460) 74438*

All sorts of useful pots from bread-crocks to mugs, hand-thrown from stoneware clay.

Open Mon–Fri 9–5.30, Sat 9–5. Closed for lunch & Xmas & Etr **C W D** ⊕

CLAPTON MILL
(Lockyer and Son) 3 m from Crewkerne on Lyme Regis rd ℘ *(0460) 73124*

Original 19th-century water-powered flour mill still in use as a commercial mill but open to visitors at weekends. Full guided tours explain the history and workings of the mill, and animal feeds and traditional stoneground flour can be purchased.

Open Jun–Oct Sat 10–6, Sun 2–6. Also open BHs 10–6. Other times by appt. **C W D** ⊕ *by appt.*

Cromer
Norfolk　　　　　　　　　　**Map 9 TG24**

NICK DEANS
(Nick Deans BA Hons Sculpture) Lake Cottage, Hall Rd, Aldborough, 6m SW of Cromer
℘ *(026377) 423*

Very unusual wood and stone carvings, plus sculpture cast in various materials ranging from bronze to concrete. Specialities are extraordinary furniture based on figures and animals, and rocking toys (sheep, pigs, horses, rhinos etc). Anything special made to order. Dead trees carved in situ.

Open any time, advisable to telephone. Closed Xmas
C W E D ⊕

E MARK JOLLIFFE
Cromer Rd, Overstrand ℘ *(026378) 488*

Traditional furniture – made chiefly in local wood – available from stock or made to customer's requirements. Fitted kitchens and specialised joinery work also undertaken.

Open Mon–Fri 9–5. Wknds by appt. Closed for lunch & Xmas **C R D** ⊕

A & J YOUNG POTTERY
Common Farm, Sustead Rd, Lower Gresham, 3 m S of Cromer ℘ *(026377) 548*

A comprehensive range of practical domestic pots in hand-thrown ovenproof stoneware. The more unusual items include lemon squeezers, cutlery drainers, colanders and bread crocks.

Open Mon–Fri am. Wknds & pm by appt. Closed for lunch & Xmas & Etr (some **C**) **W E D** ♿

Cromford
Derbyshire — Map 8 SK25
CARGO LEATHERGOODS
(Clare and Pete Ludbey) The Old Workshop, North St, nr Matlock ✆ *(062982) 4574*

Hand-made, high-quality, leather goods of all descriptions. Stock includes belts, bags, briefcases and purses: made-to-measure sandals are also available. Small production runs too.

Open Mon–Sat 10–6, Sun 2–6 **C R W E D** ♿ *by appt.*

Cropwell Butler
Nottinghamshire — Map 8 SK63
BARRATT & SWANN
(Roy Burratt and Arthur Swann) Hardigate ✆ *(06073) 2642*

Purpose-made joinery, cabinet-making and furniture-making undertaken, on a commission basis, in a variety of hard and softwoods.

Open Mon–Fri 8–4.30. Wknds by appt. Closed for lunch & Xmas & Etr **C D** ♿

Cullompton
Devon — Map 3 ST00
ALAN PETERS FURNITURE
Aller Studios, Kentisbeare, 1 m E of M5, Exit 28 ✆ *(08846) 251*

Specialist workshop producing modern craft-furniture of a very high quality. The work, ranging from single items to complete room schemes, is individually designed and made to order. There is a small showroom with a few items for sale. Fellow of the Society of Designer Craftsmen; Member of British Crafts Centre & Devon & Somerset Guilds of Craftsmen.

Open Mon–Fri 9–6 & Sats by appt. Serious visitors only please **C E D** ♿

Dartington
Devon — Map 3 SX76
VANESSA ROBERTSON & NORMAN YOUNG
Apple Barn, Week, take road to Week at Dartington church, then 1st r ✆ *(0803) 865027*

Textile artists Vanessa Robertson and Norman Young make rugs and wall hangings for individuals. Their own 'ikat' technique allows freedom to compose any shape and combination of colours, and they aim to design each piece of work with empathy towards both client and interior. The artists are happy to discuss any commission. Please telephone.

Visitors welcome by appt. only **C W E D** ♿

Dartmouth
Devon — Map 3 SX85
BELLIS STUDIO
(Jo Nicoletti) Red Lion Craft Shop, The Level, Dittisham ✆ *(080422) 401*

High-quality, pressed-flower work produced for the gift trade in a small workshop on the premises. Items include lampshades, pictures, booklets etc. There is also a shop attached to the studio which sells a variety of locally made craft work. Commissions welcome.

Open Mon–Sat 8.30–5.30. Also evngs until 9.30 & Sun 10–9.30 during summer. Closed Xmas **C W E D** ♿

Daventry
Northamptonshire — Map 4 SP56
DEVON COTTAGE CRAFTS
(G R Chaffe) 2 Daventry Road, Norton ✆ *(0327) 705691*

Many hand-made wooden items, ranging from Welsh love spoons to dressers, available from stock or to order; also made-to-measure fitted furniture. Other services include antique furniture restoration; pine-stripping; re-rushing and re-caning of old chairs, stools and other pieces of furniture; plus any type of wood-turning and inlay commissions.

Open by appt. only **C R W E D** *credit cards* ⓐ ⓥ ⓧ ⓓ ♿ *by appt.*

Dawlish
Devon — Map 3 SX97
MARBLE CRAFT
(W M Carew) Shutterton Industrial Estate ✆ *(0626) 864856/865748*

A variety of marble gifts, such as clocks, barometers, table lighters, pen holders and desk calendars are made by Marble Craft. Special commissions welcome.

Open Mon–Fri 8–5, Sat 9–12. Closed for lunch & Xmas **C R W E D** ♿

Debenham

Suffolk   **Map 5 TM16**

ASPALL CYDER
(J M and J I Chevallier Guild) Aspall Hall, nr Stowmarket ✆ (0728) 860510

Aspall Cyder House was established in 1728 and the old premises now house a shop where the original equipment is on display. Visitors can buy the products of the present-day industry, which only uses natural ingredients.

Open Mon–Fri 9–3.30. Closed for lunch & Xmas, Etr & BHs ♿

Deddington

Oxfordshire   **Map 4 SP43**

MICHAEL & HEATHER ACKLAND
Coniston House, New St ✆ (0869) 38241

Designers and makers of modern silver and gold jewellery specialising in lost-wax casting: much of the work incorporates gem stones such as amethyst and carnelian. Large stocks always on display; wedding and engagement rings made to order.

Open Tue, Wed, Fri & Sat 10–5. Closed for lunch **C D** ♿

Dent

Cumbria   **Map 7 SD78**

DENT CRAFTS CENTRE
(Brian and Matty Bradley) Helmside, between Dent & Sedbergh ✆ (05875) 400

A remarkable collection of gifts and home ideas mostly all made, restored or designed at the Centre. Pottery, old weaving-mill artefacts, dolls, knitwear, woodwork, toys and lots more. There is also a whole-food, licensed tea room (Egon Ronay recommended).

Open Etr–Xmas daily 10–6 (closed Mon) **C R W E D** 🍴 *by appt.*

COLIN GARDNER
Stone House, Cowgill, 5 m E of Dent towards B6255 ✆ (05875) 380

Cabinet-maker specialising in gun-cabinets made traditionally in solid hardwood: any specific requirements met. Also Welsh dressers, tables, chairs etc, plus commissioned items.

Open Mon–Fri 9–5, wknds 10–4. Closed for lunch & Xmas **C R D** ♿

KNITTERS OF DENT
(Janet Pigott) Main St ✆ (05875) 421

A selection of hand-knitted garments is always available, including some designer knitwear. Also a collection of stylish Knit Kits.

Open Mon–Sat. Also Sun at BH. Closed Xmas. **C W D** 🍴 *advisable to telephone*

DENNIS WOOLEY
Tubhole Barn ✆ (05875) 361

Early keyboard instruments (harpsichords, spinets, virginals) made to order in a variety of sizes and styles based on classical originals from England, France, Flanders, Germany and Italy. Also forte pianos and early grand pianos.

Visitors welcome by appt. **C R E D** ♿

Dersingham

Norfolk   **Map 9 TF63**

DERSINGHAM POTTERY
(Mrs June Mullarkey) Chapel Rd ✆ (0485) 40761

Hand-thrown practical and individual pots for sale in a variety of clays and glazes, including stoneware, porcelain and terracotta. Commemorative sprigged ware a speciality. Workshop and showroom occupy old stable buildings.

Open Mon–Sat 10–5.30. Also Sun 2–5 in summer **C D** ♿

Diss

Norfolk   **Map 5 TM17**

MOREY WOODWORK & FURNITURE
(Robert Le Besque) Oaksedge Workshop, 34 Croft La, behind Police Station on A1066 ✆ (0379) 51798

Children's chairs, Shaker furniture, boxes, kitchen-ware and small items of furniture made in wood to traditional designs. Noah's Arks and miniatures (travellers' samples) are specialities. All work made to commission.

Open Mon–Fri 10–6, Sat 10–12, by appt. **C W D** ♿

Ditchling

East Sussex   **Map 4 TQ31**

THE CRAFTSMAN GALLERY
(Jill Pryke) 8 High St, 9 m NW of Lewes ✆ (07918) 5246

The Craftsman Gallery consists of a pottery workshop, a Sussex crafts gallery and an information centre about crafts in general. Jill Pryke's earthenware pots have a soft-green glaze, and she undertakes commemorative work. The gallery's range includes batik, wood, weaving and copperware.

Open Mon–Sat 10–5 (closed Wed pm). Closed for lunch. **C W D** 🚗 by appt.

Doddington
Kent   Map 5 TQ95
PERIWINKLE PRESS
(E R, A, A L and J R Swain) Chequers Hill
✆ *(079586) 246*

The restoration of oil paintings, picture-framing and publication of reproduction prints and maps are all carried out in the workshops. In the gallery, unusual craft items, books old and new, prints, engravings and embroideries are for sale.

Open Mon–Sat 9–5. Closed Xmas, Etr & BHs
C R W D *credit cards* ⓐ Ⓥ 🚗

Dorchester
Dorset   Map 3 SY69
DORSET CRAFT GUILD SHOP
19 Durngate St, at the 'Potter-In' restaurant
✆ *(0305) 68649*

Over 60 independent craftsmen, working in or near Dorset, display their hand-made work here. They are all members of the Dorset Craft Guild.

Open Mon–Sat 10–5. Closed Xmas & Etr
C D 🚗

Draycott
Somerset   Map 3 ST45
WESTFIELD BARN
(Raymond Holloway) Wells Rd, 200 yds from Red Lion Inn ✆ *(0934) 742845*

Hand-carved oak furniture including refectory tables, dressers, chairs and four-poster beds. Also various small turned or carved country items such as bellows, butter moulds and milking stools, plus leather goods, prints and paintings. Weekend wood-carving courses available.

Open daily 9–6 but advisable to telephone. Closed for lunch & Xmas **C R W** *(some* **E***)* **D** 🚗

Drayton
Oxfordshire   Map 4 SP44
(David Pointer) 47 Sutton Wick, nr Abingdon
✆ *(0235) 31673*

Windsor chair maker specialising in high-quality items for children. These are made in the style of traditional 19th-century English Windsor elbow chairs. Limited numbers available.

Visitors by appt. only **C R E D** 🚗

Driffield
North Humberside
See under Great Driffield

Easington
North Humberside   Map 9 TA31
EASINGTON POTTERY
(Gerd Fehrling) 7 South Churchside, 21m SE of Hull ✆ *(0964) 50578*

Various hand-made domestic, garden and decorative pots in stoneware and porcelain.

Open Fri, Sat & Sun 10–5 & BHs. Closed for lunch & Etr **C W D** 🚗 *by appt.*

East Hoathly
East Sussex   Map 5 TQ51
WARNHAM COTTAGE
(Mrs Julian Akers-Douglas) ✆ *(082584) 397 (home)*

Original, unique designs for adults and children, incorporating traditional hand-smocking and surface embroidery. All the clothes are custom-made in the busy workshop. Local English wine, cider and beer sold on the premises.

Open Mon–Sat 10–4 (closed Wed). Other times by appt. Closed Xmas & Etr **C W E D** *credit cards* Ⓥ Ⓧ 🚗 *by appt.*

East Rudham
Norfolk   Map 9 TF82
FLINT STUDIO
(John and Pippa Brooker) 13m NE of King's Lynn
✆ *(048522) 303*

Individually designed and traditionally made fan-sticks in ivory and horn, as well as lace bobbins, pincushions and over 800 different beads – including hand-painted glass ones. Also a range of more than 70 assorted pottery mice, large hamster pots and money boxes.

Open flexible hours, advisable to telephone
C R D 🚗

Edenfield
Lancashire   Map 7 SD81
C WHITING
(C Whiting) 125/7 Market St, nr Ramsbottom
✆ *(070682) 4835*

A saddler marks out the seat with a hot iron

Designer-jewellery made in gold and silver, and all silversmithing work undertaken – particularly ecclesiastical plate. Also the restoration and repair of antique jewellery and silver, smelting and electroplating.

Open Mon–Fri 9–5.30. Wknds by appt. Closed for lunch & Xmas, Etr & during local holidays
C R D E ♿

Edwinstowe
Nottinghamshire   **Map 8 SK66**
CHURCH FARM CRAFT WORKSHOPS
Mansfield Rd, next to Parish Church Ⓒ *(0623) 824243*

A group of independent workshops occupy the outbuildings of the former farm. Closed Xmas, but for opening times see individual entries below **C D** ♿ *by appt.*

MAYWOODS (Linda George) – jewellery, bobbin lace, collages and gifts.

Open Wed–Sun 10.30–6 Ⓒ *(0623) 649057 (home)*

FIELD GALLERY (Dorothie Field) – fine-art specialist; paintings, prints, ceramics, sculpture, framing.

Open Thu & Fri 2–5, wknds & BHs 11–5. Also by appt. Ⓒ *(0623) 882257 (home)*

OWT IN WOOD (Bill Thirkhill) – furniture restoration and fancy wooden goods.

Open Wed–Sun 9.30–5 Ⓒ *(0623) 823331 (home)*

MANOR BRASS (Barry Bradley) – industrial and ornamental brass and bronze castings.

Open Wed–Fri 2.30–5.30, wknds 9.30–5.30 Ⓒ *(0623) 550680 (home)*

O B LAWRENCE – wood-carving, wooden signs and cast garden ornaments.

Open daily 9–5 (closed Tue & for lunch) Ⓒ *(0623) 823982 (home)*

STEAM MACHINE (George Coupe) – steam-powered models of all descriptions, made to order.

Open Mon–Fri 3–5.30, Sat 8–5.30, Sun 8.30–5.30 Ⓒ *(0623) 823325 (home)*

CLOWNAROUND TOY WORKSHOP (Margaret Thompson) – clowns, scarecrows, toys, gifts, quilted waistcoats.

Open Thu–Sun 11–5 Ⓒ *(0623) 25293 (home)*

BIT SPECIAL (Cynthia Andrews) – original designer-made knitwear.

Open Thu–Sun 11–5 Ⓒ *(0623) 24396 (home)*

WREN CRAFTSMEN
(Thomas A Rennocks) The Old School, Carburton, nr Worksop, 4 m N of Edwinstowe in Sherwood Forest Ⓒ *(0909) 483517 (workshop) 731464 (home)*

Individually designed, hand-made furniture in solid English oak and walnut, including dressers, tables and heritage stools. Also quality large toys – rocking horses, puffer trains etc – and small gift items. Church and boardroom furniture designed; searches into genealogy carried out for carved inscriptions.

Open Mon–Fri 9–5. Wknds by appt. Closed Xmas & Etr **C R D** ♿ *by appt.*

Elkesley
Nottinghamshire   **Map 8 SK67**
CHRIS ASTON POTTERY
4 High St, nr Retford, 2 m from Markham Moor roundabout Ⓒ *(077783) 391*

Attractive hand-made stoneware – ranging from tableware to one-off pieces decorated with brushwork. Also ceramic house-name plates and screen-printed presentation tankards made to order.

Open daily 10–6. Closed Xmas **C W E D** ♿ *by appt.*

Elterwater
Cumbria   **Map 7 NY30**
BARNHOWE SPINNING & WOODTURNING
(Meg and Martin Riley) Barnhowe, Lane Ends, nr Ambleside, on Elterwater Common Ⓒ *(09667) 346*

Garments, made from hand-spun yarns and hand-woven materials, include ponchos, jackets, stoles and knitwear. Spinning and weaving equipment for sale; spinning tuition and demonstrations given. Also wood-turned bowls (and some other objects) designed to emphasise the wood's grain.

Open daily mid morning–mid evng, but advisable to telephone. Closed at Xmas **C R D** 🚌 *by appt.*

Epworth

South Humberside **Map 8 SE70**

OAKLEAF CABINET MAKERS

(K Robinson and S Moore) The Old Chapel, 20 Fieldside, Crowle, nr Scunthorpe, 5m N of Epworth ✆ (0724) 711027

Specialists in hand-made reproduction furniture from oak and mahogany. Other services include repolishing and restoration work, the design and building of kitchen units, and furniture made to commission.

Open Mon–Fri 8–5, Sat 8–12, Sun 12–5. Closed Etr **C R D** 🚌

Erpingham

Norfolk **Map 9 TG13**

ALBY CRAFTS

(Valerie Alston) Cromer Rd, 6m S of Cromer, on A140 ✆ (0263) 761590/761226

Work from over 300 British craftsmen can be seen in the gallery and there are also nine resident craftsmen with workshops on the premises. These are: Lesley Thomas, lace maker; Terry Read, wood-carver; John Pooler, sculptor and artist; Julian Meaney, stained-glass artist; Ken Hooker, ceramics; Sid Colebrook, signwriter and artist; Ken Riches, silversmith and jeweller; Helen Jennings, painted silk; Karen Ford, weaver. Charles Matts has a showroom here – see entry under Aylsham. Refreshments available.

Open daily 10–5 (closed Mon). Closed Xmas & during Jan & Feb. **C R D** *credit cards* ⓐ ⓥ 🚌 *by appt.*

Eskdale

Cumbria *see under Boot*

Etal

Northumberland **Map 11 NT93**

ERROL HUT SMITHY & WORKSHOP

(N, D, P and B Smith) Letham Hill, nr Cornhill-on-Tweed ✆ (089082) 317

Ornamental wrought-iron work is produced in the smithy where welding, machining and small castings are also undertaken. In the workshop spinning wheels, small turned items, toys and furniture can be found: also spinning and plant-dyed wools and miniature steam locos.

Open daily 11–6 **C R D** 🚌 *by appt.*

Evenlode

Gloucestershire **Map 3 SP22**

EVENLODE POTTERY

(D Kunzemann) nr Moreton-in-Marsh ✆ (0608) 50804

Hand-made and hand-decorated slipware and ovenproof earthenware. Special orders taken.

Open any time. Closed for lunch & Xmas & Etr **C W E D** 🚌

Everton

Nottinghamshire **Map 8 SK69**

MILLFIELD POTTERY

(Jane Hamlyn) nr Doncaster ✆ (0777) 817723

A wide range of useful and decorative pots in salt-glazed stoneware and porcelain – all work hand-made by Jane Hamlyn who has work in the Public Collection of the V & A Museum. Prices from £5–£50. Member of Craftsmen Potters' Association.

Open daily 10–6, advisable to telephone. Closed Xmas **C W E D** 🚌

Eye

Suffolk **Map 5 TM17**

EDWIN TURNER

Home Farm, Gislingham, nr Eye ✆ (037983) 280

Manufacturers, designers and restorers of fine furniture, specialising in traditional and reproduction pieces. A range of tables, chairs and cabinets always in stock, and visitors are welcome to see any commissioned work in progress.

Open Mon–Fri 8–4, preferably by appt. Wknds by appt. only. Closed Xmas, Etr & 3rd week in Aug **C R E D** 🚌

Faringdon

Oxfordshire **Map 4 SU29**

MICHAEL BRADLEY

Unit 4, Regal Way ✆ (0367) 22316

All kinds of specialist wood-turning for domestic or trade use undertaken. Work ranges from spinning-wheels to staircase-balustrades and newel-posts.

Open Mon–Fri 9–5, by appt. Closed for lunch & Xmas, Etr & BHs **C R D** ⊕

Farmborough
Avon   **Map 3 ST66**

COLD BATH CRAFT SHOP & BUTTERHOUSE GALLERY
(Don and Anita Eatherden) Cold Bath, nr Farmborough, on A39 towards Wells ✆ *(0761) 71585*

An attractive selection of goods, nearly all made by local craftsmen, includes pottery, candles, baskets, soft toys, knitwear, embroidered items, wood-turned objects, photographs, stained-glass and enamel work. Sometimes craftsmen demonstrate in the shop. Refreshments are available.

Open daily as follows: Apr & May 10–6, Jun–Sep 10–9, Oct–Dec 10–6 **C D** *credit cards* ⓐ ⓥ ⓧ ⊕ *by appt.*

Farndon
Cheshire   **Map 7 SJ45**

BARN STUDIOS
(Iain Robertson) Top Farm Centre, High St ✆ *(0829) 270020*

Six craftsmen work from the Top Farm Centre: Iain Robertson, furniture-maker, specialising in kitchens and bathrooms; Alison Holt, textile artist – pictures, cushions etc; Robert Smith, French-polisher and furniture restorer; Pat Mitchell, knitwear from stock and commissions; Julie Brookshaw, jeweller; Conway Conservation, bookbinder.

Open Mon–Fri 9–5.30, Sat 9–4. Closed Xmas & Etr **C R D** *credit cards* ⓥ ⊕

Farnham
Surrey   **Map 4 SU84**

A HARRIS & SONS: FARNHAM POTTERIES
(E J, P J and D W Harris) Pottery La, Wrecclesham, nr Farnham. Take the Petersfield road, the A325, from Farnham and turn l after Royal Oak PH in Wrecclesham ✆ *(0252) 715318*

Hand-made earthenware pottery for the garden, plus some domestic ware. The range includes flower pots, forcing pots, wall pots, garden urns, herb pots and chimney pots. There is a resident jeweller on the premises as well (*see entry below*) and occasionally other craftwork is also on display.

Open Mon–Fri 9–5, Sat 9–4, by appt. Closed Xmas **W D** ⊕

SILVER LINING
(Ruta Brown B.A.) Craft Workshops, Farnham Potteries, Pottery La, Wrecclesham, nr Farnham ✆ *(0252) 715318*

Original designer-jewellery in gold and silver, with some use of gemstones. Special commissions also undertaken.

Open Tue, Wed, Fri 10–5. Also open some Sats, advisable to telephone. Other times by appt. **C R D** *credit cards* ⓐ ⓥ ⊕

THE HOP KILNS GALLERY
(Alan and Carolyn Wallis) Weydon La ✆ *(0252) 725812*

One-off original designs handwoven in silk, wool and other natural fibres: wraps, shawls, jackets, tops and cloth-lengths. Also hand painted silk-screened prints of many subjects. Commissions also accepted.

Open Mon–Fri 9–5, Sat 9–12. Closed Xmas, Etr &
2 wks in Aug **C D** *credit cards* (a) (v) ⊕

Farrington Gurney

Avon **Map 3 ST65**

DECOY ART STUDIO
(Bob Ridges) 11m SE of Bristol ☎ *(0761) 52075*

Decorative ducks, geese and shore birds made
both in stylised (decoy) forms and feather-
textured realistic forms. A full range of decoy
books and carving supplies is available. Britain's only school of decorative decoy carving is
based here.

Open Mon–Fri 9–5.30, Sat 9–12, also wknds by
appt. Closed for lunch & Xmas **E D** ⊕

Felmingham

Norfolk **Map 9 TG22**

BELAUGH POTTERY
(Bridget Graver and George Simmons) Church Rd,
on B1145 between Aylsham & North Walsham
☎ *(0692) 403967*

Practical oven-to-table ware, cooking pots, coffee sets, teapots, plates etc, as well as individual pieces such as lamps, vases and bells.

Everything is produced in hand-thrown stoneware; commissions are also undertaken.

Open Mon–Sat 10–5 (closed Wed pm), Sun 2–4.30
C W E D ⊕ *by appt.*

Fence

Lancashire **Map 7 SD83**

SLATE AGE (FENCE) LTD
(P A and K M Rawlinson) Fence Gate, nr Burnley
☎ *(0282) 66952*

High-quality slate gift-ware is manufactured
on the premises and sold in the separate craft
shop. Hand-crafted in a choice of green or
black slate, the range includes clocks, ther-
mometers, pen stands and lamps.

Open Mon–Fri 8–4.30, Sat 8–4. Closed Xmas &
Etr **C W E D** *credit cards* (v) ⊕

Filkins

Oxfordshire **Map 4 SP20**

CROSS TREE CENTRE
(Sir John Cripps) Cross Tree, Filkins, nr Lechlade ☎
(036786) Cotswold Woollen Weavers 491; D Collett
505; G Payne & R Poole 522; Old Stable (0367)
52573 evngs; Cross Tree Gallery 494

Cross Tree Centre comprises a woollen mill, three craft workshops, an art gallery and a tea room. See below for details, and also feature on **p.16**. *Cotswold Woollen Weavers:* spinning and weaving of wool carried on by traditional methods in converted tithe barn. Clothes, rugs and other woollen goods for sale in large mill shop. Commissions for designers, architects, etc. also undertaken. Woolmark licensee. *D. Collett & Son*, stonemasons: General masonry, fireplaces, garden ornaments etc. *Geoff Payne & Robert Poole*: wood-turners and specialists in cane- and rush-seated furniture; *Old Stable Restorations & Woodcrafts*: specialists in restoring antique furniture; *Cross Tree Gallery*: exhibits paintings, prints and crafts by local Cotswold artists.

Open: Mill Mon–Sat 10–6, Sun 2–6. Closed Xmas-New Year **C W E D** *credit cards* ⓐ ⓥ ♿; *D Collett Mon–Fri 8–4.30 closed wknds & Xmas & Etr* **C R W D** ♿ *G Payne & R Poole Mon–Fri 10–6, Sat 10–3.30 by appt. Closed Xmas & Etr* **C R W D** ♿ *Old Stable Mon–Sat 10–6, Sun 3–5 Closed Xmas & Etr* **C R D** ♿ *Cross Tree Gallery Tue–Sat 10–1, 2–5.30 Closed Xmas & Etr* **C E D** *credit cards* ⓐ ⓥ ♿

Ford

Northumberland   **Map 11 NT93**

HIGH KILN CRAFTS

(N T and A Stobbs) Heatherslaw Mill, nr Cornhill-on-Tweed, between Ford & Etal on B6354
✆ *(089082) 291 (evngs & in winter) 328 (daytime in summer)*

Engraving with diamond-point on lead-crystal glasses. All subjects undertaken, except initials and crests.

Open daily Apr–Sep 11–6. Oct–Mar by appt. only. Closed Xmas **C D** ♿

Fordingbridge

Hampshire   **Map 4 SU11**

ALDERHOLT MILL

(John and Ann Pye) Sandleheath Rd, W of Fordingbridge off B3078 ✆ *(0425) 53130*

The picturesque old watermill houses all kinds of craftwork, much of which is made in Dorset and Hampshire. Stock includes woodwork, glass, ceramics, leatherwork, wooden toys and walking sticks. Art exhibitions in the gallery change every three weeks.

Open Tue, Wed, Thu, Fri & Sun 2–6, Sat & BHs 10–6. Closed Oct–mid Nov, Xmas & Etr **C D** ♿ *by appt.*

Fotheringhay

Northamptonshire   **Map 4 TL09**

FOTHERINGHAY FORGE

(J Barry Keightley) The Forge, behind Falcon Inn
✆ *(08326) 323 day; (0780) 782918 evngs*

Hand-crafted items produced in traditional manner and style, to customers' own designs if required. Products made in the 18th-century forge include fire canopies, fire baskets, fire irons, gates, garden furniture, weathervanes etc.

Open 9–4, also Sat am. Afternoons by appt. **C R D** ♿ *by appt. Evening demonstrations by arrangement.*

Framlingham

Suffolk   **Map 5 TM26**

HECTOR MOORE

(Hector B Moore AFCL) The Forge, Brandeston, nr Woodbridge ✆ *(072882) 354*

Old family business offering traditional and modern designs and techniques in blacksmithing, metalwork (including architectural and ecclesiastical) and sculpture. Many designs available: specialists in village signs.

Open Mon–Sat 8–5. Sat by appt. Closed Xmas, Etr & BHs **C R W E D** ♿

SHASHA TOPTANI

College Rd ✆ *(0728) 724206*

Leather, suede and sheepskin clothes tailor-made to order. Items are either made to original designs, to customer's own designs or to customer's choice of existing designs made up in other materials. Leather upholstery of furniture, vintage cars and horsedrawn carriages also undertaken.

Open daily 10–6, but advisable to telephone. Closed Xmas **C R W E D** ♿ *by appt.*

Frampton-on-Severn

Gloucestershire   **Map 3 SO70**

MARTIN COULBORN RESTORATIONS

(Paul and Sandra Coulborn) Chapel House, The Green ✆ *(0452) 740334/740125*

Cabinet-maker specialising in 18th-century styles of dining-room furniture. Restoration of antique furniture, including French-polishing, also undertaken.

Open Mon–Fri 9–6 by appt. Closed for lunch & Xmas, Etr & BHs **C R W D** ♿

Freshwater
Isle of Wight **Map 4 SZ38**
ALUM BAY GLASS LTD
(Mr M Rayner FSDC) Alum Bay ✆ (0983) 753473

Decorative glassware hand-made in a variety of carefully blended colours. The work includes animals, paperweights, vases, decanters, sculptures, fashion jewellery and pieces incorporating silver or stainless-steel. Visitors watch the glassblowers from the gallery.

Open daily 9.30–5 from Etr–mid Oct, Mon–Sat 9.30–5 in winter. Closed for lunch in winter & at Xmas **C W E D** *credit cards* ⓐ ⓥ ⓧ ⓓ 🚐

GOLDEN HILL FORT
For details, see pp 12 & 14

Frome
Somerset **Map 3 ST74**
SOMERSET SMITHY
(S J and C E Field) Christchurch St West ✆ (0373) 62609

Hand-crafted ornamental wrought-ironwork. Any item, decorative or functional, can be designed to suit individual and environmental requirements.

Open Mon–Fri 8–5. Closed Xmas, Etr & 2 wks in Jul/Aug **C R W E D** 🚐

Fulbeck Heath
Lincolnshire **Map 8 SK95**
FULBECK HEATH CRAFT CENTRE
(Mr and Mrs C Lemmon) Ryland Grange Cottage, nr RAF Cranwell on A17 ✆ (0400) 61563

Hand-carved wooden rocking horses decorated in a wide range of colours, painted ceramics

A coracle-maker using a draw knife

and soft toys – all made on the premises. Repair and restoration of rocking horses also undertaken. Tea and coffee available.

Open daily 9–8. Closed 25 & 26 Dec **R E D** 🚐 *by appt.*

Gilberdyke
North Humberside **Map 8 SE82**
JERRY HARPER POTTERY
Staddlethorpe La, Blacktoft, nr Goole, approach from A63/B1230 ✆ (0430) 41082

Individual, hand-made pieces of stoneware, plus a range of sprigged domestic ware which can be decorated with customer's own choice of design: Yorkshire Rose design in stock. Commemorative badges a speciality.

Open Mon–Sat 9–5.30, Sun 11–5, by appt. Closed Xmas **C W E D** 🚐 *by appt.*

Gislingham
Suffolk **Map 5 TM07**
PAULINE A BRACEGIRDLE POTTERY & CERAMICS
Lodge Cottage, Back St, nr Eye, off A140 through Thornham ✆ (0449) 781470

Colourful earthenware and ceramics: domestic and decorative pieces; some sculptural work; house signs and commemorative plates.

Open daily 10–7 (closed Fri until 2) **C W D** *credit cards* ⓐ ⓥ ⓧ ⓓ 🚐 *by appt.*

Glastonbury
Somerset **Map 3 ST43**
DOVE WORKSHOPS POTTERY
(Paul Stubbs – potter) Barton Rd, Butleigh, nr Glastonbury, midway between Butleigh & Barton St David ✆ (0458) 50385

Raw-glazed domestic stoneware and some 'Raku' individual pieces, all hand-thrown in the studio. Also woodworking and etching workshops on the premises: the former specialising in hammer dulcimers (musical instrument). Courses in all three subjects available.

Open Mon–Sat 9–5.30. Closed Xmas **C W E D** 🚐

WORKFACE GALLERY SHOP
(Face Ltd) Market Place ✆ (0458) 33917

A spacious gallery offering an extensive selection of products made by West-Country specialist-craftsmen. Some of the many crafts on display include: lacework; leatherwork;

woodwork; pottery; designer-clothing; basketry; wrought-ironwork and lapidary work.

Open Mon–Sat 9.30–5.30. Other times by appt. Closed Xmas **C R** *(referred to individual craftworker)* **D** *credit cards* ⓐ ⓥ ⓧ ⓓ 🚗 *preferably by appt.*

Gloucester
Gloucestershire   **Map 3 SO81**
COLIN SQUIRE AND JANICE WILLIAMS
Sheldon Cottage, The Bottoms, Epney, nr Saul ✆ (0452) 740639

Hand-woven rugs, cushions, bags, decorative hangings and commissioned fabrics for furnishing or dress in natural fibres. Many embroidered articles, but specialities are canvas work and metal-thread work for commemorative and ecclesiastical use. Tuition available. Members of the Crafts Council Index of Craftsmen.

Open any reasonable time, by appt. only **C W E D** 🚗

Godalming
Surrey   **Map 4 SU94**
MG HENKE WROUGHT-IRONWORK
(Marcus Henke BA) Hambledon House, Woodlands Rd, Hambledon. Take A283 to Petworth & turn r for Hambledon. ✆ (042879) 4343

Individually designed hand-forged wrought-ironwork made to commission. Gates, railings, balustrades, ornamental screens, fire-baskets and most items of decorative ironwork. Repair and restoration also undertaken.

Open Mon–Fri 9–6.30, Sat 9–1.30, by appt. **C R D** 🚗

Godstone
Surrey   **Map 4 TQ35**
PILGRIM HARPS
(John D Hoare and Michael Stevens) Stansted House, Tilburstow Hill Rd, 2 m S of Godstone ✆ (0342) 893242

Harp makers and restorers manufacturing a range of high-quality instruments: Celtic; folk; chromatic pedal; reconditioned 19th-century Grecian and Gothic. All available with alternative finishes. Covers, cases and makers' materials supplied.

Open Mon–Fri 8–6 & wknds, by appt. Closed Xmas **C R E D** 🚗

Goring-on-Thames
Berkshire   **Map 4 SU68**
JO DANIELLI LEATHERGOODS
The Old Vicarage, South Stoke, nr Reading, 1 m from Goring on B4009 to Wallingford ✆ (0491) 873690

Fashion accessories and traditional leathergoods individually hand-made – from original designs – in a wide range of styles and colour combinations.

Open Mon–Fri 10.30–5, by appt. Closed Xmas & some other times **C W E D** 🚗

Grantham
Lincolnshire   **Map 8 SK93**
ANNEDY CRAFTS
(Christopher and Anne Armstrong) Manor Farm Barn, Hough-on-the-Hill, nr Grantham ✆ (0400) 50037/61061

Children's and adults' knitwear made-to-measure. Customers' own designs used. Commissions undertaken for embroidery, tapestry and lace-work; also motif jumpers.

Visitors welcome any time, by appt. **C R D** 🚗

Grayshott
Surrey   **Map 4 SU83**
SURREY CERAMIC CO LTD
(David Real and Philip Bates) Grayshott Pottery, School Rd, just off A3 nr Hindhead ✆ (042873) 4404

An extensive selection of plain and decorated stoneware made on the premises. The range includes cookware, table lamps, vases, pot holders and useful novelty items. A variety of other sorts of craftwork and gifts is also available in the shop.

Shop open Mon–Sat 9–5. Workshop open Mon–Fri 9–4.30, Sat 2–4.30. Closed Xmas, Etr & BHs **W D** *credit cards* ⓐ ⓥ 🚗

Great Bookham
Surrey   **Map 4 TQ15**
GRANARY CRAFTS
(Jill and Margaret Sowerbutts) Church Rd ✆ (0372) 58600

All sorts of materials for different types of craftwork for sale. Stock includes linens, threads, canvases, beads, jute, cane, pewter, candlewax, paints, liquid lead, ribbons, parchment etc. Particular requirements of teachers in the area catered for.

Open Mon–Fri 9–5 (closed Wed pm) Sat 9–4. Closed for lunch, & Xmas & Etr **D** 🚌

Great Driffield
North Humberside   Map 8 SU09

IVY HOUSE
(Kelvin and Christine Lund) Mill St ✆ (0377) 47892

Makers and repairers of leaded windows and cabinets with leaded glass doors. A range of plain and etched mirrors is also available, and small items of furniture can be made to customer's specification.

Open Mon–Fri 8.30–5, also some Sats. Evngs by appt. Closed for lunch & Xmas & Etr **C R** *(some* **W**) **D** 🚲

ENGLISH COUNTRY FURNITURE
(Patrick Smith) The Old Chapel, Kirkburn, 4 m W of Driffield on A163 ✆ (0377) 89301

Three ranges of traditional and modern furniture, hand-made in various English hardwoods, always available. Also small items such as cheese- and bread-boards and round and oval picture frames. The ash furniture inlaid with rosewood is particularly attractive.

Open Mon–Fri 8–5, wknds 9–4. By appt. Sun & evngs. Closed for lunch & Xmas & Etr **C W E D** 🚌 *by appt.*

PATRICK TITE
Galloway La ✆ (0377) 43689

Domestic furniture in English oak and mahogany; mostly dining-room suites but also individual pieces. Wood-carving decoration on all types of furniture (including church and public building items), relief carving, wood-sculpture and hand-cut lettering; honours' boards for schools and other institutions are a speciality. All work made to order.

Open Mon–Fri 9–5, Sat 9–12. Other times by appt. Closed Xmas, Etr & BHs **C D** 🚌 *by appt.*

WOLD ANTIQUES
(John M De Boen) Main St, Wetwang, 7 m from Driffield on A166 ✆ (0377) 86428

Antiques and militaria for sale. All restoration of antique furniture also undertaken, as well as pine stripping for old doors, tables and other items of wood work.

Open daily 10–6. Closed Xmas **R D** & *Trade* 🚌 *by appt.*

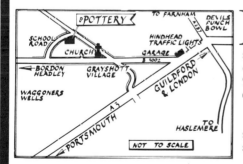

Great Dunmow

Essex   **Map 5 TL62**

JOHN RYE ROCKING HORSES
*(John and Susan Rye) 11 Rayfield Close, Barnston,
nr Gt Dunmow, off A130 Chelmsford rd ✆ (0371)
2548*

Hand-carved rocking horses made to traditional Edwardian and Victorian designs in pine
and beech. Safety stands or bow-rockers;
choice of colours; horsehair manes and tails;
leather tack. Horses also restored, made to
commission and carousel horses repaired.

Open by appt. only **C R W E D** ♿

Great Malvern

Hereford & Worcester   **Map 3 SO74**

HUGH CRAIG HARPSICHORDS
*(Hugh and Catherine Craig) Nupend House,
Cradley, just off Worcester–Hereford rd on Suckley
turn-off*

Manufacturers of fine early keyboard instruments from spinets to concert harpsichords.
Designs vary from copies of late 15th-to 18th-
century instruments to a range of 20th-century
instruments. Each piece is hand-built to
achieve the highest musical quality.

*Open Mon–Fri 10–4, Sat 10–1, by appt. Closed for
lunch & Xmas* **C R W E D** *credit cards*
ⓐ ⓥ ⓧ ⓓ ♿

LIONEL K HEPPLEWHITE
*(Lionel and Michael Hepplewhite) Soundpost, 8
North End La ✆ (06845) 62203*

Violins, violas and 'cellos hand-made in the
traditional manner to professional standards:
only the finest woods used. Commissions and
restoration work undertaken. Member of the
Crafts Council Index of Selected Makers.

Open by appt. only. Closed for lunch & Xmas & Etr
C R E D ♿

Great Missenden

Buckinghamshire   **Map 4 SP80**

'BASIA' STUDIO
*(Basia Watson-Gandy B.A. Hons, S.W.A.,
I.P.A.T.) Squirrel Court, Hare La, Little Kingshill,
turning by Nags Head PH ✆ (02406) 5441*

Hand-painted china and porcelain – especially
individually designed commissions and commemorative ware. Basia's work covers a wide
spectrum of subjects and cultures, from miniatures to historical pieces, and much of it
includes lustre and gold work.

Open by written appt. only **C W E D** *(mainly
personal orders and recommendations)* ♿

CONY CRAFTS
*(Mr S T Nowlan) Hale-Acre Workshops, Watchet
La, nr Gt Missenden ✆ (02406) 5668*

Established firm covering all aspects of antique
furniture restoration and period upholstery.
French-polishing, cabinet repairs and furniture
made to commission. Member of the Guild of
Master Craftsmen.

Open Mon–Fri 8–6, by appt. Closed Xmas **C** *(not
trade)* **R D** *credit cards* ⓐ ⓥ ⓧ ⓓ ♿

Great Ouseburn

North Yorkshire   **Map 8 SE46**

M H & J RAMPLING
*(Michael and Janice Rampling) Tarragoo, Branton
Green, nr Gt Ouseburn ✆ (09012) 3401*

Bespoke joinery and furniture made in solid
hardwoods. All types of loose and fitted furni-
ture, including windows, doors, staircases, etc.
Also a range of long-case clocks. Member of the
Guild of Master Craftsmen; Member of the
Federation of Master Builders.

Open Mon–Fri 8–5, & evngs, by appt. Closed BHs
C R D ♿

Great Strickland

Cumbria   **Map 11 NY52**

CAROL BLACK MINIATURES
Sun Hill, nr Penrith, opp. church ✆ (09312) 330

Dolls' house miniatures ($\frac{1}{12}$th scale) for collectors. The tremendous selection made in glass,
brass, copper, wood, ceramics etc, includes
work by over 40 British craftsmen, as well as by
Carol Black, whose speciality is miniature
patchwork quilts.

Open by appt. only **C E D** ♿

Great Torrington

Devon   **Map 2 SS41**

DARTINGTON GLASS LTD
School La ✆ (0805) 22321

A large selection of 24% lead-crystal glass
tableware and giftware is made at Dartington,
and every stage of the manufacturing process
can be seen in the factory.

*Tours every 30 mins 9.30–3.25 Mon–Fri (except
BHs). Factory shop open Mon–Fri 9–5, Sat 10–4.
Closed Xmas & Etr* **D** *credit cards* ⓐ ⓥ
♿ *by appt.*

WITHACOTT DRIED FLOWERS
(Andrew Payne Cook) Withacott Farm House, Langtree, nr Torrington ✆ (08055) 246

Pot-pourri, pomanders and posies in various containers are all made from the flowers and grasses grown and dried on the farm. A selection of grasses and everlasting flowers is always available, and arrangements can be made up to order.

Open Mon–Fri 10–6. **C R** *(some* **E**) **D** 🚲 *by appt.*

Grendon
Warwickshire   **Map 4 SP29**
CARTER POTTERY
(C J and J Carter) Highfields Farm, nr Atherstone, B4116 from Atherstone then turn l onto B5000 ✆ (08277) 3307

Good, hand-thrown oxidised stoneware. Tableware (vases, bowls, jugs etc) and individual pieces with a strong, lively character and an exciting use of traditional methods of decoration.

Open Mon–Fri 9–5, wknds 9–1 by appt. Closed Xmas & Etr **C W E D** 🚲

Grewelthorpe
North Yorkshire   **Map 8 SE27**
GREWELTHORPE HANDWEAVERS LTD
(M J and M B McDougall) nr Ripon, between Ripon & Masham ✆ (076583) 209

A range of English-elm handlooms and ancillary equipment for the home-weaver (produced in the workshop) is on display in the old hay-barn. Looms range from 21in-wide rigid heddle to 24in-wide four-shaft floor looms. Guided tours include demonstrations. The large craftshop on the premises has an exceptional range of gifts, a clothing department and maps, postcards etc. Refreshments are available.

Open Apr–Dec daily 10–6. Jan–Mar wknds only, or by appt. Closed Xmas **D** *credit cards* (a) (v) 🚲 *by appt.*

Guildford
Surrey   **Map 4 TQ04**
MICHAEL HEALE MUSICAL INSTRUMENTS
Market St ✆ (0483) 63096

The musical instruments made in Michael Heale's workshop are copied from antique examples of the 17th and 18th centuries: they are noted for their superb quality of performance. Most early stringed and keyboard instruments produced, but English consort viols a speciality.

Open Mon–Fri 8.30–5.30, by appt. Closed for lunch, & Xmas, Etr & BHs **C R W E D** 🚲

SCARAB KNITWEAR
(Vivien Calleja) 14 Beechcroft Drive ✆ (0483) 504942

Individually designed garments for men and women; coats, dresses, skirts, jackets, jumpers etc. Items are either hand-knitted, hand-crocheted or machine-knitted –or combinations of all three. Fair Isle patterns for hand-knitting made up and designs for electronic machines drawn. Vivien Calleja works from home but a selection of her knitwear can usually be seen at Arts of Petworth, Saddlers Row, Petworth, West Sussex.

Visitors welcome, by appt. only (some **C**) **D** 🚲

SMITHBROOK LTD
(R Cook) The Forge, Smithbrook, Cranleigh, 8 m from Guildford along A281 to Horsham ✆ (0483) 272744

Specialists in high-quality hand-made items in iron, copper and brass, with particular emphasis on lighting and traditional fireside accessories. Gates and garden furniture also made. Antiques are sold in the showroom as well.

Open Mon–Sat 8–5. Closed Xmas Etr & BHs **C R W E D** 🚲

Gunnislake
Cornwall   **Map 2 SX47**
DAVID PLAGERSON
5 Cliff View Terr ✆ (0822) 833035

Toymaker specialising in hand-made wooden Noah's Arks. These are available in mixed woods (with 14 pairs of animals), or painted (with 18 or 36 richly decorated pairs). The painted sets, which have been selected for the Design Centre, can be inscribed. Also circus, farm and wheeled toys.

Open daily 9–5, by appt. **C R W E D** 🚲

Gwithian
Cornwall   **Map 2 SW54**
DOBBIN DESIGNS
(John and Sheila Stafford) Churchtown House, nr Hayle ✆ (0736) 752536

Woodwork by John Stafford includes turned items, bowls, kitchenware, toys, rocking horses and jigsaws. Original screen prints and lithographs by Sheila Stafford and others.

Open Etr–Oct Tue–Sat 10–5. Other times by appt. Closed Xmas **C R W D** ♿

Hailsham
East Sussex   **Map 5 TQ50**
PEARTREE POTTERY
(Nigel and Christine Graham) Little Hackhurst Farm, Lower Dicker, nr Hailsham ✆ (0323) 844143

Hand-thrown stoneware for the kitchen and table. The pottery is decorated by hand in a variety of colours ranging from greenish-brown to white with blue detail.

Open Tue–Sun 10–6, but advisable to telephone **W E D** ♿

Halifax
West Yorkshire   **Map 7 SE02**
BULLACE TREES POTTERY
(K A and D E E Howley) Triangle, Sowerby Bridge, ¾ m from Sowerby Bridge on A58 towards Rochdale ✆ (0422) 832356

Specialists in making ceramic dolls, including porcelain and earthenware doll kits with full instructions. All figures are modelled by hand. Decorative earthenware and stoneware – both individually thrown pieces and cast-ware – is also made on the premises.

Open any time, but advisable to telephone. Closed 25 & 26 Dec, & week before Etr **C W E D** ♿

Hamstall Ridware
Staffordshire   **Map 7 SK11**
RIDWARE ARTS CENTRE
(Chris and Jennifer Hobbs) Hamstall Hall, nr Rugeley, app. from A515 or B5014 ✆ (088922) 351

The outbuildings of Hamstall Hall have been converted into a centre for artistic endeavour. There is an exhibition gallery and a large craft shop in the Malt House, where pottery, wood, leather, jewellery, glass, ironwork, textiles etc can be found. The centre is still developing and resident craftsmen include a picture-framer/ photographer; there are still workshops to let. Refreshments, including lunches and teas, are available at the restaurant.

Open Tue–Sun 10.30–5.30. Also open BHs. Closed Xmas **C R D** ♿ *by appt.*

A sycamore roller used for stamping shortbread

Hanbury

Hereford & Worcester   **Map 3 SO96**

JINNEY RING CRAFT CENTRE
(R and J Greatwood) nr Bromsgrove ✆ *(052784) 272* **(See also feature on p. 12)**

The following craftsmen have workshops at the craft centre: Peter Hill, stained-glass artist; Tim Bryan, leathermaker; Bridget Drakeford, potter; Bill Piper Sproat, woodcarver; Richard Greatwood, wood-turner.

Open Wed–Sat 10.30–5, Sun 2–5.30 **C R D** *credit cards* ⓐ Ⓥ 🚗

Hanley Castle

Hereford & Worcester   **Map 3 SO84**

MIDSUMMER WEAVERS
(Sigi Gonnsen) The Old School, Cross Hands, nr Upton-upon-Severn ✆ *(0684) 310045*

Hand-woven fabrics (mainly woollens of all weights) produced on 50-year-old Hattersley domestic looms. Finished items include scarves, ties, smocks and skirts, which are for sale in the craft shop together with other locally-made goods, for example, pottery, candles, jewellery etc.

Open Mon–Sat 9.30–5.30. Closed Xmas **C W E D** *credit cards* ⓐ Ⓧ 🚗

Harbottle

Northumberland   **Map 11 NT90**

SPINDLES OF HARBOTTLE
(M Krajewski) Lightpipe Hall, nr Morpeth ✆ *(0669) 50243*

Makers and restorers of spinning wheels and spinning chairs: all accessories (including fleece) and looms supplied. High-quality wood-turned items and small pieces of furniture include lamp bases and corner cabinets. Woollen garments, plus crocheted, sewn and embroidered work, also for sale. Tuition is available.

Open Apr–Sep daily 11–6. During winter, open most wknds, or by appt. Closed Xmas & Etr **C R D** 🚗

Harleston

Norfolk   **Map 5 TM28**

MILLHOUSE POTTERY
(Alan and Ann Frewin) 1 Station Rd ✆ *(0379) 852556*

Large selection of weatherproof pots ranging from cactus-size to giant tubs for trees. Many have imaginative decoration based on dragon, landscape and animal themes using half-relief and slipware techniques. Also a range of domestic ware including pie and tart plates, cider jars, jugs, mugs etc. Personalised Celebration Plates a speciality. Tea and coffee available.

Open Tue–Sun 10–5. Advisable to telephone on Sun & Tue **C W D** 🚗 *by appt.*

Harlington

Bedfordshire   **Map 4 TL03**

HARLINGTON ARMS STABLE POTTERIES
(Doug Hillyard) 7 Station Rd, nr Dunstable, 2 mins from M1, junction 12 ✆ *(05255) 2582*

Functional and decorative stoneware which has been reduction-fired in a gas kiln. Demonstrations can be given, by appointment.

Open Wed–Sun 10–6. Closed 25 Dec & Etr Mon **C D** 🚗 *by appt.*

Harrow

Greater London   **Map 4 TQ18**

GLASS BY DAVID LTD
(David Robert Smith) Unit 1, 26/28 Masons Ave, Wealdstone, nr Harrow ✆ *01-863-6918*

Manufacturers of delicate, hand-made glassware specialising in small gift items. Different ranges include flowers in pots, jewellery, perfume bottles, swizzle-sticks, drinks barrels, plus oil, salt and spaghetti dispensers. Commissions also undertaken.

Open Mon–Fri 9–5, wknds 10–4, by appt. Closed Xmas & Etr **C W E D** *credit cards* ⓐ 🚗 *by appt.*

Hartland

Devon   **Map 2 SS22**

FORD HILL FORGE
(R H Conibear) nr Bideford ✆ *(02374) 208*

Blacksmithing, agricultural repairs and farrier

work all undertaken in the forge where visitors are welcome. A range of wrought-ironwork is on sale in the showroom. One of the Hartland Workshops, see *Clovelly*.

Open Mon–Fri 9–5.30, Sat 9–1. Closed Xmas, Etr & BHs **C R W D** ⊕

Hartley Wintney
Hampshire   **Map 4 SU75**
WINCHFIELD POTTERY
(Susan Ferraby) The Chase, Winchfield, nr Hartley Wintney, by Winchfield station ✆ *(025126) 2476*

Hand-thrown domestic and decorative stoneware, plus some semi-porcelain work. Wall clocks a speciality, but also lamps, storage pots, jugs, teapots etc. The work is decorated and patterned in a Chinese style.

Open most days, but advisable to telephone. Closed Xmas **C D** ⊕ *by appt.*

Harworth
Nottinghamshire   **Map 8 SK69**
THE GALLERY
(Robert Howard) The Pottery, Tickhill Rd, village is between Tickhill and Bantry, 1 m from A1 ✆ *(0302) 743838*

Tableware, plant pots, ornamental and novelty pieces in Raku, porcelain and stoneware. Also paintings, drawings and prints.

Open Mon, Tue, Wed all day, wknds pm only. Closed Xmas **C W E D** ⊕ *by appt.*

Hastings
East Sussex   **Map 5 TQ80**
RAYMOND HARRIS
Silver Birches Cottage, Rock La, Guestling, nr Hastings, 1 m from Ore Post Office on A259 to Rye; turn 1st l after DIY store. ✆ *(0424) 431264*

Traditional fire bellows made in English elm, oak, chestnut, mahogany and pine with English leather and brass work. Faces may be decorated or plain. Martingales made from 3–4 mm hide with solid brass fittings and English horse-brasses.

Open wknds 9–5, by appt. Closed for lunch & Xmas **C R W E D** ⊕

Hatherleigh
Devon   **Map 2 SS50**
ELIZABETH AYLMER POTTERY
Widgery House, 20 Market St ✆ *(0837) 810624*

Hand-thrown domestic stoneware plus plant and garden items. Also thrown and coiled individual pots decorated with ethnic designs. Visitors welcome in the studio.

Open Mon–Fri 10–5. Also wknds by appt. **C W E D** ⊕ *by appt. only*

Hathersage
Derbyshire   **Map 8 SK28**
HATHERSAGE POTTERY
(Gordon Evans) Leach Barn, Leadmill, off B6001 Grindleford rd ✆ *(0433) 50629*

Traditionally-styled stoneware pottery designed for tourist and souvenir markets. Specialists in stamped and impressed designs and lettering: named items supplied to pubs, hotels, restaurants etc. Business gifts and promotional goods made to commission.

Open to trade only, by appt. **W** ⊕

Hatley St George
Cambridgeshire   **Map 4 TL25**
CHURCH FARM WORKSHOPS
(Anne Hysted FGA) 4 Church Farm Workshops, nr Sandy, 12 m W of Cambridge ✆ *(0767) 51482*

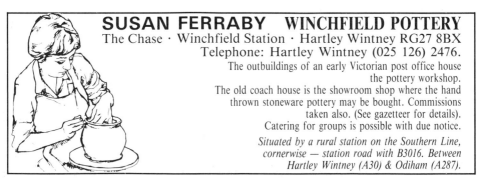

Modern designer-jewellery made in gold, silver and niobium. Special pieces designed individually to commission.

Visitors by appt. only **C R W D** ⌗

Hawes

North Yorkshire   **Map 8 SD88**

W R OUTHWAITE & SON, ROPEMAKERS
(Dr and Mrs P Annison) Town Foot, on A684 adjacent to Old Station Car Park ✆ *(09697) 487*

Rope products of all sorts are made here, using the traditional method, and visitors are welcome to watch the complete process. Products include bannister and barrier ropes; church bell ropes; ropes for agricultural and equestrian use, braids, cords and twines. Admission free.

Open Mon–Fri 9–5.30. Also most BH Mons, & most Sats in school hols 10–4. Closed for lunch & Xmas–New Year **C W D** *School parties and family-sized groups with adult(s) welcome by appt.*

WENSLEYDALE POTTERY
(Simon J B Shaw) Market Place ✆ *(09697) 594*

A full range of oven-to-table ware which can be put into dishwashers and microwaves. Many reasonably-priced gift and souvenir items, and commissions taken for commemorative pieces.

Open Mon–Sat 10–6 **C D** ⌗ *by appt.*

Hawkshead

Cumbria   **Map 7 SD39**

ESTHWAITE POTTERY
(Avis and Bernard Loshak) nr Ambleside ✆ *(09666) 241*

A good range of table and kitchen ware in oxidised stoneware. Also pots for plants

(including bonsai pots), a large variety of vases, CND brooches and mugs, and special individual pieces. Visitors are welcome to the showroom only.

In summer, showroom is open daily 9.30–6; in winter by appt or by chance. Please ring the bell. **C D** ⌗

Heighington

Co Durham   **Map 8 NZ22**

THE FORGE
(Stephen Jackson) The Forge, c/o The Dog Public House, nr Darlington ✆ *(0325) 312152/321633*

Ornamental fire baskets, gates, railings, companion sets and garden furniture. General light steel fabrication and agricultural repairs undertaken.

Open Mon–Fri 9–5. Closed for lunch & Xmas **C R D** ⌗

Helmdon

Northamptonshire   **Map 4 SP54**

MIKE GIDMAN
1 Stone Cottage, Falcutt, nr Brackley ✆ *(02805) 675*

All kinds of small wood-turned items, including lace bobbins and lace-bobbin winders, trinket boxes, door and drawer knobs, table lamps, plates, trays and tankards.

Open by appt. only **C W E D** ⌗

Helmsley

North Yorkshire   **Map 8 SE68**

WOLD POTTERY
(Jill Christie) Main St, Harome, 2 m from Helmsley off A170 ✆ *(0439) 70805*

Hand-thrown earthenware slip-decorated in blues, greens, browns and cream. Specialities are coffee and wine sets, embossed commemorative pieces and pots impressed with real leaves of various kinds.

Open Mon–Sat. Closed Xmas C W E D 🚌

Helston
Cornwall   **Map 2 SW62**
GUNWALLOE POTTERY
(Deborah Prosser B.A.) Trenoweth Farm, Gunwalloe: leave Helston on A3083 & turn r to Church Cove & Gunwalloe ✆ (0362) 240854

Barrels as garden seats or occasional tables; domestic ware; garden ware; bottles; wall hangings and tiles produced in terracotta and shiny glazed earthenware. Six different colours available, plus coloured decoration on a cream background.

Open during daylight hours, but advisable to telephone C W E D 🚌

TRELOWARREN POTTERY
(Nic and Jackie Harrison) Trelowarren, Mawgan, take A3083 from Helston, turn l onto B3293 then turn l at Garras & follow drive to Trelowarren House ✆ (032622) 583

A wide range of oven-to-table and domestic stoneware is hand-thrown in the studio where visitors are always welcome. Many individually designed pieces can also be seen in the showroom, as well as a selection of hand-woven decorative and practical rugs for the floor or wall.

Open daily 10–6 C D 🚌 *by appt.*

Henley-on-Thames
Oxfordshire   **Map 4 SU78**
OLD LUXTERS VINEYARD & WINERY
(David and Fiona Ealand) Old Luxters Farmhouse, Hambleden, nr Henley-on-Thames ✆ (049163) 330

A vineyard producing white grapes: their own 'Chiltern Valley' white wine is made on the premises.

Visitors welcome by appt. only C *(wine made)* W E D 🚌 *by appt.*

Hereford
Hereford & Worcester   **Map 3 SO54**
HILL COTTAGE POTTERY
(Wendy Nolan) Wellington, 6 m N of Hereford on A49 ✆ (043271) 236

A wide selection of ceramics ranging from garden ware, jardinières etc to teapots and tableware. The work, executed in stoneware and porcelain, is decorated with various colours and modelling techniques. House names and commemorative plates made to commission, and portraits in terracotta also undertaken.

Open daily 10–8. Closed Xmas C R W D 🚌 *by appt.*

H J & D HOBBS & CO
Karinya, Tump La, Much Birch ✆ (0981) 540516

Manufacturers of leaded-light windows, panels, lights and screens. The glass can be stained, painted, etched or blasted using both traditional and modern designs.

Open Mon–Fri 8–5.30. Closed for lunch C R W E D 🚌

KEMBLE GALLERY
(The Society of Craftsmen) 29 Church St ✆ (0432) 266049

The Gallery is the retail outlet for work by members of The Society of Craftsmen, which is a member of West Midlands Arts and a group member of the British Crafts Centre. Many crafts are represented in the shop, including ceramics, sculpture, weaving, knitting, book-

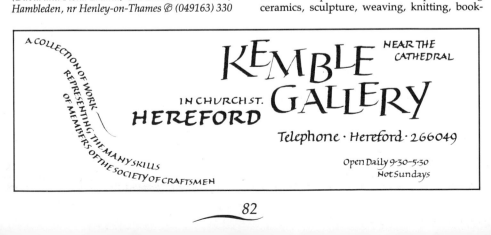

binding, woodwork, jewellery, painting and screen-printing.

Open Mon–Sat 9.30–5.30. Closed BHs **C D** *credit cards* ⓐ ⓥ

JOHN NETHERCOTT

(J W Nethercott and A D Murley) Showroom: 30 Church St ✆ (0432) 54730; workshop, Upper House, Discoed, Presteigne, Powys ✆ (05476) 369

Fine furniture made from native hardwoods in various traditional English and Welsh styles. The craftsmen's expertise in antique restoration (a service they still provide) enables them to produce pieces that are comparable to existing antiques. Items made to order.

Please telephone workshop for opening times **E D**

GERALD & VERA TAYLOR

Winforton Court, Winforton, between Hereford & Leominster on A438 ✆ (05446) 226

The farm outbuildings here are being converted into a complex for the buying, selling and restoration of fine antiques. At present clocks (both mechanisms and dials), oil paintings and furniture are restored. Long-case clocks and painted dials are a speciality, and other skills include gilding and lacquer work. There is a large showroom of antiques.

Open any time, by appt. **C R**

Herstmonceux

East Sussex **Map 5 TQ61**

PLAYSTERS

(R G Bingham) New Rd ✆ (0323) 833538

Manufacturers of traditional Sussex trug baskets ranging from 4 ins to 22 ins in length.

Open by appt. only **C W D**

SUSSEX WINDSORS

(Barry M and Mary B Murphy) Dormer's Farmhouse, Windmill Hill, just outside Herstmonceux on A271 at Windmill Hill ✆ (0323) 832388

Makers of various traditionally-styled Windsor chairs and stools (including high-chairs) in ash and elm. Several different country-style tables made from English hardwoods are available to order.

Open daily 9–5. Closed for lunch & Xmas **C D**

THE TRUGGERY

(David and Sue Sherwood) Coopers Croft, on the edge of village towards Hailsham ✆ (0323) 832314

Cabriole leg with acanthus design

Traditional Sussex trugs, made by hand in a variety of sizes, plus many sorts of English-willow baskets – shopping, log, pet etc. Various wood-turned gifts, pyrography and cane furniture also for sale.

Open Tue–Sat 10–5.30. Also open BHs. Closed Xmas **C D** *but small groups welcome by appt.*

Hesket Newmarket

Cumbria **Map 10 NY33**

MAURICE MULLINS – WOODTURNER & DESIGNER

No. 1 Brickhouse Cottage, nr Wigton ✆ (06998) 645

Maurice Mullins designs and makes a wide range of articles in a variety of woods. From miniatures to standard lamps, the designs vary from the simple to the ornate. His work can also be seen at Eden Craft Gallery, St Andrews Churchyard, Penrith and Guild of Lakeland Craftsmen, Sheepskin Centre, Lake Rd, Keswick.

Open Mon–Fri 9–5, also wknds, by appt. Closed for lunch & Xmas & Etr **C W D**

Hexham

Northumberland **Map 11 NY96**

ROBERT ARCHBOLD–VIOLINS

31 Hencotes ✆ (0434) 604694

Violins, violas and 'cellos sold, repaired and restored. Instruments in any condition purchased.

Open Mon–Sat 9–5.30. Closed Xmas, Etr & BHs **R D** *credit cards* ⓧ

BLACKSMITH SHOP
(S Pike) Bears Bridge, Whitfield, nr Hexham
✆ *(04985) 210*

High-quality ornamental ironwork, including fire grates, fire dogs, weathervanes, gates, railings and small hand-tools. Leaf-work and restoration work also undertaken.

Open Mon–Fri 8.30–5, Sat 9–4. Closed Xmas & Etr **C R W E D** ⛨ *by appt.*

BORDERCRAFT
(Mrs B Coggins) 4 Market St ✆ *(0434) 603060*

Specialists in hand-made fashion knitwear (mainly using natural fibres), Arans and Guernseys. A wide range of yarns is also for sale, and a made-to-measure service is available. Many British-made craft goods – jewellery, pottery, glass etc – are sold in the shop as well.

Open Mon–Sat 9.30–5 **C D** ⛨

AUSTIN WINSTANLEY
19b Priestpopple, in yard opp. Coach & Horses Inn
✆ *(0434) 602267*

Leatherworker and case-maker specialising in musical instrument cases, photographic gadget bags and luggage. All work is hand-made in best-quality hide and aircraft ply, and is padded and lined.

Open Mon–Fri 9–6 (approx), preferably by appt. Wknds by appt. only. Closed for lunch & Xmas & Etr. May sometimes be closed at other times **C R D** ⛨

High Wycombe
Buckinghamshire   **Map 4 SU89**

BROWNS OF WEST WYCOMBE
(D A Hines, Director) Church La, West Wycombe
✆ *(0494) 24537*

Chair-makers and specialist cabinet makers who work to commission. The restoration of antique furniture is also undertaken.

Open Mon–Fri 8.30–5.30, by appt. only. Closed Xmas, Etr & annual holidays **C R W E D** ⛨

THE GLASS MARKET
(Gerald Paxton, Managing Director) Broad La, Wooburn Green, nr High Wycombe ✆ *(04946) 71033*

A unique centre for decorative-glass processes with craftsmen specialising in stained-glass, glass-blowing, bevelling, kiln-work and sand-etching. A wide range of ornaments, lamps, mirrors etc, for sale. Materials, equipment and tuition available for stained-glass enthusiasts.

Open Tue–Sat 9.30–5. **C R W E D** *Credit cards* ⓐ Ⓥ ⛨ *by appt.*

CHARLES K HOLE
Derwent, 1 Green La, Radnage, nr High Wycombe, off A40 near Stokenchurch ✆ *(024026) 3263*

Specialist in the restoration of small pieces of antique furniture, boxes and treen – a selection of which can be purchased from stock. Also gives illustrated lectures on the restoration and history of British antique furniture.

Open by appt. only **R D** ⛨

Hilton
Derbyshire   **Map 8 SK23**

DAVID WHYMAN – CRYSTAL ENGRAVER
Willowtree Studio, Willowpit La, nr Hilton, off A516 towards Sutton-on-the-Hill ✆ *(028373) 3908*

A wide selection of engraved crystal is on display in the showroom and any subject – animals, birds, portraits etc, can be engraved to commission. Demonstrations take place in
→ **p. 89**

CRAFTSPEOPLE AT WORK

D **espite the availability** of mass-pro-
duced goods, there is always a
demand for the hand-crafted item.
Some of the crafts illustrated here are
centuries old: bookbinding, for example,
was first practised in Britain by Celtic and
Anglo-Saxon monks in the 8th century;
pipe-making, on the other hand, is rela-
tively recent, at least in Britain where
tobacco was first introduced in the 16th
century. Old or new, traditional or
specialised, all crafts share a common
characteristic: the triumph of individu-
ality over standardisation.

Fine bindings for libraries and collectors

Some traditional crafts: sculptor John Skelton *(above)* carving a shepherd's crook, and *(left)* pipe-making at the Tilshead Pipe Company near Salisbury. Church bell-ropes *(top left)* had to be made by hand because each needed to be of a different length. These ships' figureheads *(top right)* were made by Trevor Ellis in Coverdale, Yorkshire, and *(right)* tarpaulin-makers at Dobie Wyatt Ltd near Marlborough

Clare Craft Pottery

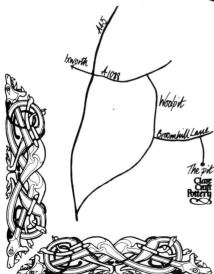

From the Earths of the Far North
From the Gases of the Buried Past
From the Metals decayed by Time,
We fashion the World of Tolkien,
of Arthur of Njalli, of Snori, the
Saga Makers of the North & the
Dreamakers of the Isle of Saints,
Finbars Lighthouse, sharp Hedins
Treasure, & Asgrims Jewels.

All can be found at Our
Workshops.

the workshop every Saturday. Paintings, pottery, furniture, metal sculptures also for sale.

Open Tue–Sat 10–5. Closed Xmas **C D** ⊕

Hindhead

Surrey   **Map 4 SU83**

COLUMBINE CRAFTS
(Gillian Rawcliffe) Crossways Rd, Grayshott, S of Hindhead off A3 ℗ *(042873) 5220*

A good range of unusual gift-items at reasonable prices. Stock includes soft toys, hand-modelled miniature houses and brooches, mobiles, wooden toys, cushions, jewellery etc.

Open Mon–Sat 9.30–5 (closed Wed pm) Closed for lunch & Xmas, Etr & BHs **C R W E D** ⊕

Holme

Cumbria   **Map 7 SD57**

ROBIN & NELL DALE
Bank House Farm, Holme Mills, Holme, via Carnforth (postal address Lancashire) ℗ *(0524) 781646*

Original hand-made and hand-painted chess sets (for example with Alice through the Looking Glass or King Arthur characters) and wooden figures depicting many different characters and costumes. Unusual commissions – of any size – welcomed.

Open (workshop only, no showroom) Mon–Fri 9–5, also wknds, by appt. Closed Xmas **C R W E D** ⊕

Holme-upon-Spalding-Moor

North Humberside   **Map 8 SE83**

ROCKING HORSE SHOP
(Anthony and Pat Dew) Old Rd ℗ *(0696) 60563*

Hand-carved traditional dapple-grey rocking horses with real horsehair manes and tails and adjustable leather tack. Complete renovation of old rocking horses undertaken and a very comprehensive stock of accessories is generally available.

Open Mon–Sat 9–6, by appt. Closed Xmas **C R E D** ⊕

Holt

Dorset   **Map 4 SU00**

HOLT CRAFT CENTRE
(M O and V S Parnell) Holt Green Farm, nr Wimborne ℗ *(0202) 887211*

Several independent craftsmen work within the 400-year-old farm's outbuildings which have been turned into a co-operatively-run craft centre. Their skills include cane-seating, wood-turning, fly-tying, taxidermy, brass-rubbing, needlework, clock-repairing. Tea room.

Open Mon–Fri 10–5, wknds 11–5. Closed Xmas & Etr **C R D** 🚗 *by appt.*

Holt

Norfolk **Map 9 TG03**

CHARLES MATTS FURNITURE
11 Fish Hill ✆ (026371) 3088

For details, see entry under Aylsham

STAINED GLASS & SCULPTURE STUDIO
(Jane and Paul Quail) Boundary Farmhouse, Gunthorpe, 6 m W of Holt on A148 ✆ (0263) 860826

Paul Quail (FMGP, FSD-C) designs and makes stained-glass, both contemporary and traditional in design, for churches and other buildings. Jane Quail sculpts in stone, ivory and wood. From small ivories to large figures, her subjects are both religious and genre. Both work to commission only.

Open by appt. **C R E D** 🚗

Using a rasp to shape a bow

P H ROBERTS & CO
27 Bull St ✆ (0263) 713803

Furniture-makers, turners and restorers of antique furniture, offering a complete service from advice to delivery. Made to individual requirements, furniture includes both modern pieces in light woods with bold inlays and fine reproductions in oak, mahogany and walnut.

Open Mon–Sat 9–5.30. Closed for lunch & Xmas & BHs. **C R E D** *credit cards* ⓐ ⓥ ⓧ 🚗

Honiton

Devon **Map 3 ST10**

CAROLINE RITCHIE – POTTERY
Shorehead, Stockland, nr Honiton, take Stockland rd; go over 1st crossroads then 1st r to Shorebottom, after ¼ m house faces you ✆ (040488) 485

Hand-thrown stoneware decorated in bright reds and blues. The range includes bowls, jugs, vases, cheese and butter bells – all in copper-red with heart and flower motifs, and bread-crocks with bread-board lids.

Open Mon–Sat 9–6. Closed Xmas **C W E D** 🚗

HONITON POTTERY LTD
(Mr and Mrs Redvers) 30 High St ✆ (0404) 2106

The pottery produces a wide range of table and gift ware, and specialises in souvenirs and commemorative plates. Visitors are able to see each stage of production. The showroom has 'seconds' as well as first-grade stock.

Factory & shop open Mon–Fri 9–4.30. Shop only open Sat. Closed for lunch & Xmas **C W E D** *credit cards* ⓐ ⓥ 🚗

Horncastle

Lincolnshire **Map 9 TF26**

PETER DAVIS
Endwood Cottage, East Rd, Tetford, nr Horncastle ✆ (065883) 228

Furniture hand-made to order, including fitted furniture. Wood-turning and antique-restoration also undertaken.

Open (workshop only, no showroom) Mon–Fri 8–6, Sat 9–1, by appt. Closed for lunch & Xmas & Etr **C R D** 🚗

Hornton

Oxfordshire **Map 4 SP34**

LIONEL W GIBBS (HORNTON) LTD
Horley Rd, between A41 & A422 nr Banbury ✆ (029587) 310

Traditional ornamental ironwork manufacture, including ornamental gates, balustrades, fire-baskets, canopies and large-scale emblems in copper, steel and stainless steel.

Open Mon–Fri 8–5, Sat 8–12, other times by appt. Closed Xmas & Etr **C R D** 🚐

Horsham
West Sussex   **Map 4 TQ13**

DREAMGLOW CANDLES
(David and Kay Wardle) Unit A, Lyons Holding, Lyons Rd, Slinfold, nr Horsham ✆ *(0403) 790885*

All sorts of candles made by hand, using both traditional and novel methods.

Open by appt. only. Closed Xmas & Etr **C W D** 🚐

SHAL DESIGN
(C M Grace Hosking) 134 Brighton Rd ✆ *(0403) 69844*

Decorative glass-topped coffee tables individually hand-painted on reverse of panel, signed and numbered by Grace Hosking. Designs (© Barbara Leslie) inspired by antique and natural sources: colours adaptable to customer's requirements. Solid mahogany bases to order.

Open by appt. only **E D** 🚐

Houghton
Cambridgeshire   **Map 4 TL27**

ALICE GREEN CRAFTS
(Alice Green and Peter Martin) Monument House, Thicket Rd ✆ *(0480) 300977*

An extensive range of Venetian-style flower jewellery in various designs and colours, plus some pyrography work (e.g. house signs). Also for sale in the shop a variety of British-made craft goods ranging from toys to sweaters.

Open daily 10–5.30 (closed Wed). Closed for lunch **C R W E D** 🚐 *by appt.*

Hove
East Sussex   **Map 4 TQ20**

EILEEN LEWENSTEIN
11 Western Esplanade, Portslade, Brighton ✆ *(0273) 418705*

Eileen Lewenstein's ceramic work has been widely exhibited and can be seen in the Victoria & Albert Museum and many other collections. She makes individual bowls and vases as well as relief panels and sculptures.

Open by appt. only **C W E D** 🚐

Hull
North Humberside   **Map 8 TA02**

MEL RIDGERS – WOOD TURNER
Corner House, Main St, Brandesburton, nr Driffield, off A165 N of Hull ✆ *(0401) 42503*

Unusual, individual wood-turned items, each designed to emphasise the unique character of various British hardwoods. Also domestic woodware such as bowls, plates etc.

Open Mon–Fri 9–6 (closed Tue pm), wknds 10–4. Closed Xmas & Etr **C R D** 🚐 *by appt.*

Huntingdon
Cambridgeshire   **Map 4 TL27**

SPICE COTTAGE CERAMICS
(Mrs Jenifer Willoughby-Fletcher) Frumetty La, Alconbury, 5 m N of Huntingdon off A1 and A604 ✆ *(0480) 891406*

Sculpted portraits of people and animals in terracotta and other clays (to order), plus 'bird-form' plant containers, garden sculpture reliefs and lettered plaques. Painted wooden clock-mounts, boxes and signs by Melanie Targett.

Open by appt. only **C R W E D** 🚐

Ickleton
Cambridgeshire   **Map 5 TL44**

DAVID AND JEAN WHITAKER
Frogge Cottage, 48 Frogge St ✆ *(0799) 30304*

Furniture-makers and wood-turners producing a selection of original hand-made furniture in English hardwoods: specialists in chair-making. Wood-turned items range from domestic ware to stools; architectural and replacement turnery is also undertaken.

Open Mon–Fri 8.30–6, Sat 9–4.30. Closed Xmas **C E D** 🚐

Ingatestone
Essex   **Map 5 TQ69**

GEO. CARFORD LIMITED
(Mr A G Careless) Ingatestone Forge, 3A High St ✆ *(0277) 353026*

All kinds of blacksmithing undertaken, including sheet metal, fabrication and security work. Traditional ornamental ironwork – gates, fire-hoods, weathervanes, lanterns etc – made mostly to commission.

Open Mon–Fri 8.30–5, Sat 9–1, by appt. Closed Xmas & Etr **C R W E D** 🚐

Ipswich
Suffolk   **Map 5 TM14**

B C M WAREHOUSE
(Mr Ray Belsher) St Lawrence St, Buttermarket
⊘ (0473) 57550

Hundreds of craft goods including basketware, mats, mugs, kitchenware, glassware, corn dollies and candles, as well as beads, posters, fancy tins, fans and earring findings.

Open Mon–Sat 9.30–5.30. Closed Xmas & Etr & BHs **D** 🚐

CHRISSY NORMAN KNITWEAR
(Peter and Chrissy Norman) 468 Woodbridge Rd
⊘ (0473) 77991

Pure new wool designer-knitwear, including a range of colourful 'fun' sweaters with motifs featuring elephants, frogs, pigs etc. Licensed to use the 'Woolmark' trade mark.

Open (wholesale trade) Mon, Tue, Thu, Fri 9.30–5 by appt. Closed for lunch & Xmas & Etr. Open Sat for retail by appt. **W E D** *credit cards* ⓐ Ⓥ 🚐

Ironbridge
Shropshire   **Map 7 SJ60**

MAWS CRAFT CENTRE
Jackfield, Telford (across river from Coalport Museum) ⊘ (0952) see individual numbers below

Several craftsmen work here and regular exhibitions are held. There is also a coffee shop. Elizabeth Crafts (883699) slatework; Tangent (882088) Tiffany lamps and shades; Sabrina Leathercrafts (883128) belts, bags and musical instruments; Winterwood Pottery (883642) decorative stoneware; Paul Sheratt, furniture designer; Dave Trainer (883909) ceramics; Countryman Decor (883480) restorers and cabinet makers; Brendan Conway (883906) stonemason; Toggles, children's knitwear; Juliet Enkel, paintings, murals and drawings; Adora Design (883552) soft toys.

Open Mon–Fri 9–5, wknds 12–6. Closed Xmas. Advisable to telephone if particular workshop wanted. **C R W E D** *(varies with each business)* 🚐

STUDIO 6
(Mrs M Dentith) Maws Craft Centre (see above) ⊘ (0952) 883565 (studio); 882121 (home)

All kinds of knitted goods which have been made on sophisticated machines using both natural and man-made yarns.

Open most afternoons, but advisable to telephone **C W E D** 🚐

Ivybridge
Devon   **Map 2 SX65**

MIRROR RESILVERING
(Michael Vaughan) Unit 4, Ermington Workshops, Ivybridge, nr Modbury ⊘ (0548) 830023

Old and antique mirrors completely restored. Old silver is removed and glass is polished to a high degree to remove blemishes, then re-silvered using a 120-year-old formula. If lettering is to be renovated, work is given to a traditional signwriter familiar with the techniques required. Michael Vaughan also runs a silversmith's workshop making all kinds of silverware, but specialising in hollow ware – cream jugs, christening mugs, boxes, drinking vessels. Also spoons, napkin rings, frames etc. For enquiries, please telephone.

Open (mirror workshop) Mon–Fri 8.30–5, Sat 8.30–12 **C R D** 🚐

Kemble
Gloucestershire   **Map 3 ST99**

WESTERN-VILLE POTTERY
(Carol L Butler) nr Cirencester, next to Kemble railway station ⊘ (028577) 651

Good, practical, domestic stoneware such as casseroles, teapots, jugs, bowls and mugs, in a variety of glazes. Also bonsai containers and a range of small, terracotta plant pots.

Open daily 9–6 **C D** 🚐

Kendal
Cumbria   **Map 7 SD59**

LAKELAND SKIRTS
(Margaret and Colin Milton) Crooklands, Milnthorpe, 5 m SE of Kendal off A65 (telephone for further directions) ⊘ (04487) 310

Lakeland Skirts operate a made-to-measure, mail-order service from their remote country workshop. The range of garments includes pure wool tweed skirts and co-ordinated hand-frame knitwear and print blouses.

Open by appt. only. Closed Xmas, Etr & annual holidays **C E D** 🚐

Kenilworth
Warwickshire   **Map 4 SP27**

SNOWGOOSE STENCILLED SILK
(Eleanor Allitt) Thickthorn Cottage, 108 Leamington Rd (cottage next to roundabout where Leamington Rd crosses A46) ⊘ (0926) 52395

Eleanor Allitt produces hand-stencilled and painted silk scarves and dress-lengths with the emphasis on quality of design and material. Her work has been widely exhibited and she lectures on textile design and gives practical workshop tuition.

Open 10–6 by appt. Closed Xmas **C E D** *credit cards* ⓐ 🏧

Kersey

Suffolk   **Map 5 TM04**

RIVER HOUSE POTTERY
(Fred Bramham and Dorothy Gorst) The Street, nr Ipswich, 2 m from Hadleigh off A1071
✆ *(0473) 822092*

A comprehensive range of hand-made tableware, vases, lamps, bowls, plates and garden pots. The work is high-fired and decorated with different glazes and techniques.

Open Tue–Sat 10–5.30, Sun 12–5. Also open BHs **C E D** *credit cards* ⓐ ⓥ ⓧ 🏧

Keswick

Cumbria   **Map 10 NY22**

BLENCATHRA STONE CRAFTS
(Mr W E Tyson) Otley Rd ✆ *(0596) 73719*

Fireplaces, coffee tables, lamps, clocks, barometers etc all made in Lakeland green slate by local craftsmen.

Open Mon–Sat 8–5. Closed for lunch & Xmas **C R W E D** 🏧

ANDREW WEBB – WORKER IN WOOD
Pack-Horse Yd, off Market Sq by Lloyds Bank ✆ *(059684) 300 (evngs)*

Furniture-maker producing simple, useful items in solid English hardwoods. Visitors welcome to view the selection on display and clients are invited to discuss their choice of timber and design with Andrew Webb.

Open Mon–Fri 9–5, & some Sats. Advisable to telephone. Closed for lunch & Xmas & Etr **C D** 🏧

Kettering

Northamptonshire   **Map 4 SP87**

V R DESIGNS
(Vivien Ridley) Lower St, Desborough, nr Kettering ✆ *(0536) 762333*

High-quality hand-forged, wrought-ironwork in traditional and original designs for the house, patio and garden. Work includes gazebos, unusually-shaped flower and climbing-plant frames, planters, gates and balustrades. Other good craftwork by cabinet-makers, sculptors, stained-glass artists, potters etc also for sale. Wrought-ironwork commissions are always welcome.

Open Tue–Fri 9.30–5.30, Sat 10–4, Sun 12–4.30. Closed for lunch, & Xmas **C R W E D** *credit cards* ⓐ ⓥ 🏧 *by appt.*

Kineton

Warwickshire   **Map 4 SP35**

KINETON GALLERY
(Miss K Smith and Miss M M Somerfield) Banbury St ✆ *(0926) 641230*

Equipment and materials for spinners, weavers, embroiderers, knitters and lacemakers. Classes in a number of crafts are held in the gallery and studio where there are looms and spinning wheels. Designer-knitwear, prints and original paintings are also for sale. Exhibitions held regularly.

Open Mon–Sat 9.30–5. Closed Thu pm & lunch **C** *(knitting only)* **D** *& mail-order credit cards* ⓥ 🏧

- Shop, Gallery and Studio specialising in supplies for the Textile Crafts
- Equipment & Materials for SPINNING, WEAVING, EMBROIDERY, LACEMAKING & DESIGNER KNITTING.
- Exhibition & Tuition
- Gift items, many from British studio workshops
- Situated in the centre of Kineton at the foot of Edgehill on the Warwickshire, Oxfordshire border

KINETON GALLERY
Banbury Street, Kineton, Warwickshire CV35 0JS
Telephone: Kineton 641230
Business Hours:
Monday to Saturday 9.30 - 1.15pm
1.45 - 5.00pm
except Thursdays 9.30 - 1.00pm
Please check for Bank Holiday opening.

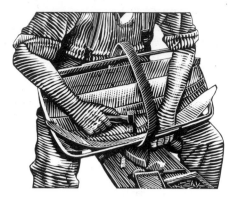

A Sussex trug-maker fixing willow boards

Kingham
Oxfordshire   Map 4 SP22

LANGSTON PRIORY WORKSHOPS
(Mr G D White) Station Rd, 200 yds from station
✆ (060871) 645

The workshops opened in 1985 and are still being developed. Several craftsmen produce furniture, leatherwork, woodwork, printing etc. Refreshments available.

Open Mon–Fri 9–5.30, wknds 9–1. Closed Xmas **C R W E D** *(varies with each business)* 🚐

King's Lynn
Norfolk   Map 9 TF62

RODNEY CRANWELL
The Forge, Stow Bridge
✆ (0366) 382600

A wide range of custom-made ornamental ironwork includes village signs, candelabras, flower stands, fire-dogs, irons and baskets and sign brackets. Traditional skills are combined with modern techniques to produce high-quality work. Period-ironwork restored.

Open Mon–Fri 8–5. Other times by appt. Closed for lunch **C R W D** 🚐

IVOR & LYN SANDFORD POTTERY
Toad Hall, Mill Rd, Wiggenhall St Germans, about 4 m S of King's Lynn W off A10 ✆ (055385) 672

Functional, domestic stoneware – tableware, kitchenware, plant-pot holders etc, plus individual pieces – all designed and hand-made. Talks and demonstrations can be arranged.

Open any reasonable hours, but advisable to telephone **C W E D** *credit cards* ⓐ 🚐 *by appt.*

Kings Somborne
Hampshire   Map 4 SU33

BARKER & GEARY LTD
Romsey Rd, nr Stockbridge, in village centre
✆ (0794) 388205

Highly-unusual elm tables and stools decorated with relief carvings of rural scenes and animals. Brasswork, wrought-ironwork, baskets, pottery and leatherware also for sale and there is a display of old tools and harness.

Open Mon–Fri 8–5, Sat 9–5, Sun 2–5. Closed Xmas **D** *credit cards* ⓐ ⓥ 🚐

Kingsteignton
Devon   Map 3 SX87

ROBERT TINNYUNT CERAMICS
96 Exeter Rd, nr Newton Abbot ✆ (0626) 61011

Local clay is used to make the wide variety of stoneware pottery on show. The work, including both domestic and individual pieces, is hand-thrown and decorated with brushwork.

Open Mon–Sat 9.30–5.30, Sun by appt. **C W E D** 🚐 *by appt.*

Kingston Bagpuize
Oxfordshire   Map 4 SU49

ROBERT LONGSTAFF WORKSHOP
(Robert and Yvonne Longstaff) Orchard View, Appleton Rd, Longworth, nr Abingdon, just N of Kingston Bagpuize off A420 ✆ (0865) 820206

Folk and early musical instruments, wooden puzzles and toys, furniture and general woodware all made on the premises. Other locally-made craftwork for sale includes batik, jewellery and leatherwork. Rare breeds of poultry and duck can also be seen here.

Open Mon–Sat 9.30–5.30, but advisable to telephone. Closed for lunch, & Xmas & Etr **C W E D** *credit cards* ⓐ ⓥ 🚐 *by appt.*

Kingston St Mary
Somerset   Map 3 ST22

CHURCH FARM WEAVERS
(John Lennon and Talbot Potter) nr Taunton (next to parish church) ✆ (082345) 267

Hand-woven tweeds, furnishing fabrics, rugs, ties and wall hangings, as well as ecclesiastical items, all made from handspun wool which has been coloured with natural plant dyes.

Open Tue–Sat 2–6, or by appt. Closed for lunch & Xmas **C D** 🚐 *by appt.*

Kington

Hereford & Worcester **Map 3 SO95**

ENGLISH OAK FURNITURE

(Terence W Clegg) 8 Headbrook ☏ (0544) 230208

Cabinet-makers producing country-style reproductions (using traditional techniques) in English oak and some mahogany and sawn-cut
walnut veneered pieces. Furniture of any period made to commission and all restoration
work concerning fine furniture undertaken –
including French-polishing. Member of the
Guild of Master Craftsmen.

Open Mon–Sat 8–5. Closed Xmas **C R D**
🚗 *by appt.*

Kirkby-in-Furness

Cumbria **Map 7 SD28**

WALL END WEAVING SHOP

*(G B and F Stone), Wall End Cottage, Wall End, on
A595 ¼ m from Commercial Inn ☏ (022989) 359*

High-quality woven goods made from British
wools and other fibres. Products range from
handbags and ties to rugs and cushion covers.

Open any reasonable time, by appt. **C W E D** 🚗

Kirkbymoorside

North Yorkshire **Map 8 SE68**

MOORSIDE WROUGHT-IRON

*(Michael Hammond and Richard Harrison) The
Workshop, Piercy End ☏ (0751) 32244*

Manufacturers of all types of wrought-ironwork, ranging from gates, railings and church
furniture to lamps and door-knockers. Michael
Hammond and Richard Harrison specialise in
restoration work.

*Open Mon–Fri 7–5, & wknds, by appt. Closed for
lunch, & Xmas & Etr* **C R E D** 🚗

Kirkby Stephen

Cumbria **Map 11 NY70**

IAN & RHONA MATHEWS

Dowgill Head, North Stainmore ☏ (09304) 465

Many items for the home such as clocks,
barometers, lamp bases and desk sets, plus
unusual studies of animals and birds, all made
in Lakeland greenstone and fossil limestone.
Also jewellery with plain stone, or stone decorated with dried flowers and coated with resin.

Open by appt. only **C R W E D** 🚗

Kirton-in-Lindsey

South Humberside Map 8 SK99

KIRTON POTTERY
(Peter and Christine Hawes) 36 High St, nr Gainsborough ✆ (0652) 648867

Traditional English slipware and majolica ware plus a wide range of reduction-fired stoneware. Commemorative plates of all kinds are a speciality.

Open Wed–Sat 9.30–5.30, Sun 2.30–5. Closed Xmas **C W E D** 🚌 *by appt.*

Knutsford

Cheshire Map 7 SJ77

D C & S BROADBENT ENGINEERING
Barnshaw Smithy, Pepper St, Mobberley, nr Knutsford ✆ (056587) 3743

All general blacksmithing work undertaken, including welding and agricultural machinery. Ornamental ironwork of high quality is also produced: gates; railings; fire-grates; cast-iron water pumps.

Open Mon–Fri 8.30–5.30, Sat 8.30–12.30. Closed Xmas & Etr **C R W E D** 🚌 *by appt.*

KEVIN P JOHNSON
Blease Farm, School La, Ollerton, 2½ m from Knutsford on A537 ✆ (056581) 2345

Traditional furniture made to a high standard using many English hardwoods. Also kitchens, custom-built to suit individual tastes, available in a wide range of finishes. Kevin Johnson is happy to discuss any furniture repair or restoration work.

Open Mon–Fri, by appt. Closed Xmas & Etr **C R E D** ♿

Kuggar

Cornwall Map 2 SW71

COACH HOUSE CRAFT CENTRE
(D C and S M Wooding) Kennack Sands, nr Ruan Minor ✆ (0326) 290661/290873

Built over 300 years ago, the stables now house several craft-workshops, selling glass ornaments, leatherwork, sculptures, pottery, furniture, model trains, wooden toys, horse-drawn vehicles and violins. There is also a large gallery selling a wide selection of sundry other crafts, as well as a well-stocked garden shop and a café serving light refreshments.

Open daily 9 am–10 pm **C D** *credit cards* ⓐ ⓥ ⓧ ⓓ 🚌 *by appt.*

Lakeside

Cumbria Map 7 SD38

WOOL GATHERERS
(Neil Hodson) Landene, nr Newby Bridge (50 yds from Lakeside Hotel behind Rose Cottage) ✆ (0448) 31021

A small cottage workshop producing high-quality, hand-framed knitwear in fine Scottish wools. Many unusual and interesting designs include a Lakeland-scene picture sweater, a sweat-shirt-styled jumper featuring the Statue of Liberty and a moon and stars pattern.

Open any reasonable time, but advisable to telephone. Closed Xmas **C W E D** ♿

Lamberhurst

Kent Map 5 TQ63

HOOK GREEN POTTERY
(Don and Ruth Morgan) Hook Green ✆ (0892) 890504

Various pieces of porcelain and wood-fired stoneware, such as vases, bowls, plates and bottles, plus a range of oven and tableware.

Open any reasonable time but advisable to telephone. Closed 25 Dec & occasionally for holidays **C W E D** ♿

Lambley

Nottinghamshire Map 8 SK64

TREVOR EMERTON C.M.B.H.I.
63 Catfoot La ✆ (060231) 3545

Clock and instrument maker specialising in the restoration of all antique timepieces, including carriage, bracket and long-case clocks, plus barometers. Complete clocks made to order. Some antique clocks are for sale.

Open any reasonable time, but advisable to telephone. Closed Xmas **C R D** ♿

PHI INTERIORS
(R A and L A Wyles) Studio 3 Green La, between B684 & A6097 NE of Nottingham ✆ (060231) 3477

High-quality work in wood and stone. Handmade furniture, individually designed to customers' own specifications, using highest-quality materials. Other items include small caskets, clock-cases and special commissions. Also work in marble, slate, granite, onyx and other types of stone – for example, fireplaces, fitted bathrooms etc.

Open Mon–Fri 9–5, Sat 9–12 by appt. only. Closed Xmas & Etr **C R D** ♿

Lamorna

Cornwall   **Map 2 SW42**

LAMORNA POTTERY
(Peter and Shirley Brown) Trewoofe, nr Penzance
℡ (073672) 330

High-fired earthenware with various glazes designed for practical use – wine sets, bowls, table lamps etc. Visitors are welcome to 'throw their own pot'. Other Cornish craftware also on sale. Refreshments available.

Open daily Apr Sep 9–sunset, Oct–Mar Mon–Fri 9–5.30. Closed for lunch & Xmas **C W E D** *credit cards* ⓐ ⓥ 🚌

Lancaster

Lancashire   **Map 7 SD46**

ROBERT DEEGAN HARPSICHORDS
Tonnage Warehouse, St Georges Quay ℡ (0524) 60186

Fine keyboard musical instruments – harpsichords, virginals, spinets and clavichords – made to a high standard of performance and finish. Restoration work also undertaken.

Open Mon–Fri 9–5. Also wknds by appt. Closed for lunch & Xmas **C R E D** 🚌 *by appt.*

Landford

Wiltshire   **Map 4 SU21**

BLACK LANE POTS
(Tony Joslin) Hamptworth, nr Salisbury ℡ (0794) 390796

Specialists in all ceramic processes, including slip-casting, hand-throwing, sculpture and individual commissions – any work in clay undertaken. The pottery is noted for its high-quality work and makes replicas for the British Museum.

Open Mon–Fri 9–5, by appt. **C W E D** 🚌
See advertisement on p. 98

Lanercost

Cumbria   **Map 11 NY56**

ABBEY MILL
(Mrs A Barker) 2 m E of Brampton ℡ (06977) 2638/ 3766

Abbey Mill, an old corn mill, has been turned into an exciting arts and crafts centre. There is a craft workshop producing dolls, toys, quilts, rugs, fabric paintings etc, and galleries where dolls, puppets, contemporary paintings, embroideries and kinetic and concrete art are exhibited. A shop sells souvenirs, prints, toys etc, plus refreshments. Abbey Mill gives priority to employing the disabled. To help visitors, there are wheelchair ramps and toilet facilities for the disabled. There is a small admission charge.

Open Tue–Sun & BHs 10–6 but closed Xmas & Good Fri **C E D** *credit cards* (a) ☞ *by appt.*

Langport
Somerset   **Map 3 ST42**
MUCHELNEY POTTERY
(John Leach) Muchelney, 2 m S of Langport ☎ *(0458) 250324*

John Leach (grandson of Bernard Leach) produces a range of exclusive one-off designs, as well as robust kitchen pots, mugs etc. All his work is characterised by the distinctive flame-finish obtained from the woodfiring. Member of the Craftsmen Potters' Association; the Art Workers' Guild; the Devon Guild of Craftsmen and the Somerset Guild of Craftsmen.

Shop open Mon–Fri 9–6, Sat 9–1. Workshop open by appt. only. Closed for lunch, & Xmas **W E D** *credit cards* (a) (v) (x) ☞

Lanivet
Cornwall   **Map 2 SX06**
ROSEHILL DESIGNS
(Catherine Hornsey and Pat Bearman) Pampas, Rosehill, nr Bodmin ☎ *(0208) 831890*

Porcelain and bone china, hand-painted with original designs ranging from delicate wild flowers to a striking dragon motif in black and gold: miniature boxes a speciality. Tiles, lamp bases etc designed to individual requirements. Tuition available.

Open by appt. only. Closed for lunch, & Xmas & Etr **C E D** ☞ *by appt.*

Launceston
Cornwall   **Map 2 SX38**
SPLATT POTTERY
(Brian and Jenny Broad) Tresmeer, nr Launceston, turn l at St Stephen's Church in Launceston towards Egloskerry & Tresmeer ☎ *(056681) 301*

Two workshops (where visitors are always welcome) produce stoneware, porcelain and hand-dyed clothing. Various cotton and silk garments are available in assorted colours with a wide choice of batik designs. Roller blinds,

lampshades etc also on display in the show-room. Special commissions for both pottery and fabrics are undertaken.

Open Mon–Sat 9–6, but advisable to telephone. Closed Xmas **C R W D** *credit cards* ⓥ 🚗 *by appt.*

Lealholm

North Yorkshire   **Map 8 NZ70**

FORGE POTTERY
(Myrna Smith) Forge House, nr Whitby ✆ *(0947) 87457*

A distinctive range of finely-thrown stone-ware, mostly decorated with hand-modelled fungi and other applied detail. Items include unusual planters, vases, pot-pourri holders etc. Also very detailed hand-modelled cottages and farmsteads for sale. Commissions for spe-cial items can be undertaken.

Open daily 10–5 **C W E D** 🚗 *by appt.*

Leatherhead

Surrey   **Map 4 TQ15**

**RICHARD QUINNELL LTD:
FIRE & IRON GALLERY**
Rowhurst Forge, Oxshott Rd, nr Leatherhead, nr M25 junction 9 ✆ *(0372) 375148*

A group of designer-blacksmiths, with Richard Quinnell Ltd as the nucleus, produce orna-mental iron and metal work of original, con-temporary and traditional design. Their work covers sculpture, lettering, seating, lighting, conservatories, weathervanes and much more. Fire and Iron Gallery (next to Quinnell's work-shops) is an exhibition and resource centre for the group, and a retail shop. Special commis-sions are also undertaken.

Open Mon–Fri 9–5, wknds 9–1, by appt. Closed for lunch, & Xmas, Etr & BHs **C R E D** 🚗

Lechlade

Gloucestershire   **Map 4 SU29**

OLD BELL POTTERY
(Keith Broley) High St ✆ *(0367) 52608*

A good range of garden pots in terracotta and stoneware, plus domestic pottery in stoneware with slip and brushwork decoration. Also a delightful line of canary sculptures.

Open daily summer 9.30–7.30, winter 9.30–5.30, but advisable to telephone **D** 🚗

Ledbury

Hereford & Worcester   **Map 3 SO73**

COLLECTION
(S B Houghton) 13 The Southend ✆ *(0531) 4641*

Lots and lots of attractive, quality goods for sale including pottery, basketry, jewellery, glass-ware, woodwork and prints. Stationery, cards and artists' materials sold as well. Some exhibi-tions held.

Open Mon–Fri 9–5.30, Sat 10–5.30. Closed for lunch, & Xmas **D** *credit cards* ⓐ ⓥ ⓧ 🚗

LEDBURY CRAFT CENTRE
(P Preston) 1 High St ✆ *(0531) 4566*

All sorts of British-made gifts are for sale in the shop, including goods from the craft work-shops on the first floor. These are: Knitcraft; Caroline Inglis Designs – china-painting; Sweetbriar Designs – patchwork; Pickpots – china restoration; Whites Farm Baskets – bas-ket makers; plus jewellery and picture-framing studios. Refreshments available.

Open Mon–Sat 9.15–5.30, also some Suns. Closed Xmas **C R D** *credit cards* ⓥ 🚗

DAVID NYE – QUALITY WOOD TURNER
2 Kimbrose Cottages, Falcon La ✆ *(0531) 3444*

Many items of wood-turnery available such as bowls, lamps, clocks, barometers, kitchenware, etc etc. Demonstrations and lectures on wood-turning and forestry given by request.

Open daily 9–5 **C R W D** *credit cards* ⓐ ⓥ ⟐ *by appt.*

MARK OWEN-THOMAS
205 The Homend ☏ (0531) 4571

Hand-thrown terracotta containers, such as wall pots, planters, strawberry tubs and simple cookware, made in styles traditional to the Hereford area yet adapted to modern needs.

Open Mon–Fri 10–5 & Sat am, by appt. Closed Xmas **C W D** ⟐

Leicester

Leicestershire	Map 4 SK50

ZION HOUSE POTTERY
(Marion Aldis) 93 Main St, South Croxton, nr Leicester ☏ (0664) 840363

Delicate stoneware pots and dishes for talc, soap, pot-pourri, jewellery etc, plus lampbases, plates and vases. Each piece is handmade and encrusted with hand-modelled flowers, painted with lustres and enamels.

Open Mon–Fri 9–5. Also wknds by appt. Closed Xmas **C W D** ⟐ *by appt.*

Leominster

Hereford & Worcester	Map 3 SO45

DUNKERTONS CIDER CO
(Susie and Ivor Dunkerton) Luntley, nr Pembridge, A44 Leominster to Kington rd & turn l at New Inn ☏ (05447) 653

Traditional ciders and perry made on the premises from locally-grown cider apples and perry pears. Draught cider available: 1-gallon jars and 5-gallon kegs or in your own container.

Open Apr–Sep Mon–Sat 10–7, Sun 12–2; Oct–Mar Mon–Fri 4–6, Sat 10–6. Closed Xmas **W D** ⟐ *by appt.*

SLOANE CARPETS
(Peter and Christine Spedding) Unit 5, Southern Ave ☏ (0568) 5863

Specialist carpet manufacturers producing hand-made rugs and carpet squares to customers' designs and colour choice. Plain carpet also made to order in any choice of colour.

Open Mon–Fri 8.30–5, & wknds, by appt. Closed Xmas & Etr **C W E D** ⟐ *by appt.*

Leverton

Lincolnshire	Map 9 TF34

LINCOLNSHIRE ARCHITECTURAL ANTIQUE SERVICES
(Peter and Pat Wise) The Cottage, Ings La, nr Boston ☏ (0205) 870751

Manufacturers of leaded windows and dealers in architectural antiques; also specialists in the repair and renovation of old, coloured, leaded windows. All paint-stripping from furniture and fittings undertaken and special commissions are welcome.

Open daily 10–8 **C R W E D** ⟐

Lewes

East Sussex	Map 5 TQ41

MARGARET FRANCES BELLAMY
Thorn House, The Street, Chiddingly, nr Lewes ☏ (082583) 872466

Margaret Bellamy specialises in work which combines the disciplines of wood-turning, sculpture and carving. This includes decorative fruits, stylised Christmas figures, candelabra, models of cats, birds etc. simple crosses and church candlesticks. She works to commission only and is a Member of the Guild of Sussex Craftsmen and on the Register of the Worshipful Company of Turners.

Open by appt. only **C** ⟐

BROOK HOUSE STUDIO
(Hamish and Maxwell Black and Fred Berwick) Novington La, East Chiltington, nr Lewes, 2nd r in Novington La ☏ (0273) 890419/890175

Brook House Studio is a partnership of three: Hamish Black is a sculptor and blacksmith whose work ranges from fire-grates to public sculptures. Maxwell Black conserves and restores antique furniture. Fred Berwick designs and hand-builds furniture.

Open Mon–Fri 8.30–5.30, by appt. only. Closed Xmas **C R D** ⟐

G W DAY & CO
(Brian Pettitt, Eileen Day and David Cox) East Chiltington Forge, South Chailey, nr Lewes ☏ (0273) 890398

Wrought-ironwork of all descriptions; gates, balustrades, fire-baskets, lanterns etc, as well as regrinding, fabrication, structural steelwork and welding repairs.

Open Mon–Fri 8–5, Sat 8–12.30. Closed for lunch & Xmas & Etr **C R D** ⟐

Leyburn
North Yorkshire **Map 7 SE19**

CHANDLER GALLERY
(Charles and Daphne Chandler) 8 Commercial Sq
℗ *(0969) 23676*

The assortment of craft goods for sale includes pottery, glass, wood, textiles, jewellery, paintings and original prints.

Open Mon–Sat 9.30–5. Also Sun 11–4 Jun–Sep. Closed Xmas & Good Fri **D** *credit cards* ⓐ ⓥ 🚐

MOORSIDE DESIGN
(Barrie, Shirley and Sarah Nichols) Moorside, West Burton, 7 m W of Leyburn off A684 ℗ *(09693) 273*

An attractive range of ceramic studies of animals (mostly cats, but also pigs, rabbits etc), and human torsos, plus some individually sculpted models of cats and the human figure. Thrown, terracotta garden-ware and domestic stoneware is made here as well.

Open Mon–Fri 9–6, wknds 10–6. Closed for lunch & Xmas **C W E D** 🚐 *by appt.*

SPENNITHORNE FORGE & CRAFTS
(Joe the Blacksmith) Spennithorne, take Bedale rd from Leyburn & turn r at Pheasant Inn. Through Harmby turn r at T-junction. Forge is 100 yds on l ℗ *(0969) 22865*

Joe the Blacksmith forges contemporary and traditional artistic ironwork. A selection of his work can be seen on display in the small gallery next to the forge.

Open Mon–Fri 10–5. Also open Sat 10–12 in summer. Closed for lunch & Xmas & Etr **C R E D** 🚐 *by appt.*

Lilford Park
Northamptonshire **Map 4 TF08**

LILFORD CRAFT WORKSHOPS
(Mrs P Fitton) Lilford Park, nr Oundle ℗ *(08015) 386/755*

Craft workshops are in the converted stable block of historic Lilford Hall. Four craftsmen and women specialise in the following crafts: hand-printed screen-prints (Carrie Akroyd); puppet- and marionette-making (Ken Barnard); wood-carving and sculpture, also village signs, house-names and numbers, private commissions and restoration work (Glyn Mould); acrylic and water-colour painting (Anna Sweeten).

Open Apr–Nov Wed & wknds 1–5 **W E D** 🚐 *by appt.*

Linton-on-Ouse
North Yorkshire **Map 8 SE46**

R WATSON & SON
(D P Watson and P R Watson) Joiner's Cottage, 10 m from York ℗ *(03474) 233*

Traditional and contemporary solid wood furniture individually designed to suit any domestic setting. Some wood-turnery, including legs, spindles, boxes and lamp-stands, undertaken. Chess tables and chessmen a speciality. Work made to commission only.

Open Mon–Fri 9–6.30, Sat 1–6, by appt.
C W D 🚐

Liphook
Hampshire **Map 4 SU83**

MILLAND POTTERY & FURNITURE WORKSHOP
(A Dannreuther, R D Carter and J Hawkins) Milland La, Milland, the pottery is 1 m off A3 between Liphook & Rake ℗ *(042876) 505*

Decorative, functional earthenware, plus a selection of terracotta plant and cooking pots made from local clay. The furniture is custom-built and includes traditional, beech-framed, upholstered sofas and chairs.

Open Mon–Fri 10–5. Also wknds 10–5 Etr–Xmas. Closed Xmas (open 24 Dec) & New Year **C R** *(furniture)* **W D** 🚐 *by appt.*

Machine-planing the felloes of a dray wheel

Litchborough
Northamptonshire Map 4 SP65

CRISTINA – ORIGINAL KNITTED FASHION
(Susan Cristina Morley) Bay Tree, Towcester Rd
✆ *(0327) 830130*

Top-quality exclusive knitwear (ladies' suits, coats, jackets, sweaters and dresses) with the emphasis on unusual textures. All the designs are available from stock or can be ordered.

Open Mon–Fri 10–4, but advisable to telephone. Also wknds, by appt. **C D** *credit cards* Ⓥ ⇔

Littlebourne
Kent Map 5 TR25

LITTLEBOURNE CRAFTS
(Mrs Jackie Payne) 6/8 High St, nr Canterbury
✆ *(0227) 721716*

Traditional corn dollies of all kinds are hand-made on the premises and a selection of other craft goods is on display in the shop.

Open most days, but advisable to telephone. Closed Xmas **C W E D** ⇔ *by appt.*

London
See entries under Brockley and Harrow For Designer Bookbinders (Philip Smith) see entry under Merstham

Longframlington
Northumberland Map 11 NU10

D G & E M BURLEIGH
Rothbury Rd, nr Morpeth ✆ *(066570) 635*

Makers of Northumbrian small pipes – the county's traditional instrument. Visitors can see the pipes being made and can hear them being played. Local music and records for sale. Tea and coffee available.

Open Mon–Sat 8–5 & Sun, by appt. Closed for lunch & Xmas **C R D** ⇔ *by appt.*

Longnor
Staffordshire Map 7 SK06

FOX COUNTRY FURNITURE
(George W Fox) Sunnyside, Church St, 6 m S of Buxton on B5053 ✆ *(029883) 496*

Solid elm and oak furniture made to simple, clean-cut designs. The range includes tables, telephone benches, chairs and video cabinets, but any piece can be made to order.

Open Mon–Fri 9–5, & Sat by appt. Closed for lunch & Xmas & Etr **C W D** ⇔

Louth
Lincolnshire Map 8 TF38

ALVINGHAM POTTERY
Alvingham, 3 m NE of Louth ✆ *(050782) 230*

A wide range of both domestic and decorative hand-thrown earthenware is on display in the gallery. Potters can be seen at work daily.

Open Mon–Sat 9–5, Sun 2–5. Closed Xmas **C W D** ⇔

HARVEST POTTERY
(Keith and Mary Green) Brinkhill, nr Louth
✆ *(05216) 702*

Terracotta garden pottery in a wide variety of sizes and designs, including large planters, strawberry-growers and wall pots. Also a good range of kitchen ware at competitive prices.

Open daily 10–10 **C W D** ⇔ *by appt.*

Lowestoft
Suffolk Map 5 TM59

EARTH POTTERY
(Giles and Carol Cattlin) 94 Norwich Rd ✆ *(0502) 511396*

Hand-thrown stoneware available in several different coloured glazes and decorated with a variety of patterns. The range includes plant pots, kitchenware, lamps, candle holders, plus celebration plates. There is also a stall in the craft village at Pleasurewood Hills Theme Park at Corton near Lowestoft.

Open Mon–Sat 9–6 Closed at Xmas, Etr & BHs **C W D** ⇔

Ludgershall
Buckinghamshire Map 4 SP61

PETER H BLOMFIELD – CABINET MAKER
Willow-Wood, Bit La, nr Aylesbury (take no through rd opp. Bull & Butcher PH & bear l at bottom) ✆ *(0844) 238278*

Traditional and modern furniture made in any timber to suit customers' requirements, using a combination of hand and machine techniques. One-off items and complete room schemes.

Open Mon–Fri 9–5, by appt. Workshop & showroom 'open day' 1st Sat in each month 9–5. Closed Xmas & Etr **C R E D** ⇔

Ludlow

Shropshire   **Map 7 SO57**

DAVID ACKROYD
Bleathwood Manor Farm, Bleathwood (leave Ludlow on Temeside & Steventon New Rd, continue towards Tenbury Wells on unclass. rd for 4 m to red-brick farmhouse on l @ *(0584) 810726*

High-quality furniture traditionally made in fine woods, such as satinwood, rosewood, ebony and walnut: each item is designed to order. Specialist joinery work and all aspects of antique restoration also undertaken, including inlay, marquetry, fretwork and boule work.

Open daily 9–7, by appt. **C R D** 🚗

COTTAGE INDUSTRY HAND-MADE FURNITURE
(Graham Hayes) 4 Quality Sq @ *(0584) 5363*

A small group of independent craftsmen produce high-quality items of furniture which can be seen in the Quality Square Showroom. Most of the work is in oak or mahogany and the traditional styles range from a 17th-century coffee table to a 19th-century Windsor chair.

Open Mon–Sat 10–5. Closed Xmas & Etr Sun **C W E D** 🚗

WOODSTOCK HOUSE CRAFT CENTRE
(Hugh and Wendy Rulton), Brimfield, 5 m S of Ludlow on A49 @ *(058472) 445*

The old coaching house of Woodstock House has been turned into a fully-equipped fabric craft centre where Wendy Rulton sells her own work and runs holiday courses in embroidery, dress-making and soft furnishings. Specialist courses are also available.

Open daily 9–9. Closed Xmas & 2 wks in Jan **C R D** 🚗 *by appt.*

Lustleigh

Devon   **Map 3 SX78**

OXSHOTT POTTERY
(Rosemary D Wren ARCA and Peter M Crotty) Mill Cottage, Mill La, nr Newton Abbot @ *(06477) 231*

Ceramic sculptures of many different English birds and animals. Each piece is made entirely by hand and coloured with oxides and stoneware glazes. Prices range from £14 for a small bird to £350 for a bull.

Open daily, but advisable to telephone. Closed Xmas **C W E D** 🚗

Lydford

Devon   **Map 2 SX58**

LYDFORD GORGE WOODCARVER
(Rodney Smith) Larrick Cottage, ¾ m S of Lydford in lane W of Gorge road @ *(082282) 288*

Rodney Smith specialises in deep-relief woodcarvings – either pictures or free-standing tableaux – which depict birds or animals set in their natural surroundings: he will also undertake carvings of customers' pets or homes. He has won three gold medals at 'Woodworker Shows' and has twice been awarded the 'Henry Taylor Award for Woodcarving'.

Open anytime, but advisable to telephone **C D** 🚗
See advertisement on p. 104

Lydney

Gloucestershire   **Map 3 SO60**

BRAMBLES CRAFT SHOP
(Gillian Benham) Bailey Hill, Yorkley, 2½ m from Lydney @ *(0594) 562780 (mornings & evenings)*

Specialists in spinning, weaving and natural-dyeing supplies, as well as the repair of spinning wheels and looms. A wide selection of local crafts always for sale, plus pot-pourri, essential oils, orris root etc.

Open daily 2 5.30 (closed Wed). Closed Xmas **C R W D** 🚐 *(limited parking space)*

Lyme Regis

Dorset   **Map 3 SY39**

ENGLISH WILLOW BASKETS
(Peter Benson) 6A Cobb Rd @ *(02974) 5330*

Traditional and original baskets made from the best Somerset-grown willow. Among the range are baskets for logs, linen, shopping, gardening, toys, babies, cats, bread, paper, fishing.

Open daily 9–9 in summer, 9–5 in winter **C R W E D** 🚗

Lyndhurst

Hampshire   **Map 4 SU20**

ANGELS FARM POTTERY
(Joanna Osman) Pinkney La, on Lyndhurst one-way system, SP Bournemouth @ *(042128) 2185*

An attractive range of simply-decorated reduction-fired pots for table and kitchen use. Also some flower pots and vases available.

Open Mon–Fri 9.30–4.30, Sat 10–4. Closed Xmas **C W D** 🚐 *by appt.*

Lytchett Matravers

Dorset　　　　　　　　**Map 3 SY99**

STONEY DOWN POTTERY

(Adrian Lewis-Evans) Pottery is just E of A350 Poole–Blandford rd at cross-roads to Lytchett Matravers ✆ (0202) 622392

Flame-fired stoneware pottery decorated with a variety of beautiful glazes. The many unusual and attractive items include pitchers, tankards, Dorset 'owl' cider flagons, ikebana, bonsai and wall-pots. All sorts of pottery can be made to order.

Open Mon–Fri 9–6. Also many evngs & most wknds. Closed 25 Dec & Good Fri **C R W E D** 🚌 *by appt.*

Maiden Newton

Dorset　　　　　　　　**Map 3 SY59**

WARWICK PARKER – POTTERY

The Dairy House, nr Dorchester ✆ (0300) 20414

A wide range of domestic stoneware pottery, plus individual pieces of a functional nature.

Open Mon–Fri 9–5.30, Sat 9–12, but advisable to telephone. Closed Xmas **C W E D** 🚌

Maldon

Essex　　　　　　　　**Map 5 TL80**

OAKWOOD ARTS CENTRE

(Oakwood House Ltd) 2 High St ✆ (0621) 56503/ 52317

There are five craft studios at the Arts Centre: Shuttlewood Studio (Nina Shuttlewood, see also entry below) – spinning and weaving; Many Hands Needlecraft Co-operative; Friars Pottery (Sue Smith) – hand-built slipware; David Goodship – jewellery; Manor Frames and Pictures (Jan and Les Palmer). Refreshments are available in the Acorn Café.

Open Mon–Fri 10–5 (closed Wed), Sat 9–5. Closed Xmas **C R D** 🚌 *preferably by appt.*

SHUTTLEWOOD STUDIO

(Nina Shuttlewood) Friars Walk, Friars La ✆ (0621) 55349

Designer knitwear hand-made in both commercial and hand-spun yarns using natural fibres such as wool, silk, mohair and cotton. Many designs are exclusive to Shuttlewood Studio. Spinning wheels and all fibres and equipment used in hand-spinning also for sale. Tuition available.

The Lydford Gorge Woodcarver

Rodney Smith's studio is at Larrick Cottage on the lip of Lydford Gorge, one of Devon's most attractive beauty spots. Clients are welcome.

"Fisherman's Tale", a carved tableau in Lime, 18″ × 14″.
Winner of the Henry Taylor Best-in-Show Award, Woodworker Show, London, 1984.

Open Tue–Sat 9–5. Closed Xmas & Etr **C W E D**
credit cards (a) (v) 🚌

Mansfield
Nottinghamshire   **Map 8 SK56**

PETER REVELL – CERAMIST
Bridge House Farm, Cuckney, nr Mansfield
✆ *(0623) 842381*

Peter Revell creates models of individual
homes in porcelain. Each one is hand-made
and very detailed – often incorporating plants,
outbuildings, statues etc. The overall size
varies, but most models are about six inches
high. Every piece is signed and dated.

*Open Mon–Fri 9–5 & wknds, by appt. Closed
Xmas & Etr* **C D** 🚌

Market Bosworth
Leicestershire   **Map 4 SK40**

BOSWORTH CRAFTS
(Mr R Thorley) 23 Main St ✆ *(0455) 290869
(evngs)*

Visitors can see leather items being made in
the shop. Stock includes belts, purses, bags,
bellows etc, but anything can be made to order.
Also other locally-made craftwork for sale such
as pottery and patchwork.

*Open Mon–Sat 9–5. Also open Sun 2–5.30 May–
Sep* **C R W E D** *credit cards* (a) 🚌

COUNTRY CRAFTS
*(B T and M Sturgess) Main St, at rear of No 9, the
Coffee Shop* ✆ *(0530) 72469 (evngs)*

English country baskets and babies' cradles
hand-made from willow. All types of rush and
cane seating also undertaken and any kind of
wickerwork can be completely restored. Member of the Basket Makers' Association and the
Guild of Master Craftsmen.

*Open Mon–Fri 10–4, wknds 10–5, but advisable to
telephone. Closed at Xmas* **C R W E D** 🚌 *by appt.*

MIDDLEWAY
*(David and Carole Herbert) Old Village Hall,
Shenton, nr Market Bosworth, close to Bosworth
Battlefield* ✆ *(0455) 212372*

Clock cases individually designed and hand-
made from the finest materials: commissions
welcomed. Also some turned furniture, and
the restoration of cane and rush seating is
undertaken.

Open Mon–Wed & wknds. Closed Etr & BHs
C R E D *credit cards* (a) (v) (x) 🚌

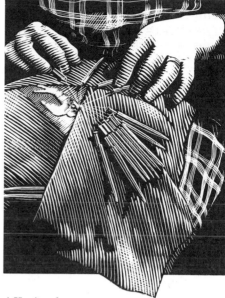

*A Honiton lace-
maker at work*

Market Harborough
Leicestershire   **Map 4 SP78**

QUORN POTTERY
*(J W and Mrs A E Brookes) 46–48 Scotland Rd,
Little Bowden, off A6 out of Market Harborough*
✆ *(0858) 31537*

An unusual range of slip-cast earthenware
includes post-box teapots, teapot clocks, light-
bulb cruets, children's sandals etc. There is
also a selection of simpler containers with air-
brushed decoration.

*Open Mon–Fri 10–5.30, Sat 10–5. Closed Xmas &
for annual holidays* **C W E D** 🚌

ROSEMARY COTTAGE STUDIO
*(Cliff Hayhurst) 23 West St, Welford, nr Market
Harborough, on A50 between Leicester &
Northampton* ✆ *(085881) 284*

Hand-made stoneware decorated with unusual
glazes. The standard lines include patterned
bowls and large decorative plates, complete
table lamps, cheese, hors d'oeuvre and soup
dishes and jugs of all sizes, plus many amusing animal models. Some individual figure
sculptures.

Open daily 8.30–8.30, but advisable to telephone
C W D 🚌 *by appt.*

Markyate

Hertfordshire   **Map 4 TL01**

CLARE STREET
Gosslow, nr St Albans, 3 m SE of Dunstable
🕾 *(0582) 840378*

Precious-metal jewellery (mostly yellow gold) ranging from modest pieces to exclusive designs is available from stock and items can be designed to commission. Seals are engraved to order on rings, cufflinks and fobs.

Open by appt. only Mon–Fri 8–7 & Sat am. Closed Xmas & Etr **C E D** 🚗

Marton

Warwickshire   **Map 4 SP46**

PAUL GANDY CERAMICS
Marton Farm House 🕾 *(0926) 632923*

Most of Paul Gandy's striking ceramic sculptures are based on architectural and landscape themes. His work, mainly high-fired and matt-glazed, combines the techniques of throwing, slabbing, extruding and modelling. Member of the Crafts Council Index of Artist-Craftsmen.

Open Mon–Fri 9–5, but advisable to telephone. Also other times & wknds by appt. Closed Xmas **C W E D** 🚗 *by appt.*

Masham

North Yorkshire   **Map 8 SE28**

UREDALE GLASS
(Tim and Maureen Simon) The Market Place, nr Ripon, 🕾 *(0765) 89780*

A studio workshop where coloured glassware is hand-blown and formed. A wide range of vases, bowls, plates, paperweights and scent bottles is produced.

Open Mon–Fri 9–5, wknds 10–5. Closed Xmas & Jan **C W E D** 🚗

Matlock

Derbyshire   **Map 8 SK36**

CRICH POTTERY
(Diana and David Worthy) Market Place, Crich, nr Matlock 🕾 *(077385) 3171*

Hand-thrown domestic stoneware distinguished by unusual designs and bold use of colour. The range is very wide and includes salad bowls, punch sets, casseroles, jugs, teapots etc.

Open (seconds shop only) Mon–Fri 8.30–5.30, Sat 9–5.30, Sun 10–5.30. Closed Xmas **C W E (D** *seconds & commissions only)* 🚗

Mawgan Porth

Cornwall   **Map 2 SW86**

ST EVAL LEATHERCRAFTS
(A R Dennis) Downhill, St Eval, nr Mawgan Porth
🕾 *(06374) 860357*

Hand-stitched leather goods such as bags, purses, belts and many other small items. Also presentation tankards, music cases, chessboards and clogs. Also hand-cut and carved medieval leather vessels and bellows.

Open Mon–Fri 8.30–4.30 **C R D** *credit cards* ⓐ ⓥ 🚗

Mayfield

East Sussex   **Map 5 TQ52**

GRETA E CHATTERLEY
Timewell Cottage, South St, 9 m S of Tunbridge Wells on A267 🕾 *(0435) 872435*

All types of carving, sculpting and letter-cutting undertaken in wood. Work includes human and animal models, ecclesiastical figures, crosses, house-signs, memorial plaques, club shields, coats of arms and collectors' caddy spoons. Repairs to furniture carving as well.

Open at any reasonable time, but advisable to telephone **C R D** 🚗

Melksham

Wiltshire   **Map 3 ST96**

A M ENGINEERING
(Andrew Missen) Old Forge, 206 Woodrow Rd, Lower Forest, between Melksham & Lacock
🕾 *(0225) 704230*

Traditional ornamental ironwork of all kinds, including gates, fire-baskets, lamps, canopies, security grills, room dividers and balustrades. Special commissions undertaken.

Open daily 8–5. Closed Xmas & Etr **C R D** 🚗

Melmerby

Cumbria   **Map 11 NY63**

VILLAGE BAKERY
(Liz and Andrew Whitley) between Penrith & Alston on A686 🕾 *(076881) 515*

The work of several craftsmen (mostly from the locality) can be seen on the first floor of the Village Bakery licensed restaurant. Among the goods for sale are toys, pottery, ceramic animals, dolls, woodcuts, photographs, knitwear.

Open Tue–Sat 8.30–5, Sun 9.30–5. Closed Xmas– Etr **D** 🚗 *by appt.*

Mentmore

Buckinghamshire **Map 4 SP91**

STABLE YARD CRAFT GALLERY
(Terry and Diane Payne) Stable Yd, nr Leighton Buzzard ✆ (0296) 668660

A fascinating selection of original, hand-made work from craftsmen throughout Britain. Goods include pottery of all kinds, basketry, patchwork, wooden toys and puzzles, dried flowers, blown- and stained-glass, dolls and wood-turned items.

Open Wed–Sun 10–6. Also open BHs. Closed Xmas **D** 🚗 *by appt.*

Merstham

Surrey **Map 4 TQ25**

PHILIP SMITH
Contact through: Designer Bookbinders, 6 Queen Sq, London WC1N 3AR ✆ 01-254-1521 (Hon. Sec. Miss L Bath)

Philip Smith works mainly to commission producing artistic hand-bindings for books, in leather and other materials. The finished products are collectors' items, functional, but also exhibition pieces. Books can be presented in special or sculptured containers. He can be contacted care of the above address.

Open any reasonable time by appt. **C E D** 🚗

Methwold

Norfolk **Map 5 TL79**

PHILIP ISERN
Crosshill House, 1 Old Feltwell Rd, off B1106 between Brandon & Stoke Ferry ✆ (0366) 728573

Goldsmith and silversmith, designing and making a wide range of unusual jewellery and silverware, based on animals, birds, plants and people.

Open Sun–Fri 10–6, Sat 10–11.30 am. Closed Xmas **C R W E D** 🚗 *by appt.*

Middleham

North Yorkshire **Map 7 SE18**

OLD SCHOOL ARTS WORKSHOP
(Peter and Judith Hibbard) nr Leyburn ✆ (0969) 23056

Run as a study centre for sculpture, woodwork, modelling and other visual arts, the Old School also has a gallery where paintings, ceramics, prints, sculpture, carvings, books etc, are for sale. Picture-framing, furniture-making, repairs and specialist casting in GRP

and concrete undertaken. Residential short courses available.

Open daily 10–5 in summer. Advisable to telephone in winter. Closed Xmas **C R W E D** 🚗

MIDDLEHAM FURNITURE COMPANY
(W and J Bishop and M R Phillips) Market Pl ✆ (0969) 22703

Cabinet-makers producing a small range of copies of 18th-century country furniture. Each piece is made individually and a variety of timbers is used. Commissions for both traditional and contemporary designs undertaken. Some turnery and treen available.

Open Mon–Fri 8–5.30, Sat 9–1, by appt. **C R W E D** 🚗

Middle Tysoe

Warwickshire **Map 4 SP34**

CRAFT FACTORY
(Amanda Evans) Main St ✆ (029588) 705

Traditional English clogs, hand-smocked dresses and traditional shepherds' smocks made to order. Also an attractive range of children's clothes, toys, dolls, house-signs, gifts and souvenirs for sale, plus a small museum of bygones.

Open Mon–Thu 9.30–5, Sat 9.30–12.30, Sun 2–5 Closed Jan–Etr **C R D** *credit cards* Ⓥ 🚗

Midsomer Norton

Avon **Map 3 ST65**

ROY WILTON
The Priory, Church Sq, ✆ (0761) 418982

Roy Wilton makes mechanical musical manikins. All the figures are hand-carved from wood, dressed in a variety of traditional costumes, and move to a musical accompaniment with the aid of electricity.

Open by appt. only **C R E D** 🚗 *by appt.*

Milford

Surrey **Map 4 SU94**

THURSLEY TEXTILE DESIGNS
(Zoë O'Brien) 1 Moushill La, nr Godalming ✆ (04868) 24769

Hand-woven articles, tapestries and designer knitwear are made (mostly to commission) in the Weaving Workshop. A wide variety of craftsmen-made original textiles is sold in the shop, including house furnishings, clothes and toys. Exhibitions are held regularly.

Open Mon–Sat 10–5.30. Also other times by appt. Closed Xmas & Etr **C D** *credit cards* ⓐ ⓥ ⓓ 🚌 *preferably by appt.*

Millom
Cumbria **Map 7 SD18**
SCHÖNE LEDER MODE
(G Schönfelder) Newton St/King St 🕾 *(0657) 2761*

Suede, leather and sheepskin garments made-to-measure in any style and any size. Customers' own designs can be made up.

Open Mon–Fri 9–5, Sat 10–12. Closed for lunch & Xmas & Etr **C R W D** 🚌

Minehead
Somerset **Map 3 SS94**
YARDE OAK POTTERY
(Geoffrey and Susan Grimshaw-Bevan) Yarde, Williton, nr Taunton. Turn off A39 Minehead/Williton road at Washford transmitter onto B3190 to Bampton. Take next l onto B3188. Pottery is on r. 🕾 *(0984) 40032*

Traditional pots to eat from, useful pots for cooking in, unglazed pots for planting things, imaginative pots for fun, decorative pots for pleasure – all in high-fired earthenware.

Open Mon–Fri 9–6, Sat 9–1. Closed Xmas **C W E D** 🚌 *by appt.*

Mistley
Essex **Map 5 TM13**
MISTLEY QUAY WORKSHOPS
(Messrs Cooper, Pearson, Rendell and Tucker) Swan Basin, nr Manningtree 🕾 *(0206) 393884*

The workshops offer high-quality work at reasonable cost. Con Rendell makes 'cellos and lutes; Bennett Cooper RCA makes domestic pottery with slip decoration; Graham Pearson works with wood to customer's requirements; Anne and Ian Tucker follow traditional working methods in the making of harpischords, virginals and spinets.

Open daily 10–6. Closed Xmas **C R D** 🚌

Modbury
Devon **Map 3 SX65**
WOODTURNERS (SOUTH DEVON) CRAFT CENTRE
(Mr and Mrs J and Miss H Trippas) New Rd 🕾 *(0548) 830405*

Visitors are welcome to watch the craftsmen and women at work making all sorts of wooden things for the home, from egg-cups to furniture. Other locally-made crafts for sale in the showroom include pottery, silverwork, baskets, pressed-flower pictures etc.

Open Mon–Sat 10–6. Closed Xmas **C R D** 🚌

Moretonhampstead
Devon **Map 3 SX78**
GULL STUDIO
(Gerald and Ulla Owen) 29 Cross St 🕾 *(0647) 40671*

Gold and silversmiths specialising in making silver spoons to both traditional and modern designs. A wide range of jewellery of all styles is always available, and items can be made to commission. Many original oil paintings of Dartmoor and other subjects, hand-made cards, bookplates and prints also for sale. Member of the Devon Guild of Craftsmen.

Open Mon–Fri 9.30–6.30, wknds 10–6.30 **C R D** 🚌

PATRICK B HAWKSLEY – SILVERSMITH
Old Wool Store, Bow La 🕾 *(0647) 40850*

Many articles traditionally made to modern designs include table silverware, silver and gold jewellery, boxes and photo frames, plus a range of solid-silver cats. All the work is carried out in sterling silver, hallmarked in London. Member of the Devon Guild of Craftsmen.

Open daily 9–5. Closed Xmas & Etr **C R W E D** *credit cards* ⓐ 🚌

Setting the scrolls in a wrought-iron gate

Moreton-in-Marsh

Gloucestershire   **Map 4 SP23**

COTSWOLD FURNITURE MAKERS LTD
(Richard Bagnall and David O'Donnell) 93 Northwick Business Centre, Blockley, nr Moreton-in-Marsh ✆ (0386) 700801

Quality upholstered sofas and chairs which have been hand-made using traditional methods and natural materials. Each design is available with fixed or loose covers made from a wide choice of fabrics. Repairs and re-upholstery also undertaken.

Open daily 10–4. Closed Xmas **R W E D** *Finance credit available 🚐 by appt.*

Morpeth

Northumberland   **Map 11 NZ28**

CHANTRY SILVER
(Alan Le Chard) The Chantry, Chantry Pla ✆ (0670) 58584

Silver jewellery of all descriptions, incorporating precious and semi-precious stones, always in stock. Also numerous paintings in many different media for sale. Glass engraving on presentation items undertaken.

Open Mon–Sat 9.30–5. Closed Xmas, Etr & BHs **C R W D** 🚐

TAILOR'S WORKSHOP
(Miss V E Godwin) Cambo, 12m W of Morpeth ✆ (067074) 217

Pure wool garments available in a choice of over 40 colours and over 70 designs, including extra-warm double-knitted sweaters, ladies' suits and dresses. All items are hand-finished to a high standard. A selection of ready-to-wear garments can be seen at the workshop.

Open Mon, Tue, Wed, Sat 9–1, Thu & Fri 2–5. Other times inc BHs by appt. Closed for lunch & Xmas & Etr **C W E D** 🚐

Mosterton

Dorset   **Map 3 ST40**

SHEPHERD'S WELL POTTERY
(David, Benjamin, Simon and Caroline Eeles) nr Beaminster, on A3066 ✆ (0308) 68257

A family business producing hand-made, wood-fired stoneware and porcelain. Work includes good functional table and kitchen ware, as well as large and small individual pieces. Many coloured glazes are used imaginatively with fluent brushwork decoration.

Open Mon–Sat 10–6, Sun 10–5. Closed Xmas **C W E D** 🚐 *by appt.*

Much Birch

Hereford & Worcester   **Map 3 SO53**

COTTAGE CLOCKS
(David and Barbara Firks) Bryn Garth Cottage ✆ (0981) 540419

An attractive selection of wall-clocks, made from pine, or lathe-turned in a variety of other woods. The faces are hand-painted in floral designs chosen to complement any decor.

Open Mon–Sat 9–6, Sun 10–6 **D** *credit cards* ⓐ 🚐

Much Cowarne

Hereford & Worcester   **Map 3 SO64**

STRAW CRAFTS CENTRE
(Mr R M and Mrs M Bradbury) The School House, nr Hereford ✆ (043278) 317

All straw-crafts are practised here; craft work includes corn dollies, rick finials, straw marquetry, hats and furniture. Residential summer schools are run in July and August, and at other times there is a studio, with holiday accommodation, to let. Member of the Herefordshire Guild of Craftsmen.

Open by appt. **C R D** 🚐

Muker-in-Swaledale

North Yorkshire   **Map 7 SD99**

SWALEDALE WOOLLENS LTD
(David and Grizel Morris) Strawbeck, nr Richmond ✆ (0748) 86251 (shop); 4768 (office)

A cottage industry specialising in products made from the local Swaledale wool. These are on display at the Centre in Muker and include crocheted garments, sweaters, ties, tweeds and wool for home knitting. Mail order service.

Open Mon–Sat 11–5.30, Sun 1–5.30. Closed Sun & Mon Jan–Mar **E D** *credit cards* ⓐ ⓥ 🚐 *by appt.*

Mullion

Cornwall   **Map 2 SW61**

SHOOGLY LUMS FOLK TOYS
(Anthony and Judy Peduzzi) Southernwood, Predannack Wartha, nr Mullion, telephone for directions from Mullion ✆ (0326) 240273

A comprehensive range of unusual and traditional moving folk toys, magical illusions and jig-dancing dolls – all made in wood, brightly painted, highly entertaining and suitable for all ages. The authors' book, *Making Moving Wooden Toys*, is available at the workshop.

Open all hours all year **C W D** 🏠

NORMAN UNDERHILL
Collectors' Corner, Trecarne, Meaver Rd ✆ *(0326) 240667*

Original and humorous character studies in earthenware. There are about 40 pieces in the range at present; each one is hand-modelled – using a coffee spoon and a small knife – and signed by Norman Underhill.

Open daily 10–10 **C D** *credit cards* ⓐ ⓥ ⓧ 🏠

Nantwich
Cheshire   **Map 7 SJ65**

FIRS POTTERY
(Joy and Ken Wild) Sheppenhall La, Aston, 4 m from Nantwich on A530 to Whitchurch ✆ *(0270) 780345*

A large selection of functional and decorative hand-built and thrown stoneware: grass-holders, lamp-bases and shades, planters, coffee-sets, mirrors and salt pigs, plus a range of cookware suitable for microwaves and dishwashers.

Open most days, but advisable to telephone **C W D** 🏠

Netherfield
East Sussex   **Map 5 TQ71**

LILIAN FORSHAW
'Potters', Darwell Hill, 1 m from Netherfield towards Heathfield on B2096 ✆ *(042482) 300*

Headquarters of a cottage industry making high-quality suede garments sold through mail order. Samples of work can be seen at Potters, and some ready-to-wear items are available 'off the rail'.

Open Tue & Thu 10–4, by appt. Closed for lunch **C** *(R on own work)* **E D** *credit cards* ⓐ ⓥ 🏠

Nether Stowey
Somerset   **Map 3 ST13**

QUANTOCK WORKSHOPS
(Sue and Crispin Aubrey) Hockpitt Farm, nr Bridgwater, up & over Castle Hill ✆ *(0278) 732921*

A converted stone barn provides working space for local craftsmen selling enamelled, bead and silver jewellery, designer knitwear and knitting kits, and imaginatively hand-

dyed yarns. Residential craft courses in summer and craft weekends in Sept. Please write for leaflet.

Open daily 10–5 **C R D** 🏠 *by appt.*

Newark-on-Trent
Nottinghamshire   **Map 8 SK75**

TUDOR ROSE ANTIQUES & BYGONES
(Christine and David Rose) Yew Tree Farm, Carlton-on-Trent, 6 m N of Newark on A1 ✆ *(0636) 821841*

Traditional furniture, mostly in oak and yew, and other country items of interest are made on the premises and can be seen in the showroom. Specialists in antique restoration.

Open Mon–Fri 8–5, wknds 9–5. Closed Xmas **R W D** 🏠 *by appt.*

Newbury
Berkshire   **Map 4 SU46**

ECCHINSWELL POTTERY
(Geoffrey Eastop) Ecchinswell, 5m S of Newbury off A339 ✆ *(0635) 298220*

Geoffrey Eastop works in porcelain, stoneware and earthenware, making mostly individual pieces, thrown on the wheel, with an emphasis on sculptural character. He is also well known for his richly coloured and decorated earthenware dishes.

Open most days or evngs by appt. Closed 25, 26 Dec **C W E D** 🏠 *by appt.*

SANDLEFORD PRODUCTS
(Graham Smith) Old Buildings, Sandleford Farm, Newtown Rd ✆ *(0635) 32624*

Specialist wood-workers undertaking turnery work, furniture-making and restoration, plus vehicle-coachwork building and repair – including the restoration of vintage vehicles.

Open Mon–Fri 8.15–5, Sat 9–12. Closed for lunch & Xmas **C R W E D** *credit cards* ⓐ 🏠 *by appt.*

STAN WARD'S SADDLERY
(C W Wordsworth) East Ilsley, 8m N of Newbury ✆ *(063528) 226*

An old-established workshop specialising in racing saddlery for the local training stables. Any kind of leatherwork can be made to order.

Open Mon–Fri 8–5, wknds 8–12. Closed Xmas & Etr **C R D** 🏠

Newmarket
Suffolk   **Map 5 TL66**
DOREEN SANDERS
Pippin Cottage, Wood Ditton ✆ (0638) 730857

A selection of textured wall-hangings, rugs, cushions and clothing made chiefly from natural yarns – including wool from many different breeds of sheep.

Open by appt. only **C E D** ⬛

Newquay
Cornwall   **Map 2 SW86**
HIDEBASHER LEATHER
(Andrew David Parkin and Timothy Chitty)
Crantock St ✆ (06373) 77785

Manufacturers of Ugg Boots – a range of unique sheepskin boots for the whole family, as well as many styles of sandals hand-made in traditional 'oak-bark' tanned leather. Leather goods of most descriptions made and a range of gift items is available. Saddlery repairs undertaken.

Open daily 10–6. Also 7 pm–10 pm Jun–Aug. Closed for lunch **C R W E D** *credit cards* ⓐⓥⓧⓓ⬛

LORNA WILES DESIGNS
(Lorna Wiles and Bob Cann) Wesley Yd ✆ (06373) 6840

Attractive and unusual co-ordinated summer skirts, tops, dresses and jackets, plus table linen, cushions and scarves – all made from hand-printed textiles. Special commissions are also undertaken.

Open Mon–Fri 8–5. Also Sat 10–4 Jun–Aug. Closed Xmas & Etr **C W E D** ⬛ *by appt.*

Nordelph
Norfolk   **Map 5 TF50**
WILLOW FORGE
(Jonathan Hurlock) High St ✆ (03668) 351

Makers of decorative, hand-forged wrought ironwork such as gates, garden furniture, staircases, fire-irons etc. Commissions welcome.

Open Mon–Sat 8–5, preferably by appt. **C R W D** ⬛ *by appt.*

Northampton
Northamptonshire   **Map 4 SP76**
P E M LINDSLEY LCG
27 Thornton Rd, Kingsthorpe, outskirts of Northampton ✆ (0604) 710590/890111

Joiners and cabinet-makers producing all types of quality free-standing and fitted furniture. Using solid timber, traditional or modern designs are made to customers' requirements.

Open by appt. only. Closed for lunch & Xmas & Etr **C R W** *(some* **E***)* **D** ⬛

PHOENIX MODEL DEVELOPMENTS LTD
(B L and S G Marlow) The Square, Earls Barton, 6m E of Northampton ✆ (0604) 810612

Miniature figurines and other scale models produced in kit form. Series range from the Georgian period to the fantasy figures of 'The Lost World of Atlantis' and all are cast in 'white metal' or English pewter. Free quotations for completed models, special trophies and commissioned work.

Open Mon–Fri 9–5, by appt. Closed Xmas, Etr & BHs **C R W E D** *credit cards* ⓐ ⬛

Northbourne
Kent   **Map 5 TR35**
PAUL HARRISON – SILVERSMITH
New Mill, Mill La, between Deal & Eastry, ✆ (0304) 373460

A wide selection of jewellery and silverwork designed and produced on the premises: some items incorporate hardwoods and other relevant materials. Work includes cutlery, gifts and articles for home, church and business use.

Open Mon–Fri 10–6. Also wknds by appt. Closed Xmas **C R W E D** ⬛

North Tawton
Devon   **Map 3 SS60**
GILL TREGUNNA CRAFT GALLERY & WORKSHOP
5 The Square ✆ (083782) 513

Gill Tregunna specialises in sculptural ceramics and her work can be seen in several major galleries. The subjects include cats, goats, hedgehogs, seahorses, dragons and warriors. Etchings, water-colours and textiles by local artists also on view.

Open Tue–Sat 10–6 **C E D** ⬛

North Walsham
Norfolk   **Map 9 TG23**
CAT POTTERY
(Ken and Jenny Allen) 1 Grammar School Rd, nr Black Cat Garage ✆ (0692) 402962

Traditional workshops where up to life-size, life-like pottery cats with glass eyes are made, together with phrenology heads, classical heads and skulls. A collection of 'railwayana' and other curiosities also to be seen here.

Open Mon–Fri 9–6. Closed Xmas & Etr **C W E D** 🚫 *by appt.*

MICHAEL VIRDEN ENGRAVED GLASS
Folgate Rd, Laundry Loke Industrial Estate, on bypass ✆ *(0692) 404417*

A selection of good-quality glass – drinking glasses, bells, plates, ashtrays etc – engraved with a wide variety of designs. Personalised engraving available.

Open Mon–Fri 9–5. Also Sat by appt. Closed Xmas **C W E D** *credit cards* ⓐ ⓥ 🚫 *by appt.*

Norwich
Norfolk   **Map 5 TG20**

LENHAM POTTERY
(Mrs A G Funnell) 215 Wroxham Rd, on the A1151 to Wroxham ✆ *(0603) 419065*

Slip-cast, semi-porcelain models of dogs, cats and goats, plus horses (available in four sizes and choice of colour) to order. Dolls'-house China made to $\frac{1}{12}$ scale. All parts for model horse-drawn vehicles supplied. Mail-order catalogue.

Open Mon–Fri 9–6, & wknds, by appt. Closed for lunch **C R W E D** 🚫

RENCRAFT STUDIOS
(Alistair S Rennie) Hazlemere Cottage, Langley, Loddon, 9 m SE of Norwich ✆ *(0508) 20302*

Miniature figures sculpted in metal, particularly 14th-century medieval knights. About 100 mm high, each one is hand-painted and the armour and heraldry are totally accurate.

Open by appt. only. Closed for lunch & Xmas & Etr **C W E D** 🚫

SIMON SIMPSON – CABINET MAKER
Cotenham Barns, Panxworth, 7 m E of Norwich on B1140 ✆ *(060549) 270*

A country workshop concentrating on high-quality, traditionally-styled furniture in a variety of hardwoods, but anything made to order. Specialist joinery and antique restoration also undertaken. Other crafts also on sale.

Open Mon–Sat 9–5.30, Sun 11–5. Closed Xmas **C R W E D** 🚫 *by appt.*

DAVID VAN EDWARDS
89 Rosary Rd ✆ *(0603) 629899*

Lutes, archlutes, theorboes and chitarrones made to authentic designs from the medieval, renaissance and baroque periods, plus renaissance and baroque bows for violin and viola-da-gamba instruments. All instruments are hand-made to the player's requirements in a variety of woods.

Open by appt. only **C R E D** 🚫

Nuneaton
Warwickshire   **Map 4 SP39**

JOHN LETTS SCULPTURES
(John Letts and Keith Lee) The Old School, Church La, Astley, nr Nuneaton ✆ *(0676) 42073*

Both artists can be seen working in the studio where their sculptures are for sale. John Letts' work is fluid and romantic whereas Keith Lee concentrates on character studies and men at work. The pieces are modelled in clay and cold-cast in bronze. The sculptors make both limited editions as well as original pieces. Special commissions are undertaken.

Open Mon–Sat 10.30–6. Also Sun, by appt. Closed Xmas **C W E D** *credit cards* ⓐ ⓥ 🚫 *by appt.*

Oakamoor
Staffordshire   **Map 7 SK04**

DOT MERRY
10–11 The Square , nr Alton Towers ✆ *(0538) 702744*

Artist specialising in equine, horticultural and domestic-animal portraiture. Free self-catering holidays available to anyone who would like their pet's portrait.

Open any time, preferably by appt. **C E D** 🚫 *by appt.*

Oakham
Leicestershire   **Map 4 SK80**

RUTLAND FOLK CRAFTS
(David and Sylvia Fish) 27 Thistleton Rd, Market Overton, nr Oakham ✆ *(0572) 83344*

Original, detailed paintings of birds on selected slices of naturally polished semi-precious agates, complete with display stand. Also a range of hand-painted decorative glass: doors and windows to customer's specification and many 'ready-to-hang' circles, shields, mirrors etc, plus lamps.

Open by appt. only **C W D** *credit cards* ⓐ ⓥ 🚫

Oakington

Cambridgeshire **Map 5 TL 41**

MARK BURY'S WORKSHOP
*(M E P Bury, AFGE) 53 Longstanton Rd ✆
(022023) 2401*

Mark Bury, a former pupil of David Kindersley, specialises in glass engraving, stone-carving and lettering, sculpture and design work for printing. Much of his work is commissioned and clients include the Perse School, Cambridge, and Corpus Christi College, Cambridge as well as many private customers.

Open Mon–Fri 9.30–5.30, Sat 10–4. Closed for lunch & Xmas & Etr **C R D** ♿

Odiham

Hampshire **Map 4 SU75**

BARTLEY HEATH POTTERY
(Lesley and Michael Dixon) North Warnborough, nr Odiham ✆ (025671) 2163

Hand-made domestic stoneware and various garden pots in terracotta.

Open Mon–Sat 9–6. Also some Suns. Closed 25 Dec–2 Jan. Advisable to telephone between Xmas & Etr **C W D** 💬 *by appt.*

Old Cleeve

Somerset **Map 3 ST04**

JOHN WOOD
(John Wood and Son (Exmoor) Ltd) Linton, between Minehead & Watchet ✆ (0984) 40291

Sheepskin tannery manufacturing coats, jerkins, rugs, hats, moccasins, toys etc. Factory tours take in every stage of the process. Many bargains in the showroom and 'seconds' shop.

Free guided tours Apr–Oct Mon–Fri at 10.45, 11.30, 2.15 & 3. Showroom open Mon–Fri 9–4.30 all year. Also Mar–Dec Sat & BHs 10–4. Closed Xmas **C W E D** *credit cards* Ⓐ Ⓥ 💬 *by appt.*

Oldham

Gtr Manchester **Map 7 SD90**

ACORN CRAFTS
(Janice Oakes) Unit 15, Alexandra Craft Centre, Uppermill (5 m from Oldham) ✆ (061652) 9637

Appliquéd quilted jackets for both adults and children in original designs. Individual clothes for children made to match the stories on the jackets. Nursery soft furnishings and paintings on nursery walls to a choice of themes.

Open Wed–Fri 11–4, wknds 11–5. Closed Xmas **C W D** *credit cards* Ⓥ 💬 *by appt.*

ARTISAN
(Anne Hamlett) 3 King St, Delph, nr Oldham in Saddleworth area ✆ (04577) 4506

Anne Hamlett works in the gallery creating her fantasy castles, dragons and figures out of clay. There is always a selection of other items of craftwork on display as well, including glassware, ceramics, paintings and sculpture. Also special exhibitions and demonstrations from time to time.

Open Thu–Sat 10.30–5.30, Sun 2–5. Also open BHs, & other times by appt. Closed Xmas (after 24 Dec) **C W E D** 💬 *by appt.*

Ollerton

Nottinghamshire **Map 8 SK66**

T S BARROWS & SON
(Rex, Norman and John S Barrows) Hamlyn Lodge, Station Rd ✆ (0623) 823600

Cabinet-makers, antique restorers and studio potters. A range of stoneware pottery, hand-made furniture and antiques is on display in the showroom here. The workshops are not on the premises.

Open Tue–Sat 10–5, Sun 12–5. (Oct–Mar Sun 12–4). Also open BHs. Closed 25 & 26 Dec & 1 Jan **C R W E D** *credit cards* Ⓐ Ⓥ 💬

Olney

Buckinghamshire **Map 4 SP85**

OLNEY POTTERY
(Deborah Hopson) Holes La ✆ (0234) 712306

Functional stoneware glazed with smooth, matt blues and greens and decorated with raised ribs, incised lines and inlay work. Named and commemorative commissions welcome.

Open any reasonable time, but advisable to telephone. Closed Xmas **C W E D** ♿

Otterburn

Tyne & Wear **Map 11 NY89**

REDESDALE SHEEP DAIRY
(Mark and Marijke Robertson) Soppitt Farm ✆ (0830) 20276

The Robertsons have revived the ancient tradition of milking sheep and keep several different breeds for the purpose. All the products are completely natural and include cheeses, with or without herbs, yoghurts, biscuits, quarg, riccotta and whey drinks.

Open at any reasonable time **C W D** ♿

Oundle
Northamptonshire　　　　　**Map 4 TL08**
OLD SCHOOL POTTERY
(Geraldine Doughty) Aldwincle, Kettering, nr Oundle ✆ (08015) 359

Hand-thrown and coiled pottery. The range includes oven-to-table ware, mugs, jugs, vases and plant pots. Christening and anniversary dishes, made to order, a speciality. Also house name and number plaques.

Open by appt. only **C D** ♿ *by appt.*

Over
Cambridgeshire　　　　　**Map 5 TL37**
LITTLE LEAD SOLDIERS
(P Davis) Unit 11A, Over Industrial Park, Long Stanton Rd, 9 m NE of Cambridge ✆ (0954) 30690

A large range of small lead military figures made and painted to a very high standard on the premises. Some casting can be done on the spot. Retail sales for large orders only.

Open Mon–Fri 9–4.30, Sat 9.30–12, by appt. Closed for lunch & Xmas & Etr **C W E** *(sometimes* **D**) ♿

Over Kellet
Lancashire　　　　　**Map 7 SD56**
THE WOOD REVOLUTION
(Malcolm Cobb) 'Thie-ne-Shee', Moor Close La, off B6254 E of Carnforth ✆ (0524) 735882

Wood-turner principally making turned components for new furniture, antique repairs and internal decorative joinery, e.g. newel posts. Work undertaken from architectural or engineering drawings and other illustrations. Medium production runs considered. Some gift-ware produced.

Open Mon–Sat 9–9, Sun 9–1, preferably by appt. Closed odd half days. **C R W E D** ♿

Oxford
Oxfordshire　　　　　**Map 4 SP50**
JOHN BYE – WOODWORKER
Springfield, 42 North Hinksey La, North Hinksey, and Old Estate Yd, Fyfield, Abingdon ✆ (0865) 721814 or Frilford Heath 390521

Wood-carver and cabinet-maker specialising in church carving and furnishings, letter-cutting and heraldry, plus upholstery and reproduction furniture.

Open Mon–Sat 8–5, but advisable to telephone. Closed Xmas **C R E D** ♿

GEOFFREY HARDING – GOLDSMITH & SILVERSMITH
31 The Green, Steventon, S of Oxford just off A34 ✆ (0235) 831371

Hand-wrought silver and gold ware for any domestic, ceremonial or ecclesiastical use. Special commissions undertaken.

Open all reasonable times, by appt. only. Closed for summer holiday **C D** ♿

GERALDINE KNIGHT
The Studio, Overford Farm, Wytham, off western Oxford ring road ✆ (0865) 250811

A varied selection of animal sculptures modelled and cast in many different materials.

Open most days, but advisable to telephone **C R E D** ♿

CYNDY SILVER – GOLDSMITH
19 Cumnor Rise Rd ✆ (0865) 862295

Gold and silver jewellery, incorporating precious and semi-precious stones, individually designed: client's own stones can be used. Any item made to customer's specification, or to special commission. Pearls and bead necklaces inventively restrung.

Open by appt. only **C** *(some* **R**) **W E D** ♿

Paddock Wood
Kent　　　　　**Map 5 TQ64**
WHITBREAD HOP FARM
(Whitbread and Co plc) Beltring ✆ (0622) 872068/ 872408

The country-crafts centre occupying one of the old oast houses has a selection of good-quality work made by the craftsmen who have workshops on the premises: Bill Wood, pottery; Louise and Hilary Whipp (0732) 842666, patchwork and soft furnishings; Louis J. Harvey (04747) 3075, metalwork; Tricia Miller (089272) 2829, pressed-flower work; E.T. Robins (0634) 240375, woodcraft; Amaltheus Designs (01-777) 0017, toys and mobiles. Refreshments available.

Open Tue–Sun 10.30–5 Apr–Oct. also open BHs. Craft Centre open by appt. in winter. **C R W E D** *credit cards* ⓐ ⓥ ⓧ *(varies with each business)* ♿ *by appt.*

Pailton

Warwickshire   **Map 4 SP48**

PAILTON POTTERY
(Sylvia Edon Langham) 12 Lutterworth Rd, nr Rugby ✆ (0788) 832064

A large selection of kitchen and tableware suitable for ovens, microwaves and dishwashers. Also many different ornamental animals and a range of decorative vases, wine sets etc.

Shop open Mon–Sat 9–6, Sun 12–6. Closed for lunch **C D** ⬥

Par

Cornwall   **Map 2 SX05**

MID CORNWALL CRAFT CENTRE & GALLERIES
(Margaret and Graham Could) Biscovey, nr Par, 3 m E of St Austell ✆ (072681) 2131

A comprehensive collection of individual work by West Country artists and craftsmen, including paintings, ceramics, glass, textiles, furniture and jewellery. Major one-man and mixed-media exhibitions held regularly. Also available: pottery and china-painting materials; tuition in fine-china painting; commemorative china.

Open Mon–Sat 10–5. Closed 25 Dec–1 Jan **C R D** *credit cards* Ⓐ Ⓥ ⬥ *by appt.*

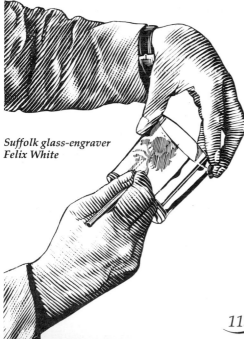

Suffolk glass-engraver Felix White

WELL STREET STUDIO
(Sarah Couch) 6 Well St, Tywardreath, nr Par ✆ (072683) 2437

Fine bone china and porcelain pieces individually hand-painted with delicate, naturalistic designs. Each item is unique. Special commissions accepted. Tuition and demonstrations in the art of china-painting.

Open Mon–Fri 9–4. Also other times if there **C W E D** ⬥

Pateley Bridge

North Yorkshire   **Map 7 SE16**

RICHARD BRAY & THE HOUSE OF GLASS
High St, 10m NW of Harrogate ✆ (0423) 711109

High-quality glassware exclusively hand-engraved to commission only – thimbles, goblets, lamps, prisms, scent flasks, vases and many other unusual items, plus mirrors, windows, table tops, terrariums etc. All commemorative work undertaken. Sculptured designs in blocks of crystal a speciality.

Open Mon–Sat 9–5, Sun 11–4.30 **C** *(R chipped glass)* **D** *credit cards* Ⓐ Ⓥ Ⓧ ⬥ *by appt.*

Penrith

Cumbria   **Map 11 NY53**

EDEN CRAFT GALLERY
(Eden Craft Association) Old Grammar School, St Andrew's Churchyard

The 16th-century school buildings provide an attractive setting for the comprehensive collection of craft goods for sale. All made by local craftsmen belonging to the Eden Craft Association. The range includes many unusual crafts.

Open Mon–Sat 9–5. Closed Jan–Mar Mon & Wed **C R D** *credit cards* Ⓐ Ⓥ ⬥

WEATHERIGGS COUNTRY POTTERY
(Jonathan and Dorothy Snell) Clifton Dykes, 4 m S of Penrith off A6 ✆ (0768) 62946)

Nineteenth-century pottery buildings now housing a pottery workshop, a weaving shed and gallery and a forge. The shop displays a full range of their work which includes traditional slipware, tiles and commemorative ware, goods woven from Jacob and Herdwick fleece and hand-forged ironwork. Other craft goods also for sale. Refreshments available.

Open daily 9–5.30. Closed Xmas **C R W E D** *credit cards* Ⓐ Ⓥ ⬥ *by appt.*

Penzance
Cornwall   **Map 2 SW43**

SANCREED STUDIOS
(Michael Truscott) Sancreed House, Sancreed, 2 m from Penzance on A30 ⊘ (073672) 450

All kinds of restoration work and cleaning of paintings is undertaken in the studios.

Open Mon–Fri 9–4.30, by appt. Closed for lunch & Xmas, Etr & BHs **C R** 🗑

SPINNING JENNIE STUDIO
(Naomi Gray Wallis) The Warehouse, Bread St ⊘ (0736) 61843

High-quality hand-made knitwear, needlework and soft toys. Specialists in one-off designs in natural fibres and hand-spun yarns, adults' and children's smocks and smocked garments, traditional teddy bears in character dress and toys such as the mice from Beatrix Potter's stories. Also spinning supplies, equipment and tuition.

Open Mon–Sat 10–5 (closed Wed pm). Closed for lunch **C R E D** 🗑

WEST CORNWALL WOODWORK
(Graham and Maureen Davey) Unit 4D, Longrock Industrial Estate, Poniou Rd, Long Rock ⊘ (0736) 69248 (home)

Contemporary-styled furniture made from woods such as oak, ash and elm available in a variety of finishes. A selection of furniture – tables, chests, cupboards, mirrors etc – can be seen at the studio.

Open Mon–Fri 9–5, Sat 9–12. Closed Xmas **C W D** 🗑

WOLF AT THE DOOR
(D Prosser, L Simmons, A Sicher, D McIntosh, S Marshell) 5/7 Bread St ⊘ (0736) 60573

Goods on display – all made by professional craftsmen – include pottery, *crêpe-de-Chine* garments, furniture, jewellery, basketry, model boats, rugs, rocking horses and lots more. Also a corner for selling children's work.

Open Mon–Sat 9.30–5.15 (closed Wed). Closed Xmas **C** *(occasionally* **R***)* **W E D** *credit cards* ⓥ 🗑 *by appt.*

Pershore
Hereford & Worcester   **Map 3 SO94**

JENNIE HILL GALLERY OF LOCAL ARTS
86 High St ⊘ (0386) 553969

All varieties of local art and craft work. Jewellery, engraved glass, pottery, woodwork, metal sculpture, smocked dresses, leatherwork, model soldiers, paintings etc, etc. Special emphasis on promoting young or unknown craftsmen and artists.

Open Mon–Sat 10–5.30. Closed Thu pm, for lunch & Xmas & Etr **C R D** *credit cards* ⓐ ⓥ 🗑

Peterborough
Cambridgeshire   **Map 4 TL19**

CHESTNUT COUNTRY CRAFTS
(Mrs Brenda Whaley and Mrs Audrey Walker) 90 North St, Stilton, 6 m S of Peterborough ⊘ (0733) 240636/240016

Stationery, toys, pottery, preserves, pressed-flower work, pictures, wooden items, patchwork, macramé etc, all made by East Anglian craftsmen, are sold in the shop.

Open Tue, Thu, Fri & Sat 10–4.30. Closed for lunch & Xmas **C D** 🗑 *by appt.*

R TAYLOR – THE WOODWORKER
Eastgate Cottage, Deeping St James, 7m N of Peterborough ⊘ (0778) 343381

Solid hardwood furniture made to customers' requirements. All types of woodwork undertaken, including production and site work. Member of the Guild of Master Craftsmen and the Guild of Woodworkers.

Open any time, but advisable to telephone **C R W E D** 🗑 *by appt.*

Peterchurch
Hereford & Worcester   **Map 3 SO33**

CRAFT INN
(Mr and Mrs J Hughes) High St ⊘ (09816) 651

Manufacturers of dried- and pressed-flower pictures using a variety of frames and flowers, e.g. roses, dahlias, begonias. Special pictures made to order using bridal bouquets etc. General picture-framing also undertaken.

Open Mon am, Tue–Sat and Sun pm. Closed for lunch **C R W E D** 🗑

PINE FACTORY
(Robert Norman and Andy Myatt) Old Forge Industrial Estate, on B4348 between Hereford & Hay-on-Wye ⊘ (09816) 527

Manufacturers of solid pine furniture. Welsh dressers, wardrobes, chests of drawers, tables etc, based on traditional designs and available in a range of coloured finishes at factory prices.

Open daily 10.30–4.30 by appt. Closed Xmas **D**
credit cards ⓐ Ⓥ Ⓧ 🚾

Petersfield
Hampshire   **Map 4 SU72**
EDWARD BARNSLEY WORKSHOPS
Cockshott La, Froxfield, nr Petersfield ✆ (073084) 233

All types of domestic, church and boardroom furniture individually designed and hand-made by master craftsmen and apprentices.

Open Mon–Fri 8–5.30, & wknds by appt. Closed Xmas & Etr **C D** 🚾

Petworth
West Sussex   **Map 4 SU92**
GRAFFHAM WEAVERS LTD
(Gwen and Barbara Mullins) Shuttles, Graffham, nr Petworth ✆ (07986) 260

All sorts of hand-woven products such as floor rugs (flat and pile), saddle blankets, cushions, bags, stoles and scarves made on the premises.

Open daily 10–5 by appt. Closed Xmas & for annual holiday **C D E** 🚾 by appt.

Pevensey
East Sussex   **Map 5 TQ60**
GLYNLEIGH STUDIO
(Sam Tanaroff) Peelings La, Westham, nr Pevensey ✆ (0323) 763456

A variety of work in non-ferrous metals such as brass and copper undertaken. Plates, dishes, jugs, lamps, candlesticks, bowls, etc made, plus church work of any description. Also antique restoration involving metal.

Open Mon–Fri 9 5.15, by appt. Closed for lunch & Xmas, Etr & BHs **C R D** 🚾

Pickering
North Yorkshire   **Map 8 SE78**
CROPTON CRAFTS
(Veronica and Russell Fletcher) The Old Manor House, Cropton, nr Pickering ✆ (07515) 607

The work of both amateur and professional craftsmen from North Yorkshire can be seen in the Old Turf House behind the Manor House. Woollens made from hand-spun yarn and hessian figures are made on the premises. Other goods include woodwork, jewellery, pottery, basketry, dried flowers, cards and gifts.

Open daily May–Oct & Dec **C D** 🚾

YORKSHIRE WOOLLENS
(Barry and Nancy Ward) Whitbygate, Thornton Dale, 2 m from Pickering on Scarborough rd ✆ (0751) 72468

A cottage industry specialising in high-quality, made-to-measure garments for ladies, but gents' suits etc also undertaken. Motifs on knitwear designed to customers' requirements. Hundreds of accessories on show, ranging from socks to hats.

Open daily 9–6 **C R W E D** credit cards ⓐ Ⓥ 🚾

Plaistow
West Sussex   **Map 4 TQ03**
PLAISTOW PLACE
(Ronald Hoad) ask in village for directions ✆ (040388) 212

Specialist in the repair and restoration of old clocks. Day or residential courses in repair and restoration techniques held at Plaistow Place. Mature apprenticeship schemes available. Clocks can be made to customers' specification.

Open almost any time, by appt. Closed Xmas **C R D** 🚾

Polperro
Cornwall   **Map 2 SX25**
POTTERY SHOP
(Mr and Mrs P Bishop) The Quay ✆ (0503) 72307

A wide choice of ceramic work hand-made by West Country craftsmen, plus other craft items. Casseroles, tea-sets, pottery cottages, dinner services, wooden and soft toys, silver and pewter jewellery, heraldic plaques, slate pictures, and so on.

Open daily 10–9 during summer season. Other months Mon–Sat 10–4, but advisable to telephone. Jan–Mar by appt. **D** credit cards ⓐ Ⓥ Ⓧ Ⓓ 🚾

Polstead
Suffolk   **Map 5 TL93**
H W ANGER & SON LTD
(D W Anger and Mrs D E Anger) 1 Mill La, 9 m N of Colchester ✆ (0206) 262274

A selection of over 300 tools for clay modelling and ceramic work. They are all hand-made from wood or metal and range from 5 in to 12 in in length, covering a wide spectrum of shapes and styles.

Open Mon–Fri 9.30–4.30 by appt. Closed for lunch & Xmas, Etr & 2 wks in Jul/Aug **W E D** 🚾

Polzeath

Cornwall   **Map 2 SW97**

ORIGINAL LEATHERWORK

(Steve Walton and Jane Thornton) 'Chy-an-Mor',
take turning to Tristram car park, then 1st l into
private rd ✆ (020886) 2567

High-quality leatherwork hand-made to
unique designs: bags, domed boxes, belts with
hand-made buckles, sandals and various small
items. Speciality is a range of unusual sculptural masks, also in leather, and special commissions are welcome.

Open Mon–Fri 8.30–6, Sat 8.30–5.30 Closed
Xmas **C R D** ♿

Pontrilas

Hereford & Worcester   **Map 3 SO32**

PARADISE FORGE

(Graham Perkins) ✆ (0981) 240374

Ornamental and functional hand-forged ironwork, ranging from candlesticks to church
gates, in modern or traditional designs. Special
commissions also undertaken.

Open daily 9–6 (usually), by appt. Closed for lunch
& Xmas & Etr **C R D** ♿

ROWLSTONE POTTERY

(Michael Tovey) Rowlstone (1½ m from Pontrilas off
A465) ✆ (0981) 240759

Domestic stoneware, garden pots and studio
pottery in rich, natural colours, or decorated
with an 'oak leaf' design. Stock ranges from
mugs to breadcrocks, and any commemorative
piece can be inscribed to order.

Please telephone for opening times. Closed Sun
C W D 📻

Portland

Dorset   **Map 3 SY67**

WELLBELOVED YARD POTTERY

(Carenza Hayhoe) Church Ope Rd, follow A354
into Wakeham. Pottery is beyond Museum
✆ (0305) 820237

Attractive and unusual pottery, including the
special 'Wildacre' range decorated with delicate landscape designs. Also hexagonal dishes
and pots, jars and bottles in the oriental tradition, teapots, cheese-dishes etc. Anniversary
clocks and plates designed to order.

Open Tue–Sat 2–5. Closed 24 Dec–Good Fri but
open to Trade buyers by appt. only. Closed for lunch
C W E D ♿

Postbridge

Devon   **Map 2 SX67**

POWDERMILLS FORGE & POTTERY

(M B Cutler and S Stevens) Blue Cottage,
Powdermills Farm, 2m from Postbridge on B3212
towards Two Bridges ✆ (0822) 88217

Ceramic figures and domestic ware hand-
made in the studio pottery; ornamental
wrought-ironwork, such as fire baskets and
implements, gates, and railings, produced in
the forge. There is an interesting display of old
country-craft items. Refreshments available.

Open Mon–Fri 10–6.30, wknds 10–5.30. Closed
Xmas **C R E D** *credit cards* Ⓥ 📻 *by appt.*

Praze an Beeble

Cornwall   **Map 2 SW63**

PRAZE AN BEEBLE GLASS BLOWING

(Norman Stuart Clarke) Homefield, nr Camborne
✆ (0209) 831325

Beautifully-coloured, decorative, freeblown
glassware with an iridised, lustrous finish:
vases, goblets, tankards, perfume bottles,
paperweights and tableware.

Open daily 9–6. Closed for lunch, wknds 9–6,
closed 1–3, & Xmas **C W E D** 📻 *by appt.*

Preston on Stour

Warwickshire   **Map 4 SP24**

OLD CARPENTERS SHOP

(Dennis Tomlinson) Alscot Park, nr Stratford-
upon-Avon ✆ (078987) 588

Cabinet-maker and joiner specialising in furniture and custom-made kitchens using old pine
and pitch pine.

Open daily. Closed Xmas **C W D** ♿

Princes Risborough

Buckinghamshire   **Map 4 SP80**

PETER WILDER – CABINET MAKER

Lydebrook, North Mill, Bledlow, nr Princes
Risborough ✆ (08444) 2213

High-quality furniture designed to suit customers' requirements. Mostly based on 18th-
and early 19th-century designs, work has included bureaux, chairs, glass-fronted book-
cases and pedestal dining tables. Any unusual
item undertaken. Producer of the Lute and
Cittern Kits.

Open Mon–Fri 8–8, wknds 8–1, by appt. Closed
Xmas **C R W E D** ♿

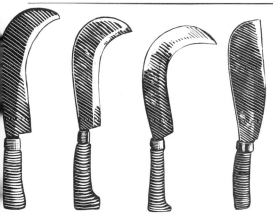

Billhooks used for spar-and hurdle-making

Puddletown

Dorset   **Map 3 SY79**

JACKY'S KNITWEAR
(Jacqueline and David Selby) Dairy Cottage, Admiston Farm, nr Dorchester ℰ (030584) 423 (after 6.30 pm)

Individual knitwear designs available ready-to-wear or made-to-measure. Jumpers, dresses, suits etc, can be made in a wide choice of yarns and colours. Pattern books provided for browsing. Customers' own designs can be made up to order.

Open Tue–Sat 10–4. Closed for lunch & Xmas & Etr **C D** 🚗 *by appt.*

Quainton

Buckinghamshire   **Map 4 SP72**

W G RUSHWORTH
Fieldside Farm, nr Aylesbury ℰ (029675) 500

Specialists in the production of glass-fronted gun cabinets. Any of the designs on show, made in solid hardwood, can be adapted to customer's specific requirements. Other cabinets, tables, bookcase units and one-off pieces made, plus steel safes for firearms. Member of the Guild of Master Craftsmen.

Open Mon–Fri 8.30–5.30, Sat 9–1, by appt. Closed for lunch & Xmas **C D** 🚗

Queen Camel

Somerset   **Map 3 ST52**

RIDGE POTTERY
(Douglas Phillips) High St, nr Yeovil ℰ (0935) 850753

Useful pots of all shapes and sizes in stoneware and porcelain – all hand-made, wood-fired and colourfully decorated. Douglas Phillips runs summer workshop courses at the pottery: enquiries welcome.

Open Mon–Fri 9–6, Sat 9–1, by appt. Closed Xmas **C W D** 🚗

Quendon

Essex   **Map 5 TL53**

QUENDON POTTERY & CRAFTS
(Russ and Brenda Smith) Cambridge Rd, between Stansted & Newport on B1383 ℰ (079988) 439

A wide collection of craftwork made mostly in East Anglia: English-willow baskets, pottery, paintings, prints, glass, wood, textiles, soft toys, ironwork, brass, candles, pot-pourri, sculptures, lace etc.

Open Wed–Sun 10–5.30 & BHs **C D** *credit cards* ⓐ ⓥ 🚗

Radstock

Avon   **Map 3 ST65**

FAULKLAND GARDEN GATES & COUNTRY CRAFT SHOWROOM
(M J Horler) The Forge, Home Farm Workshops, Ammerdown, nr Bath, private road SP Faulkland Garden Gates off B3139 ℰ (0761) 35305

Ornamental wrought-ironwork forged on the premises. Many other craft goods made in Avon and Somerset also for sale, including engraved glass, wooden house-plaques, chopping boards, trinket boxes, toys, turned bowls and light-pulls.

Open Mon–Fri 9–5, Sat 9–1, Closed for lunch, & for 1 wk in summer **C R W E D** *credit cards* ⓐ 🚗 *by appt. to see blacksmith at work.*

Ravenshead

Nottinghamshire   **Map 8 SK55**

LONGDALE RURAL CRAFT CENTRE
(Gordon C Brown) Longdale La ℰ (0623) 794858/ 796952

The Centre has a gallery selling a huge range of craftwork, workshops where some of the goods are made, and a display of old craft tools and equipment. Just some of the crafts represented are leatherwork, pokerwork, pottery, modelmaking, weaving, furniture-making and bookbinding. Refreshments available in the licensed restaurant.

Open daily 9–6. Closed Xmas **C R E D** 🚗 *by appt.*

Ravenstonedale

Cumbria   **Map 7 NY70**

BECKSIDE GALLERY & WORKSHOP
(John Hawkins) Scar Cottage, nr Kirkby Stephen
℡ (05873) 259

Fine furniture traditionally made by hand in all types of hardwood. Designs are based on traditional-English and period styles. Special commissions welcomed. All forms of antique restoration undertaken.

Open Mon–Sat 9–6 in summer, 10–5 in winter, & Sun 11–5. Closed 25 & 26 Dec **C R W E D** ⌖

Reeth

North Yorkshire   **Map 7 SE09**

PHILIP BASTOW – CABINET MAKER
Stonegate, Back La, nr Richmond ℡ (0748) 84555

A small firm concerned with designing and manufacturing solid wood furniture and specialist joinery. Small, turned gift-items, including wall clocks, also for sale. Special commissions are welcome

Open daily 9–8. Closed Sun in winter **C R W D** ⌖ *by appt.*

Retford

Nottinghamshire   **Map 8 SK78**

LEE SINCLAIR – DESIGNER/CRAFTSMAN
Endon House, Main St, Laneham, between Retford & Lincoln on R Trent ℡ (077785) 303

A small workshop producing individually designed modern furniture ranging from upholstered items to cabinet work; from domestic pieces to special contract designs for architects and interior designers The work is sculptural in style and aims to be both practical and attractive. The hardwoods used are kiln-dried on the premises.

Open by appt. only **C D** ⌖

Ringwood

Hampshire   **Map 4 SU10**

BURLEY POTTERY
(M Crowther) 3 Ringwood Rd, Burley, nr Ringwood ℡ (04253) 3205

A selection of table and oven ware, ceramic pictures and sculptures, plus original paintings and macramé work.

Open Tue–Sun 10–5.30. Also open Mon in Jul & Aug **C D** ⌖

Roadwater

Somerset   **Map 3 ST03**

RIVERDEN CRAFT WORKSHOP
(Bill, Margit and Stella Poirrier) nr Watchet, 400 yds from Valiant Soldier PH ℡ (0984) 40648

Fire-forged metalwork of a functional yet decorative nature; hand-made ornamental candles in many shapes, sizes and colours; hand-knitted garments made from hand-spun Exmoor and Jacob sheeps' wool.

Open Mon–Fri 9–5.30. Also wknds, by appt. **C R W E D** ⌖ *by appt.*

Rockhampton

Avon   **Map 3 ST69**

CAROLE FORD PAPERWEIGHTS & MINIATURES
The Old Post Office, nr Berkeley ℡ (0454) 260498

An attractive range of hand-painted glass paperweights and gilt-framed wall miniatures – including some pen and ink drawings. Many subjects are depicted, but local scenes a speciality. Personal, business and trade commissions undertaken.

Open any time by appt. **C R W E D** ⌖

Romsey

Hampshire   **Map 4 SU32**

LITTLE LONDON SPINNERS
(Fran Benton) 7 Tee Court, Bell St ℡ (0794) 516026

A full range of spinning supplies, including wheels, fleece, fibre and patterns, plus unusual hand-spun yarns for hand-knitting and a selection of garments. Spinning lessons, demonstrations and talks by arrangement.

Open Mon–Sat 9.30–5 (closed Wed pm). Closed BHs **C** (**R** *wheels*) **W E D** *credit cards* ⓐ ⓥ ⓧ ⓓ ⌖ *by appt.*

MICHELMERSH BRICK CO LTD
(D A and Q Hill) Hillview Rd, Michelmersh, turn r off A3057 4 m N of Romsey ℡ (0794) 68506

Manufacturers of hand-made, kiln-fired bricks. Briquettes, paviors (paving bricks), sawn-gauged arches and specially-shaped bricks all available in a range of four colours. Also fireplace kits and fittings in a variety of distinctive designs.

Open Mon–Fri 9–5, Sat 9–12. Closed Xmas & Etr. Telephone at BHs **C R W E D** *credit cards* ⓐ ⓥ ⌖ *by appt.*

THE THATCHER'S ART

Thatching is said to be the oldest of all the building crafts practised in Britain. The earliest materials used for thatching were certainly wild plants such as reed, rushes, broom, heather and bracken. Today, however, thatchers mostly use either wheat long straw, combed wheat reed or water reed. Thatch made of water reed is assessed by CoSIRA as lasting on average from 50–60 years; next comes combed wheat reed, at 25–40 years; and lastly long straw at 10–20 years. A list of Master Thatchers' local associations is given on p. 124.

Thatched cottage at Furzey Gardens, Minstead in Hampshire

Special machines (above) can be used for harvesting to get the straw or reed of a workable length, and it is then prepared for use by combing (top). When working on a roof, the thatcher usually keeps his tools in the thatch for convenience, as in the display from Knuston Hall near Northampton (left). A skilled thatcher (opposite, above and right), who lays the thatch properly, ensures a long life for the roof

Master Thatchers Association
Local Secretaries *(in county order)*
F J PURSER (Beds & E Midlands)
34 Bradford Rd, Toddington, Dunstable, Beds
℡ (05255) 3610

MJ MINCH (Berks, Bucks, Oxon)
The Rookery, Church Hanborough, Oxon
℡ Freeland (0993) 882152

I ROSE (Cornwall & Devon)
The Coach House, Ashley Manor,
Atherington, Umberleigh, Devon
℡ High Bickington (0769) 60410

D SYMONDS (Dorset)
Dormer Cottage, Chideock, Bridport, Devon
℡ (029789) 644

S R HARRIS (Gloucs, Heref & Worcs, Warwicks)
19 Brookend La, Kempsey, Heref & Worcs
℡ Worcester (0905) 820010

The traditional Devon village: cob and thatch cottage at Branscombe

J H GALE (Hants, Wilts)
17 Greyfriars, Eastgate St, Winchester, Hants
℡ (0962) 67389

MRS A JARVIS (Kent, Surrey, Sussex)
Malling Place, Middle Way, Kingston Gorse,
East Preston, Sussex
℡ Rustington (09062) 6104

M FRANKLIN (Leics, Rutland)
3 Maltings Yd, Exton, Oakham, Leics
℡ (0572) 812763

G DUNKLEY (Northants)
25 Little La, Yardley Hastings, Northants
℡ (060129) 280

E H PARKS (Somerset)
Mead House, 104 Periton La, Minehead,
Somerset
℡ (0643) 4939

R YATES (Suffolk)
Lake Farm House, Rougham,
Bury St Edmunds, Suffolk
℡ Sicklesmere (028486) 365

Ross-on-Wye

Hereford & Worcester   **Map 3 SO62**

BLADES JEWELLERS
(T W Blades) 54 High St ✆ *(0989) 64560*

All types of jewellery designed and manufactured in precious metals. Specialists in titanium jewellery, with a wholesale range of over 60 designs. Repairs and commissions undertaken in autumn and winter only.

Open Mon–Sat 9–5.30. Closed for lunch & Xmas **C R W E D** *credit cards* ⓐ ⓧ ⇪

MOREL & PARTNERS
(K Mooney, P Russell, H Eldridge) Old Gloucester Rd ✆ *(0989) 67750*

Cabinet-makers specialising in custom-built furniture for kitchens and bedrooms; tables; chairs; display cabinets and fire-surrounds.

Open Mon–Fri 8–5.30, Sat 9–4 **C D** ⇪

MULTI-CRAFTS
(Mr G K and Mrs M Peckham) 25 High St ✆ *(0989) 62438*

High-quality pine furniture for kitchens, bedrooms, bathrooms etc hand-made on the premises. Items made to order. Examples of many other crafts also for sale in the shop.

Open Mon–Sat 9–5 (closed Wed pm). Closed Xmas **C D** *credit cards* ⓐ ⓥ ⓧ ⇪

J ARTHUR WELLS – CRAFTSMAN IN WOOD
Gatsford, 400 yds from end of M50 on A449 ✆ *(0989) 62595*

Furniture-maker and wood-turner producing purpose-made woodwork of all descriptions. A selection of turned items always in stock.

Open daily 9–9 **C R D** ⇪

Rothbury

Northumberland   **Map 11 NU00**

LEIF DESIGN
(Anthony J Hope) Tumbleton House, Cragside Estate, on Rothbury to Alnwick rd ✆ *(0669) 21036*

Jewellery and silversmithing workshop producing a wide range of gold jewellery (gem-set and plain) and silverware. Commissions undertaken for designing and making any item in precious metals – trophies, sculptures etc: individual pieces or production runs.

Open by appt. only. Closed Xmas **C R W E D** *credit cards* ⓐ ⓥ ⓧ ⓓ ⇪

Rotherwick

Hampshire   **Map 4 SU75**

CRAFTY ANNE
(John and Anne Sheppard) village is just N of Hook ✆ *(025672) 2461*

A wide range of ceramic ware, engraved glass and tapestry kits all produced and sold on the premises. Day and evening classes available.

Open Mon–Fri 9–7 (closed Wed pm), Sat 9–6, Sun normally 10–2 **C D** ⇪ *by appt.*

Routh

North Humberside   **Map 8 TA04**

D F HALL – JOINER
(workshop is on Beverley to Hornsea rd) ✆ *(0401) 42314*

A selection of garden furniture available, including seats, tables, flower boxes, bird tables and dog kennels. Also gates to order.

Open Mon–Fri 9–5 & most wknds. Closed Xmas **C D** ⇪

Rowlands Castle

Hampshire   **Map 4 SU71**

OLD FORGE POTTERY
(Harry and Pam Clark) 37 Durrants Rd ✆ *(070541) 2632*

Simple, functional stoneware glazed with warm, natural colours. Ranging from dinner services to individually designed pots, the work is all hand-thrown and personally signed. Large decorative platters and uniquely-styled clocks are specialities of the pottery.

Open Mon–Fri 9–5, wknds 10–4.30. Closed Xmas **C D** ⇪

Royston

Hertfordshire   **Map 5 TL34**

FOXHALL STUDIO
(Gill Rennison) Kelshall, nr Royston, off Baldock rd, turn l after ¾ m. Follow SP Kelshall ✆ *(076387) 209*

Stained-glass artist Gill Rennison uses modern and traditional techniques in her rural studio workshop. As well as windows, the range of items she produces includes Tiffany-style lampshades, table and wall lights, terrariums, sun-catchers, mirrors, butterflies and jewellery boxes.

Open Mon–Fri 8–6, wknds 9–6, but advisable to telephone. Closed Xmas **C R D** ⇪

M D GRATCH
(Betty and David Gratch) The Maltings, 99 North End, Meldreth, off A10 between Royston & Cambridge ✆ (0763) 61615

Furniture, wood-carvings and turned work made from solid hardwoods. The showroom has a range of modern furniture based on traditional styles, wooden utensils and carved items. Commissions welcomed.

Open Mon–Fri 8.30–5.30, Sat 8.30–4. Closed for lunch & Xmas, Etr & BHs **C W E D** *credit cards* Ⓥ ⊞ *by appt.*

Ruddington
Nottinghamshire   **Map 8 SK53**

O J BLOOD – BLACKSMITH
43–45 Church St ✆ (0602) 211842

Ornamental ironwork such as gates, weathervanes and flower-holders. All general blacksmithing work also undertaken.

Open Mon–Fri 9–5, Sat 9–12, by appt. Closed for lunch & Xmas & Etr **C R D** ⊞

Rudyard
Staffordshire   **Map 7 SJ95**

DAISYBANK POTTERY
(Raymond Victor Mee) Old Post Office, Lake Rd, nr Leek ✆ (053833) 656

A studio pottery where a range of both practical and decorative stoneware is hand-thrown.

Open Tue–Fri 10–7 in summer, 10–5 in winter. Also open wknds. Closed Xmas **C E D** ⊞

Rushlake Green
East Sussex   **Map 5 TQ61**

GEOFF CHASE – WOODTURNER
Thorneyfold Cottage, Bodle Street Green, nr Rushlake Green ✆ (0435) 830598

Geoff Chase produces hand-turned quality woodware in a wide variety of home-grown English hardwoods. His range includes nutcrackers, butter dishes and knives, pen stands, candlesticks, bud vases and wooden eggs for collectors.

Open Mon–Sat 9.30–6, by appt. **C W D** ⊞

Ryde
Isle of Wight   **Map 4 SZ59**

G & M JEWELLERY
(Guy and Menna Morey) 123 High St ✆ (0983) 611232

Jewellery designed and made to order: many gem-stones in stock or customers can supply their own materials. All kinds of repair work undertaken, including re-stringing, replacing stones and restoring antique pieces. Old jewellery remodelled into new designs.

Open Mon–Sat 9.30–5 (closed Thu). Closed for lunch **C R W E D** *credit cards* Ⓥ ⊞

Rye
East Sussex   **Map 5 TQ92**

DOROTHY CARTER HOME-MADE PRESERVES
(Gerald and Dorian Campbell) Oxenbridge Cottage, Readers La, Iden, nr Rye ✆ (07978) 212

Home-made preserves – jams, jellies and marmalades – made to old family recipes by traditional methods. Freshly-picked locally-grown fruits, including damsons, medlars, loganberries and quinces used, with no colouring or preservatives.

Open daily 9–6. Closed Xmas & Etr **C W E D** ⊞ *by appt.*

FIELD'S HOUSE GALLERY
(Frank Page) Udimore, 3½ m W of Rye on B2089 ✆ (0424) 882142

Finishing the rim of a laundry basket

Designer knitwear in pure Shetland wool for men, women and children. All made on hand-frame machines and hand-finished. Sweaters, pullovers, waistcoats and cardigans are available in a range of original designs and choice of attractive colours. Mail-order catalogue.

Open Tue–Sat 10.30–5.30 **C W E D** 🗘

DAVID SHARP CERAMICS
(D T Sharp and D M Sharp) 55 High St ✆ (0797) 222620

Specialist in ceramic signs and plaques, hand-made and painted to order. The studio also makes birds, animal-figurines, wall-tiles and pictures, and there is always a large selection of number signs, mugs, jugs etc in stock. There is a world-wide mail-order service for plaques.

Open Mon–Fri 9.30–5, wknds 10–5. Closed Xmas & Etr **C W E D** *credit cards* Ⓐ Ⓥ Ⓧ Ⓓ 🗘

SYNTOWN MINIATURES
(Mr C R Coxon) Knellstone Lodge, Udimore, 3 m from Rye on B2089 towards Broad Oak ✆ (0797) 223388

Designers and manufacturers of metal model soldiers which are usually sold in kit form. Figures can be painted with oils to customer's specification. All repair and restoration work concerning model soldiers undertaken, as well as the restoration of most types of militaria.

Open daily 9–6, by appt. Closed lunch & Xmas & Etr **C R W E D** 🗘

Saffron Walden
Essex   **Map 5 TL53**

DAVID H COLEMAN & DAVID PRUE
26 Radwinter Rd ✆ (0799) 22558

Craftsmen cabinet-makers who specialise in producing exact replicas of antique English period furniture, particularly William and Mary and Queen Anne pieces in English walnut.

Open Mon–Fri 8–5.30, & wknds, by appt. Closed Xmas & Etr **C W E D** 🗘

St Briavels
Gloucestershire   **Map 3 SO50**

ST BRIAVELS POTTERY
(Gill and Rob McCubbin) nr Lydney ✆ (0594) 530297

Studio potters producing a wide range of stoneware. Most of it is for domestic use and, apart from the plates, is oven- and freezer-proof.

Records are kept so that any piece can be repeated if required.

Open daily 9–8, but advisable to telephone. Closed for lunch & Xmas **C W D** 🗘

St Germans
Norfolk

See entry under Wiggenhall St Germans

St Ives
Cambridgeshire   **Map 4 TL37**

HAND-ENGRAVED GLASS BY JOHN BRITTON
(John and Lyn Britton) 20 East St ✆ (0480) 61065

Hand-engraved glassware and crystal for every occasion. Souvenirs, gifts, trophies, prizes etc, to order or available from stock. Over 200 lines to choose from, each item individually designed. Customers' own glass can be engraved, if suitable.

Open Mon–Sat 9–5.30 (closed Thu pm). Closed Xmas **C D** *credit cards* Ⓐ Ⓧ 🗘

GEM GARDENS GLASS ART
(Geoff Copping) Allgood Glass, 18 East St, Robb's Yd ✆ (0480) 301660

Stained-glass windows, screens, lampshades, jewellery boxes, terrariums etc, in stock and made to order. Doors with company logos a speciality. Tools, books and materials for the hobbyist sold.

Open 8.30–5, Sat 9–4. Closed BH Mons **C R W E D** 🗘

L'BIDI STUDIO
(Lindsay and Margot Beedie) 40 The Broadway ✆ (0480) 66886, also 81 High St, Buckden, nr Huntingdon ✆ (0480) 810545

Hand-painted silks, scarves, tops, cushions, cards – produced in the studio and sold with other quality British-made items in wood, metals, clay, textiles and glass. There is a gallery displaying work by local artists.

Open Mon–Sat 10–5.30 (closed Thu), Sun 2–5. Closed Xmas **C R** *(W silk only)* **E D** *credit cards* Ⓐ Ⓥ 🗘

St Ives
Cornwall   **Map 2 SW54**

ANCHOR POTTERY
John Buchanan Gallery, The Custom House, Wharf Rd ✆ (0736) 795078/796192 ext 5

A good selection of stoneware, porcelain, water-colour and oil paintings, plus various other quality gift-items.

Open Jan–Sep Mon–Fri 10–5.30. Also open wknds in high season. Closed for lunch C W D *credit cards* ⓐ ⓥ ⊟

LEACH POTTERY
(Janet Leach) Upper Stennack, nr St Ives ☎ *(0736) 796398*

Janet Leach studied pottery in Japan for two years and this influence is reflected in her unusual and distinctive work. It has been widely exhibited and has a place in many public and private collections. She runs the pottery founded by her late husband, Bernard Leach.

Open Mon–Fri 9–5. Also Sat in summer. Other times by appt. Closed Xmas C W E D *credit cards* ⓐ ⓥ ⓓ ⊟ *by appt.*

St John's Chapel
Co Durham **Map 11 NY83**

WEAVERS
(Michael and Mary Crompton) Forge Cottage, Ireshopeburn, nr St John's Chapel ☎ *(0388) 537346*

Specialists in traditional hand-loom weaving. Rugs, fabrics, bags, belts, soft furnishing etc for sale. Also tapestries woven from mixed yarns: some natural dyes used. Spinning and weaving equipment sold and repaired. Tuition available.

Open daily 10–4 (closed Thu). Closed Xmas C R W E D ⊟

St Merryn
Cornwall **Map 2 SW87**

HARVOSE WOODCRAFT
(Peter Ian Rutherford) Harvose, nr St Merryn ☎ *(0841) 520567*

Wood-turned house-signs, stools, teapot stands, bowls, lamps, coffee tables, cheeseboards, platters and miniatures for sale. Any item can be made to order. Tuition available.

Open all reasonable hours except Sun pm C R W E D *credit cards* ⓐ ⓥ ⓧ ⓓ ⊟

PYDAR CRAFTS
(Mary Lunnen and Joan Nunn) 9 Trelantis ☎ *(0841) 520755*

Copper-enamel work produced mainly for the wholesale trade: jewellery (earrings, pendants, brooches etc); bowls; boxes. Also pure silk scarves hand-dyed in an endless variety of colours and patterns.

Visitors by appt. only W *(some* D*)* ⊟

Salisbury
Wiltshire **Map 4 SU12**

CASTLE GALLERIES
(John Lodge) 79 Castle St ☎ *(0722) 333734*

Examples of Colin Stanton's dioramas and period house models (built to a scale of about 4 mm: 1 ft) can be seen at the Galleries. The dioramas are framed and boxed false-perspective models of scenes which give an illusion of great depth: there is no restriction on the subject matter. Photographic references can be used for both types of work.

Open Mon–Sat 9–5.30 (closed Wed). Closed for lunch & Xmas & Etr C D *credit cards* ⓐ ⓥ ⊟

AXEL KEIM – WOODCARVER
43 Russell St, Wilton, nr Salisbury ☎ *(0722) 744143*

Cabinet-making, figurative and ornamental wood-carving and turned work – including ecclesiastical work. Pattern-making also undertaken.

Open Mon–Fri 8–6, Sat 8–1. Closed Xmas & Etr C R W E D ⊟

TILSHEAD PIPE COMPANY LIMITED
(Kennedy Barnes) 19–20 Candown Rd, Tilshead, 14 m NW of Salisbury on A360 ☎ *(0980) 620679*

Hand-made briar smoking pipes which have been individually turned from solid blocks of naturally-dried Greek plateau briar. Several styles, all based on traditional English shapes, are available.

Open Mon–Fri 8.30–5.30. Closed Xmas & Etr C R W E D ⊟ *by appt.*

Sampford Peverell
Devon **Map 3 ST01**

DAVE REGESTER
Millstream Cottage, Higher Town ☎ *(0884) 820109*

Wood-turner making bowls to be used and looked at in English hardwoods. Wood with burrs (swirly natural patterns) a speciality. Other individually designed domestic and ornamental items turned to customers' specification. Inscriptions carved or pyrographed.

Open Mon–Fri 8.30–5 by appt. Closed for lunch & Xmas & Etr C D ⊟

Sandbach
Cheshire   **Map 7 SJ76**

WARMINGHAM CRAFT WORKSHOPS & GALLERY
(Graham and Barbara Moores) The Mill, Warmingham, nr Sandbach ✆ (027077) 246/304/366

Resident craftsmen and artists are Simon Darton, wood-worker (see separate entry below); Tony Robertson-Suggett, jigsaw maker; Roger Hounslow, silversmith; Andy and Steve, potters; Eileen and Janet, Warmingham Woollen Constructions; David Robinson, artist; Mike Scott, creative woodcraft; Anne Claxton, farrier. The gallery displays their work, plus many other craft goods.

Gallery open Wed–Sun 11–5.30. Also open BHs. Closed Xmas **C R W D** *credit cards* Ⓐ Ⓥ 🚌 *by appt. Workshops vary.*

STUDIO 1 – WARMINGHAM CRAFT WORKSHOPS
(Simon Darton) The Mill, Warmingham ✆ (027077) 304

Traditional and modern furniture, plus many turned wooden items such as hand- and table-mirrors, stools, walking-sticks and hand-spinning accessories. Also carved house-signs made from a choice of hardwood boards.

Open at varying times so advisable to telephone. Closed Xmas **C R W E D** 🚌

Sandwich
Kent   **Map 5 TR35**

HOMEWEAVES
(Sally Gordon Boyd) 53 New St ✆ (0304) 617272

All sorts of hand-woven and knitted items in natural fibres such as wool, cotton and mohair. The range includes sweaters for men, women and children, rugs, cushions, bags, gloves, hats etc and anything can be made to order. Mail-order catalogue.

Open Tue, Thu, Fri & Sat 10–5. Other times by appt. Closed Xmas **C R W E D** *credit cards* Ⓐ Ⓥ 🚌 *by appt.*

Saxmundham
Suffolk   **Map 5 TM36**

BRUISYARD WINES LTD
(Mr and Mrs I H Berwick) The Winery, Church Rd, Bruisyard, nr Saxmundham ✆ (072875) 281

A working vineyard and winery where wine can be tasted free. The shop sells wines, vines,

souvenirs, local crafts, books etc. 1½-hour group tours available by appointment.

Open May–mid Oct daily 10.30–5 **W E D** *credit cards* Ⓐ Ⓥ 🚌 *by appt.*

Scarborough
North Yorkshire   **Map 8 TA08**

VALLEY HOUSE CRAFT STUDIO
(Enid M Taylor) Ruston, nr Scarborough ✆ (0723) 862426

Lace-making, lace bobbin-making and embroidery work are demonstrated and taught in the studio where visitors can either just watch, or participate. Various hand-made items made by other craftsmen are for sale.

Open Etr–Spring BH wknds 2–6; Spring BH–end Sep daily 10–6; Oct–Etr Mon, Tue & Thu 1.30–4.30. Sometimes closed for classes **C D** 🚌

Scawby Brook
South Humberside   **Map 8 SE90**

JOHN RICHARD COLLINSON
Lilly Grove 1m W of Brigg ✆ (0652) 53436

Traditional domestic and ecclesiastical furniture hand-made in English oak with an original adzed finish. Various small items ranging from ashtrays to cheese-boards are also for sale.

Open Mon–Fri 9–6, wknds 10–5. Closed Xmas **C R E D** *credit cards* Ⓐ Ⓥ 🚌

Seaborough
Dorset   **Map 3 ST40**

HILL FORGE
(Michael Henderson) Mount Pleasant, nr Beaminster ✆ (0308) 68781

A wide range of traditional hot-forged, wrought-ironwork items usually in stock. Fireside and domestic fittings individually made to order.

Open Mon–Fri 9–6. Closed Xmas **C R D** *credit cards* Ⓐ Ⓥ 🚌

Seale
Surrey   **Map 4 SU94**

MANOR FARM CRAFT CENTRE
¼ m off Hog's Back (A31) between Guildford & Farnham

Blown-glass by Deborah Fladgate ✆ (02518) 2101; woodturning by Bob Cordell ✆ (02518) 2103/3661; stained-glass and jewellery by

Helen Walker ✆ (02518) 3661. Refreshments available in Herbs Restaurant.

Open Tue–Sat 10–5, Sun 2–5. Restaurant closed in Jan C R W E D ✉ by appt.

Sedbergh

Cumbria   **Map 7 SD69**

PENNINE TWEEDS
(Bryan and Carol Hinton) Farfield Mill, 1 m E of Sedbergh on Hawes rd ✆ (0587) 20558

Commercial weavers of high-quality all-wool tweeds and worsteds, specialising in mohair, Jacob and Herdwick woollens. Hats, slippers, ties, scarves, rugs, skirts and jackets, plus some hand-knitted garments, for sale in the showroom. Tours of the mill by arrangement.

Open daily 9–8 C W E D credit cards ⓐ ⓥ ✉

Sennen Cove

Cornwall   **Map 2 SW32**

ROUND HOUSE
(P A and M P Coxon) Sennen Cove, 2 m from Lands End

A collection of some of the best work produced in Cornwall from over 100 artists and crafts-men. More unusual items include kites, crab pots, knot-boards and folk toys, as well as pottery, glass, toys, sculptures, silk etc, etc. Demonstrations given during the summer.

Open Mon–Sat 10–10 in summer, 10–5 in winter. Closed Jan & Feb C E D credit cards ⓐ ⓥ ✉

Sessay

North Yorkshire   **Map 8 SE47**

ALBERT JEFFRAY – WOODCARVER & CRAFTSMAN
nr Thirsk ✆ (0845) 401323

Hand-carved, English-oak dining-room and occasional furniture, plus church furniture and carvings. Different sizes and designs from those in stock made to order. Smaller items also usually available.

Open Mon–Fri 8–5, Sat 10–5. Other times by appt. Closed Xmas C R W E D ✉ by appt.

Shaftesbury

Dorset   **Map 3 ST82**

CAMELOT CRAFT GROUP
Town Hall, High St ✆ Barbara Harrison (07476) 2954

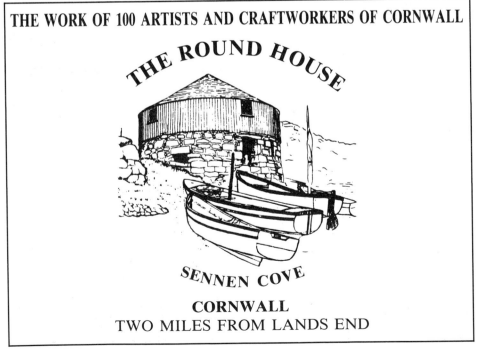

A hurdle-maker starting a new weaving rod

A regular Craft Market has been held in Shaftesbury for some years. Crafts always to be found include needlework, enamelled jewellery, basketry, weaving, wood-turning and glass-engraving. Potters, coppersmiths, leather and iron workers, plus others, attend intermittently.

Open 10.30–4.30, May–Dec two or more Fris per month. Telephone for precise dates. **C R D** 📠

COUNTRY FURNITURE
(David and Denise Plimmer) 12 Bell St 🕾 *(0747) 3121*

Cabinet-makers specialising in traditionally-styled fitted furniture. A selection of antiques and gift-ware also for sale. Special commissions undertaken.

Open Mon–Sat 9–5. Closed Xmas **C R E D** *credit cards* (a) (v) 📠

FONTMELL POTTERIES
The Old Brewery, Fontmell Magna, nr Shaftesbury 🕾 *(0747) 811597*

Manufacturers of pottery giftware and kitchenware. Several lines available with various designs featuring birds, flowers, butterflies, fruit and animals. Special ranges to order.

Open Mon–Fri 8–4.30. Closed Xmas **C W** 📠

STUDIO POTTERY WORKSHOP
(Anne Chase BA) 15 Bell St, behind bookshop, opp. car park 🕾 *(0747) 2198 (home)*

Unusual, delicate pieces of fine porcelain reminiscent of toadstools, water lilies, seed-heads, rock pools, standing stones etc. Some larger pieces, mainly in stoneware, and a few domestic items as well. All hand-made.

Open Mon–Sat 9.30–6 in summer, 10–4 (closed Wed) in winter. Closed Xmas (after 24 Dec) & New Year **D** 📠

WING & STAPLES
(John Wing and Les Staples) The Forge, Motcombe, nr Shaftesbury 🕾 *(0747) 3104*

Practical and decorative hand-forged ironwork; fire and door furniture, lanterns, gates, grilles, garden furniture etc, plus replicas of medieval weapons. All kinds of repair work and horse-shoeing undertaken.

Open Mon–Fri 9–5, Sat 9–1, preferably by appt. Closed for lunch & Xmas & Etr **C R D** 📠 *by appt.*

Sheringham
Norfolk   **Map 9 TG14**
SHERINGHAM POTTERY
(H L, A C and I J Farncombe) 30 Church St 🕾 *(0263) 823552*

Glazed earthenware pottery made by slab, coil and pinch-pot methods only, which produce a wide range of non-symmetrical forms. Lots of tableware, pots, vases, lamps etc, plus some white-porcelain, sculptured pots.

Open daily 9–5, but advisable to telephone **C D** 📠 *by appt.*

Sherrington
Wiltshire   **Map 3 ST93**
MATTHEW BURT
Albany Cottages, nr Warminster 🕾 *(0985) 50531*

Fine contemporary furniture designed and made by Matthew Burt. Principally using English hardwoods – fruitwoods in particular – his commissions have ranged from Japanese bridges to a 14 ft boardroom table, including many domestic pieces. Items from a small batch-produced range are available at shorter notice.

Open daily 9–6, by appt. Closed Xmas & Etr **C E D** 📠

Shilbottle
Northumberland   **Map 11 NU10**
SHILBOTTLE GLASS STUDIO
(Paul Manson) West End, nr Alnwick 🕾 *(066575) 521*

Free-blown, hand-finished glassware (using colour) made from 24-per-cent lead glass. The range includes goblets, jugs, plates, bowls, etc, as well as individual pieces. Reproductions, commissions and engraving all undertaken. Cards and other studio glass are also for sale. Refreshments available.

Open Tue–Sat 10–5.30, Sun 10.30–5.30. Also open BHs **C R W E D** *credit cards* ⊗ 🚌

Shillingstone
Dorset **Map 3 ST81**
CECIL COLYER MA, FSD-C
Orchardene, Candys La, nr Blandford Forum, opp. Methodist Church ✆ *(0258) 860252*

Furniture of all sorts and turned items such as bowls, mirrors and mazers made from rare or special hardwoods. Also church and domestic silverware: wedding and anniversary presents a speciality. Most work to commission.

Open by appt. only. Closed for lunch **C D** 🚌

Shipham
Somerset **Map 3 ST45**
GEOPEG GEMS
(Geo W H and Kate E P Reed) Hawthorn Cottage, Hollow Rd ✆ *(093484) 2609*

Unusual, hand-crafted gifts made from minerals and semi-precious stones; gemstone trees, agate clocks, shell and gemstone jewellery, pen sets, book-ends and polished mineral specimens. Engraved nameplates to order.

Open Mon–Fri 9–6, wknds 10–5 **C W D** 🚌

Shrewsbury
Shropshire **Map 7 SJ41**
ST JULIAN'S CRAFT CENTRE FOR SHROPSHIRE
(Andrew S N Wright) St Alkmunds Sq, entrance in High St ✆ *(0743) 53516*

Permanent studios make/sell/undertake: hardwood toys, printing, shoe-making, picture-framing, jewellery, spinning and weaving, pine goods, stained-glass and mirror-work, pottery and craft supplies. Also three separate art galleries, plus a market every Saturday with lots more crafts.

Open Mon–Sat 10–5 (closed Thu). Closed 25, 26 Dec & Etr Mon **C R D** *(varies with each studio)* 🚌

Silverdale
Lancashire **Map 7 SD47**
WOLF HOUSE GALLERY
(Edward and Denise Dowbiggin) Gibraltar, nr Carnforth ✆ *(0524) 701405*

High-quality work from British artists and craftsmen, including original paintings, traditional wooden toys, hand-blown glass, wood-carvings and textiles. Pottery workshop on the premises. Craft demonstrations sometimes given and residential and non-residential tuition offered. Home-made refreshments are also available.

Open summer Tue–Sun 10.30–5.30 (closed for lunch wkdys only). Winter: wknds only 10.30–5.30 **C W E D** *credit cards* ⓐ ⓥ ⓧ ⓓ 🚌 *evngs only, by appt.*

Simonsbath
Somerset **Map 3 SS73**
SIMONSBATH POTTERY
(R A Billington) Pound Cottage (on Exmoor) ✆ *(064383) 443*

Casseroles, mugs, jugs, vases, garden pots and lamp bases made on the premises. Other crafts and paintings for sale in the gallery include silverware, hand-blown glass and prints.

Open Mon–Fri 9.30–6, Sat 9–12, Sun 10–5. Closed Tue Nov–Mar, & Xmas **C W D** *credit cards* ⓐ ⓥ 🚌

Skegness
Lincolnshire **Map 9 TF56**
NEWTON NEWTON FLAG GALLERY & WORKSHOP
(Clifford and Georgina Ann Newton) Bishop Tozer's Chapel, Middlemarsh Rd, Burgh le Marsh, 2½m W of Skegness off A158, turn l at Croft crossrds ✆ *(0754) 68401*

A 19th-century chapel and schoolroom houses this small manufacturer of flags and banners. All are made by the appliqué (Sewn) method and the range includes national, state and provincial flags, as well as civic, regimental, school, society, club and guild flags and banners. Also golf-green flags, burgees, pennants and international signal code flags.

Open all reasonable times by appt. Closed Xmas & Etr **C W E D** *credit cards* ⓐ ⓥ ⓧ ⓓ 🚌 *by appt.*

Slaidburn
Lancashire **Map 7 SD75**
PEBBLE ISLAND PROJECTS (Falkland Islands)
(Consultants: John and Eileen Huckle) Dale Head, B6478 to Tosside. After 3 m turn l onto unclassified rd to Clapham. Farm is on r after 3½ m ✆ *(02006) 294*

Souvenirs and gift-goods from the Falkland Islands, including paperweights – polished stones from the islands' beaches decorated with an enamel crest, and jewellery – pendants, brooches etc, made from Pebble Island or other Commonwealth stones. Hand-embroidered items made to commission.

Open Mon–Fri by appt., wknds 9–5. Closed Xmas
C W E D ♿

Sleaford
Lincolnshire   **Map 8 TF04**

ANWICK COUNTY FORGE
(Richard Geoffrey Powell) 62 Main Rd, Anwick, nr Sleaford ✆ *(0526) 832176*

Specialists in traditional hand-forged, wrought-ironwork. Gates, screens, balustrades, spiral staircases, ornamental garden ironwork and fireside furniture all made to a high standard of craftsmanship.

Open Mon–Fri 9–6, Sat 12–6, Sun all day. Closed Xmas **C R D** 🚌 *by appt.*

JOHN BANGAY PUBLICATIONS
12 Sleaford Rd, Cranwell, 4 m N of Sleaford ✆ *(0400) 61275 or home (0522) 25516*

Prints, stationery, tableware and framed pictures featuring the drawings of John Bangay. Using pen and ink and some water-colour, his subjects are buildings in the East Midlands, e.g. Lincoln Cathedral, various windmills, Gainsborough Old Hall and general townscapes.

Open by appt. only **C W E D** ♿

Snettisham
Norfolk   **Map 9 TF63**

SNETTISHAM STUDIO
(Mrs Carole Grace) 1 Lynn Rd ✆ *(0485) 41167*

Woven and hand-spun garments, wall hangings, soft furnishings etc, and all equipment and supplies for spinning, weaving and dyeing for sale. Tuition in these crafts available. Lots of other goods from toys to patchwork sold as well.

Open daily 10–5. Closed Xmas **C W E D** 🚌 *by appt.*

Somerby
Leicestershire   **Map 8 SK71**

VIPA DESIGNS LTD
(Peter Crump and Vivia Bremer-Goldie) Chapel La ✆ *(066477) 439*

An original range of modern gold and silver jewellery produced by lost-wax casting. Sold in retail outlets throughout Britain.

Open 9–5.30 & wknds by appt. Closed Xmas & Etr
C W E D ♿

Somersham
Cambridgeshire   **Map 4 TL37**

SOMERSHAM POTTERY
(Stuart Marsden BA (Hons) LSD-C) 3 & 4 West Newlands, nr Huntingdon ✆ *(0487) 841823*

Hand-made stoneware, terracotta and porcelain. Specialities include mugs with medallions for clubs, pubs etc, house plaques, commemorative plates and a large selection of plant-pot holders, vases and planters.

Open daily 9–5. Closed 25 Dec to New Year
C R W E D 🚌

Soudley
Gloucestershire   **Map 3 SO61**

DEAN HERITAGE MUSEUM TRUST
See also feature on pp. 13 & 15.
Camp Mill, nr Cinderford ✆ *(0594) 22170*

The resident craftsmen at Soudley produce wrought-ironwork, pottery, engraved glass, pokerwork, knitwear, leather goods and brightly-painted wooden articles. Visitors are welcome to watch them at work. A wide choice of souvenirs, paintings and other craft work is available in the gallery.

Open daily 10–6. Closed 25 Dec **C R W D** 🚌 *(appt. preferred).*

South Littleton
Hereford & Worcester   **Map 4 SP04**

THE BASKET MAKER
(Russell A Rogers) Main St, nr Evesham ✆ *(0386) 830504*

Traditional English-willow and cane baskets of a very high quality are made on the premises. There is a wide selection in the showroom, and any special commissions are welcomed.

Open Mon–Sat 9–6. Other times by appt. Closed Xmas & Etr **C R D** 🚌 *by appt.*

South Molton
Devon   **Map 3 SS72**

SANDY BROWN POTS
(Sandy Brown and Takeshi Yasuda) 38 East St ✆ *(07695) 2829*

Two potters producing their own distinctive, highly-individual pots. Sandy Brown's work is exuberant and colourful with abstract designs; Takeshi Yasuda's is softly-thrown, strong and warm.

Open by appt. **C W E D** ⊞

South Newington
Oxfordshire   **Map 4 SP43**
P GIANNASI
The Close, nr Banbury ✆ *(0295) 720703*

Craftsman in metal and wood. Hand-forged wrought-ironwork from garden furniture to fire-furnishings (mostly to commission) and turned items in British woods, including bowls, complete lamps, goblets, skittles and croquet sets. Many designs incorporate both materials, e.g. nutcracker bowls.

Open at all reasonable times **C R D** ⊞

Southwell
Nottinghamshire   **Map 8 SK75**
J D & M WATTS
Unit R, Maythorne Mill, off Lower Kirklington Rd ✆ *(0636) 815149*

All kinds of cabinet-making and wood-turning undertaken.

Open Mon–Fri 7.30–4.30, by appt. Closed for lunch & Xmas. Open Etr by appt. **C R D** ⊞ *by appt.*

Clinching nails in a cleft-oak gate

Spalding
Lincolnshire   **Map 8 TF22**
MOULTON SERIES OF MINIATURES
(Alfred Herring) 4 Seas End Rd, Moulton Seas End, nr Spalding

Model-maker specialising in miniature horse-drawn vehicles built to a 1/12 scale, as well as dolls' houses and miniature furniture. Many models can be seen at this address, and brochures are available by post.

Visitors by appt. only **C R W D** ⊞

Stalham
Norfolk   **Map 9 TG32**
SUTTON WINDMILL POTTERY
(Malcolm Flatman) Church Rd, Sutton, nr Stalham ✆ *(0692) 80595*

A small workshop producing an extensive selection of hand-thrown, reduction-fired stoneware in a variety of glazes. The range includes all sorts of domestic ware from dinner services to lamps, plus individual pieces. Visitors welcome in the workshop.

Open most of the time, but advisable to telephone. Closed Xmas & Etr **C W D** ⊞ *by appt.*

Stamford
Lincolnshire   **Map 4 TF00**
TINWELL FORGE
(David O'Regan) Tinwell, 2 m W of Stamford on A6121 ✆ *(0780) 56341*

All types of hot- and cold-forged, decorative ironwork undertaken. The varied range of stock in the shop attached to the forge includes plant-troughs, hay-racks, door-knockers, candlesticks, fencing, and hanging baskets. Barbecues, weathervanes, streetlights etc to order.

Open Mon–Fri 8.30–5.30, wknds 9–5.30. Closed for lunch & Xmas **C R W E D** ⊞

Standon
Hertfordshire   **Map 5 TL32**
S R SMITH – CABINET & CLOCK MAKERS
Mill End, nr Ware ✆ *(0920) 822685*

Clocks and furniture made in solid wood, particularly mahogany, English oak and walnut. All items are hand-finished and French-polished. Specialists in long-case, bracket and wall clocks with traditional English movements, Welsh dressers and chests.

Open Mon–Fri 9–5. Wknds by appt. Closed Xmas, & 2 wks annual holiday **C D** ⊕

Staveley

Cumbria   **Map 7 SD49**

PETER HALL WOODCRAFT
Danes Rd, W side of village on A591 between Kendal & Windermere ℗ *(0539) 821633*

Cabinet-makers, antique furniture restorers and wood-turners producing high-quality, hand-made work; dining tables and chairs, coffee tables, corner cupboards, dressers, chests, bowls (inlaid or plain) lamp bases, ring boxes, tea caddies etc. Member of the Guild of Lakeland Craftsmen.

Open Mon–Fri 9–5, Sat 9–12. Closed Xmas **C R E D** *credit cards* ⓐ ⓥ ⊕ *by appt.*

Sleeple Bumpstead

Suffolk   **Map 5 TL64**

ANN WRIGHTSON
The Pottery, North St, ℗ *(044084) 552*

Stoneware decorated with slip and sgraffito work. Most of the range is for domestic use, but there are also some individual pieces and models of animals.

Open Mon–Fri 10–6.30. Wknds by appt. Closed for lunch & Xmas & Etr **C W D** ⊕

Steyning

West Sussex   **Map 4 TQ11**

GORDON LAWRIE
Hammes Farm, Washington Rd ℗ *(0903) 814056*

Interesting, figurative jewellery made in gold, silver and titanium. Designs are inspired by the landscape, myths, magic, the Celts and the Dark Ages. Gordon Lawrie's work has been widely exhibited in the UK and abroad.

Open Mon–Sat 9.30–5, but advisable to telephone. Other times by appt. Closed 25 Dec **C E D** ⊕ *by appt.*

GERALDINE ST AUBYN HUBBARD
2 Charlton Court Cottages, Mouse La ℗ *(0903) 814204*

Hand-woven and block-printed textiles, using some hand-spun yarns, dyed and made in the workshop. Finished items include simple clothes, scarves and ties in silk, wool or cashmere, and block-printed ties and cushions.

Open any time, but advisable to telephone **C W E D** ⊕

Stockland Bristol

Somerset   **Map 3 ST24**

RON & OLIVE HAMILTON
Cherry Trees, nr Bridgwater off A39. Hinkley Point rd at Cannington, then 3rd r. ℗ *(0278) 653176*

Furniture designed and made to suit individual requirements. A small range of country-style furniture, such as tables, dressers and benches, is available in a variety of timbers.

Open Mon–Fri 9–5, Sat 9–12, preferably by appt. Closed for lunch & Xmas & Etr **C D** *credit cards* ⓐ ⊕

Stockton

Warwickshire   **Map 4 SP46**

NEVILLE NEAL
(Neville and Lawrence Neal) 22 High St, nr Rugby ℗ *(092681) 3702*

The old village craft of making ash-chairs with rush seats is continued by Neville Neal and his son. Locally-grown ash poles and rushes are used to make a range of spindle and ladder-back chairs and stools.

Open Mon–Fri 8–5.30; Sat 9–12 or by appt. Closed for lunch, Xmas & Etr **C R E D** ⊕ *by appt.*

Stogumber

Somerset   **Map 3 ST03**

YELLOW POTTERY
(David Winkley) Lower Vellow, Williton, 1 m off A358 just S of Williton, nr Stogumber ℗ *(0984) 56458*

Robust, decorative, oven-proof pots and dishes to cook in, serve from and eat off. A very wide selection in stoneware or porcelain.

Open Mon–Sat 8.30–6. Closed Xmas **C W E D** *credit cards* ⓐ ⓥ ⊕ *by appt.*

Stoke St Gregory

Somerset   **Map 3 ST32**

WILLOW CRAFT INDUSTRY
(C B and M A Coate) Meare Green Court, 8m E of Taunton ℗ *(0823) 490249*

An old family business engaged in willow-growing, processing and basket-making in the traditional manner. Visitors to the workshop can also see willow charcoal for artists being produced. Dozens of baskets available in the shop, plus a display concerning the industry.

Open Mon–Fri 9–5. Closed for lunch & Xmas, Etr & BHs **R W E D** ⊕ *by appt.*

Stonham
Suffolk   **Map 5 TM15**

BROOK CRAFT MARKET
(Mrs V A Belsher) Ascot House, Norwich Rd, Earl Stonham, nr Stowmarket ✆ (0449) 711495

A good collection of assorted craft goods and gifts, including corn dollies, jewellery, clothes, pottery, pictures, toys, mobiles, basketware, mats, cards. See also entry under Ipswich.

Open Tue–Sun 10–5 (closed Mon–Wed Jan–mid Jun). Closed for lunch **D** 🚌

Stourton Caundle
Dorset   **Map 3 ST71**

CAUNDLE CHAIR RENEW
(Mrs Alison Leslie-Jones) The Old Vicarage, nr Sturminster Newton ✆ (0963) 62453

All chair re-caning and re-rushing work undertaken in any pattern.

Open any time, but advisable to telephone. Closed Xmas **C R** 🚌

Stowmarket
Suffolk   **Map 5 TM05**

COMBS TANNERY SHOP
(Mrs N Portway) Combs Tannery, 1½ m S of Stowmarket ✆ (0449) 674656

Sheepskin rugs, plus skins and offcuts from the 18th-century tannery are sold in the shop at factory prices. Also a complete range of sheepskin coats, jackets and accessories, as well as a new line in suede and leather clothing.

Open Mon–Fri 9.30–5 in summer, 9.30–5.30 in winter. Also open Sat Sep–Mar. Closed for lunch & Etr **D** *credit cards* ⓐ ⓥ 🚌

MUSEUM OF EAST ANGLIAN LIFE
✆ (0449) 612229

Demonstrations of many different East-Anglian crafts can be seen on certain days between April and October. They include: riven-ash hurdle-making; butter-making; lace-making; natural dyeing; spinning; bee-keeping; blacksmithing; wood-turning; basket-making.

Museum open Apr–Oct Mon–Sat 11–5, Sun 12–5. Closed Nov–Mar **D** 🚌 *preferably by appt.*

Stow-on-the-Wold
Gloucestershire   **Map 4 SP12**

HART VILLA INTERIORS
(Richard Bagnall) Sheep St ✆ (0451) 30392

An interesting collection of work hand-made from natural materials by craftsmen or small businesses: furniture, rugs, pottery, lamps, pictures, sculpture, carvings and taxidermy.

Open Mon–Sat 10–5 (closed Wed). Closed Xmas **C R W E D** *credit cards* ⓐ ⓥ ⓧ 🚌

Stratford-upon-Avon
Warwickshire   **Map 4 SP25**

PETER DINGLEY GALLERY
(Peter Dingley and Guido Marchini) 8 Chapel St ✆ (0789) 205001

A gallery specialising in high-quality work from a number of British artists and craftsmen – both well known and less so. One-man exhibitions are held in spring and autumn, and a ceramic display in summer.

Open Mon–Sat 9.30–5.30 (closed Thu pm). Closed for lunch & Xmas & Etr **D** 🚌 *by appt.*

STRATFORD-UPON-AVON POTTERY
(Gareth Richards) Firs Farmhouse, Lower Quinton, nr Stratford ✆ (0789) 720703

Visitors are welcome in the workshop where a wide range of domestic stoneware is hand-thrown. Mugs, vases, honey-pots, storage jars, goblets, flower pots, coffee-sets, bread crocks etc and porcelain, for sale in the showroom.

Open daily 10–5. Closed Xmas **C W E D** 🚌 *by appt.*

TORQUIL POTTERY
(Reg Moon) 81 High St, Henley-in-Arden, 8 m N of Stratford ✆ (05642) 2174

Pots of all shapes and sizes for practical and ornamental purposes. All hand-thrown and decorated in stoneware and porcelain.

Open Mon–Sat 9–6. Closed for lunch, & Xmas & Etr **W D** *credit cards* ⓐ ⓥ 🚌 *by appt.*

Street
Somerset   **Map 3 ST43**

SIMPLE WAY
(David Price) Unit 5, The Tanyard ✆ (0458) 47275

Manufacturers of 'do-it-yourself' leather shoe- and handbag-kits. Each one contains everything needed to make the shoes or bags, plus full instructions; only assembling and stitching is involved. A made-to-measure service is available. Mail-order catalogue.

Open Mon–Fri 9–5, wknds 9–1. Closed Xmas **W E D** *credit cards* ⓐ ⓥ 🚌 *by appt.*

Stroud

Gloucestershire   **Map 3 SO80**

PATENI POTTERS & CERAMIC SCREEN PRINTERS
(John and Susan Howard) High St, South Woodchester, nr Stroud (at old post office)
℗ *(045387) 2562*

Indirect screen-printing for the decoration of ceramics and silk-screening in ceramic enamels, plus art and camera work, are all undertaken on the premises.

Open any time, by appt. Closed for lunch, & Xmas & Etr **C W E D** 🚐

MAXINE RELTON
5 The Street, Horsley, nr Stroud ℗ *(045383) 2597*

Many unusual and attractive wooden items all individually designed and hand-turned, chiefly in local hardwoods. Also a wide selection of reasonably-priced original etchings, engravings, water-colour paintings and drawings, including Cotswold landscapes.

Open daily, by appt. **C D** 🚐

Sturminster Marshall

Dorset   **Map 3 SY99**

NIGEL PAIN PRODUCTS (WESSEX) LTD
(Nigel and June Pain) 2 Bailey Gate Industrial Estate, opp. Churchill Arms, just off A350
℗ *(0258) 857737*

Souvenir Victorian-style glass paperweights, using prints and photographs, are made on the premises. Customers' own pictures can be made up on the spot. A selection of over 300 on display in the showroom, including Caithness, Isle of Wight and Medina Glass paperweights.

Open Mon–Fri 9–5. Closed Xmas & Etr **C W E D** *credit cards* ⓐ ⓥ 🚐 *by appt.*

Sturminster Newton

Dorset   **Map 3 ST71**

RALPH HAMPTON
Grenestede Farm, Kingston, Hazelbury Bryan, nr Sturminster Newton ℗ *(02586) 7116*

Cabinet-maker specialising in traditional Chinese-style furniture using solid hardwoods and natural finishes.

Open by appt. **C E D** 🚐

Sutton

Norfolk   **Map 9 TG32**

SUTTON WINDMILL POTTERY
(Malcolm Flatman) Church Rd, nr Stalham
℗ *(0692) 80595*

A small independent workshop in a Broadland village, producing a wide range of practical domestic stoneware pottery, both single items, sets, and complete dinner services. Also lamps and commissions in a range of glazes.

Open any reasonable time, but telephone call advisable. Closed Xmas & Etr, **C W D** 🚐 *by appt.*

Swaffham

Norfolk   **Map 5 TF80**

BRECKLAND WOODCRAFTS
(Brian Elliott) Unit 4, Old Station Yd ℗ *(0760) 24282*

Craftsmen specialising in fine, wood-turned work, using English and exotic timbers, and in hand-made wall- and mantle-clocks and small items of furniture. Wholesale trade only.

Open Mon–Fri. 9.30–5.30. Closed Xmas **C R W** 🚐

THE GOODSHED CRAFT GALLERY
(Emma Woodrow and Willa Emerson) Little Dunham, 6 m NE of Swaffham ℗ *(0760) 22348*

A small gallery housed in a converted Victorian railway building where prints, textiles, glassware, furniture, wooden toys, ceramics, wood carvings and turnery are on display. Cy Woodrow, designer and furniture maker, works on site (see below).

Open Wed–Sun 10–5. Closed Xmas **C D** 🚗 *by appt.*

CY WOODROW & EMMA – DESIGNERS & MAKERS OF FURNITURE
The Goodshed, Little Dunham, 6 m NE of Swaffham 🕾 *(0760) 22348*

Fine furniture made to order in various English hardwoods. All types of work – from individual designs to replicas of period pieces – undertaken.

Open daily 9–5. Other times by appt. Closed Xmas **C D** 🚗 *by appt.*

Swanage
Dorset   **Map 4 SZ07**

THE OWL POTTERY
(Leslie Gibbons) 108 High St 🕾 *(0929) 425850*

Highly decorated hand-thrown and moulded earthenware. Specialities include individual dishes with pictorial motifs or intricate designs in majolica and slip, ceramic jewellery, small animals and hand-decorated tiles – a small selection of artwork is for sale.

Open Mon–Sat (closed Thu pm), but advisable to telephone. Closed for lunch & Xmas & Etr **D** 🚗 *school visits by arrangement*

WEST COUNTRY CRAFTS
(Pauline and John Neil) 6 Station Rd 🕾 *(0929) 423879*

An extensive display of quality craftwork which includes dolls with feather-stitched clothes, toys, pottery, kitchenware, table mats, glass, dried flowers etc.

Open Mon–Sat 9.30–5.30. Closed Xmas **D** *credit cards* ⓐ Ⓥ 🚗

Tatham
Lancashire   **Map 7 SD66**

WILL TYERS – CABINET MAKER & TIMBER SUPPLIERS
The Workshop, Moorhead Farm, nr Wray 10 m NE of Lancaster. (Please ring for directions) 🕾 *(0468) 21292*

Good-quality country furniture. Everything is hand-made in solid wood using traditional methods of construction. A small selection of original designs is available from stock but work is mostly made to order. Suppliers of English hardwoods and pitch pine.

Open Mon–Sat 8–6, by appt. Closed for lunch & Xmas **C W E D** 🚗

Taunton
Somerset   **Map 3 ST22**

FITZHEAD STUDIO POTTERY
(J Watt and V A Jones) Fitzhead, ½ m E of village at Higher Fitzhead. 8 m W of Taunton 🕾 *(0823) 400359*

High-quality stoneware and porcelain ranging from domestic ware to sculptural pieces. Also an attractive selection of batik pictures, lampshades and scarves. Classes and courses are available.

Open most of the time, but advisable to telephone **C W D** 🚗

THE ENGLISH BASKET CENTRE
(Nigel Hector) The Willows, Stoke St Gregory, nr Taunton 🕾 *(0823) 69418*

Basketware of all kinds, including furniture, can be found in the showroom. Everything is made by craftsmen using home-grown willow which has been processed in the workshop. Hurdles and artists' charcoal are also produced.

Open Mon–Fri 9–5, Sat 9–12 **C R E D** 🚗 *by appt.*

MAKERS
7A Bath Place 🕾 *(0823) 51121*

A co-operatively-owned shop where several craftsmen sell their work. The range, which is of consistently high quality, includes jewellery, silverware, pots, leather bags and belts, silks, paintings, knitwear, sculpture and woodwork.

Open Mon–Sat 9–5.30 **C R D** *credit cards* ⓐ Ⓥ 🚗

PERRY'S CIDER MILLS
(H W Perry) Dowlish Wake, nr Ilminster, 15 m from Taunton 🕾 *(04605) 2681*

Various ciders – made on the premises every autumn from locally-grown apples – can be bought in the shop where stone jars, mugs, corn dollies, pottery etc are also for sale. The 16th-century barn houses a fascinating collection of country bygones.

Open Mon–Fri 9–5.30, Sat 9–4.30, Sun 9.30–1. Closed for lunch & Xmas & winter BHs **W D** 🚗 *by appt.*

QUANTOCK DESIGN
(R A Billington) Chapel Cottage, West Bagborough, 9 m from Taunton ✆ (0823) 433057

Domestic and decorative stoneware. Specialities are casseroles of all shapes and sizes and matching vases and lamp-bases decorated with designs of local wild flowers. Other crafts are also for sale in the showroom.

Open Mon–Fri 8–6, Sun 11–5. Closed Xmas **C W E D** *credit cards* (a) (v) ⬆

SHEPPY'S FARMHOUSE CIDER
(R J Sheppy and Son) Three Bridges, nr Bradford-on-Tone, between Taunton & Wellington ✆ (082346) 233

Producers of good-quality, traditional Somerset cider which is for sale at the shop. Visitors are welcome on the farm and there is an interesting farm- and cider-museum on the premises. Guided tours by arrangement.

Open Mon–Sat 8.30–dusk, Etr–Xmas Sun 12–2. Closed Xmas **W D** ⬆ *by appt.*

Tenbury Wells
Hereford & Worcester   Map 7 SO56

RESTORATIONS UNLIMITED
(Robin Plowright and David Dyche) Yew Tree Cottage, Upper Rochford, nr Tenbury Wells ✆ (058479) 567

Specialists in traditionally-made leaded windows. All work made to individual requirements.

Open Mon–Fri 9–5, by appt. only. Closed Xmas **C R D** ⬆

Tetbury
Gloucester   Map 3 ST89

MARTIN WHITE (JEWELLERS)
(Carrie and Martin White) 25a Church St ✆ (0666) 53819 (day) 54030 (evngs)

Original designs in gold and silver using precious (and some semi-precious) stones. Diamond engagement rings using different coloured golds a speciality. Work mostly made to commission.

Open Mon–Sat 9–5.30 (closed Thu pm). Closed for lunch **C R W E D** *credit cards* (a) (v) (x) (d) ⬆

Tetsworth
Oxfordshire   Map 4 SP60

THE FORGE
(R and M Crockett) Back St ✆ (084428) 200

All types of ornamental and functional wrought-ironwork made. The showroom has a display of gates, lights, fire-dogs and baskets, flower stands etc, plus of brassware and pottery.

Open Mon–Fri 8–5.30, Sat 8–1, Sun 2–5. Closed for lunch & Xmas & Etr **C R D** *credit cards* (v) ⬆

Tewkesbury
Gloucestershire   Map 3 SO83

BECKFORD SILK
(James and Marthe Gardner) The Old Rectory, Beckford, nr Tewkesbury ✆ (0386) 881507

All the processes involved in the hand screen-printing of silk can be observed in the print shop. The finished articles, all exclusively designed and made to a high standard, are available in the Silk Store next door: they include dresses and a range of accessories.

Open Mon–Sat 9–5.30. Closed for lunch & 24 Dec–2 Jan **C W D** *credit cards* (v) ⬆

Thame
Oxfordshire   Map 4 SP70

BATES & LAMBOURNE
(Richard Bates & David Lambourne) The Camp, Milton Common, nr Thame, ✆ (08446) 8978

Furniture-makers specialising in Windsor chairs and traditionally-styled English country furniture. All their work is executed in British hardwoods such as elm, oak, ash and yew.

Open Mon–Fri 9–6, Sat 9–1, by appt. Closed Xmas & Etr **C W E D** ⬆

THE FORGE
(David Moss) 71 High St ✆ (084421) 5979

Hand-made forged metalwork of any description undertaken, plus all repair and restoration work of iron, steel, copper, brass etc.

Open daily 9–6. Closed Xmas **C R D** ⬆ *by appt.*

J H HARRIS-ANTIQUE FURNITURE RESTORATION
Crabapple Cottage, Shabbington, nr Aylesbury (3 m from Thame) ✆ (0844) 201553

Most kinds of restoration work to antique and hand-made reproduction furniture undertaken. Skills include veneering, French polishing, carving, turning and gilding. Small pieces of reproduction furniture, e.g. Pembroke, card and tilt-top tables, made to commission.

Open Mon–Fri 8–5, & wknds, by appt. Closed Xmas, Etr & for annual holidays **C R** ⬆

Thaxted

Essex   **Map 5 TL63**

GLENDALE FORGE
(F M Tucker) Monk Street, nr Thaxted ✆ (0371) 830466 telex 817164

Blacksmiths producing traditionally-forged ornamental wrought-ironwork: gates, light fittings, pokers, candlesticks, fire hoods etc, plus blacksmiths' tools and equipment ranging from tongs to forges (catalogue available). There is a display of half-size and scale-model vehicles.

Open Mon–Fri 9–4.30, Sun 10–12. Closed Xmas, Etr & BHs **C R W E D** 🚐 *by appt.*

Thirsk

North Yorkshire   **Map 8 SE48**

DESIGN IN WOOD
(Andrew James) The Old Coach House, Chapel St ✆ (0845) 25103

A small but very flexible range of traditionally-made contemporary furniture and cabinets for domestic and office use. Individually designed built-in cabinet work also undertaken. Special commissions welcomed.

Open Mon–Fri 9–5. Also wknds, by appt. Closed Xmas & New Year **C D** 🚐

ROBERT THOMPSON'S CRAFTSMEN LTD
(Mr R T Cartwright) Kilburn, 7 m E of Thirsk beneath the chalk White Horse ✆ (03476) 218

The business begun by famous furniture-maker Robert Thompson continues in the same tradition today. All the furniture – domestic, church and boardroom – is hand-made from naturally-seasoned English oak, as are the carved animals and various other small articles. Everything bears the well-known 'Mouse' trademark.

Open Mon–Thu 8–5, Fri 8–3.45, Sat 10.30–12. Closed for lunch & Xmas, Etr & BHs **C D** 🚐 *by appt.*

TRESKE LIMITED
(John Gormley) Station Works ✆ (0845) 22770

There are four showrooms here full of domestic furniture made in solid English ash, elm and oak. The range is extremely wide – from beds to desks – and features both traditional and modern designs which have won Treske a number of awards. Church work is also undertaken. Visitors welcome in the workshops.

Open Mon–Fri dawn–dusk, wknds 9–5 **C W E D** *credit cards* Ⓐ Ⓥ 🚐

Thornbury

Avon   **Map 3 ST68**

TYTHERINGTON WORKSHOPS
(Don White and Keith Bunting) The Old School, Tytherington, nr Thornbury ✆ (0454) 411467

Turned wooden items and etched brassware is produced on the premises. Work includes bowls in burr-woods and unusual grains; boxes in a variety of exotic woods, fingerplates; picture frames and jewellery. Also regular exhibitions of work from some of the West Country's leading craftsmen and artists. Don White is a member of the Somerset and Gloucestershire Guilds of Craftsmen.

Open most wkdys & some wknds, advisable to telephone. Closed Xmas **C R W E D** 🚐

Thornby

Northamptonshire   **Map 4 SP67**

ISLAY WOOL SHOP
(Kate Harrison) ✆ (0604) 740221

Specialist in hand-made knitwear made to traditional designs in Icelandic, Falkland,

Aran, Pure Breed and Donegal wools, or mohair. Tweed skirt-lengths, rugs, scarves etc also available in pure wool. All the yarns and patterns used can be purchased for home knitting.

Open Mon–Fri 8–5.30 (closed Tue), wknds 2.30–5.30. Closed for lunch & Xmas **C W E D** *credit cards* ⓐ ⓥ 🚲 *by appt.*

Thursby

Cumbria   **Map 10 NY35**

THE JEWELLERY WORKSHOP

(Michael John King) Oakleigh Cottage, Todd Close, Curthwaite, nr Wigton, ¾ m from Thursby off A595 ✆ *(0228) 710756*

Fine jewellery hand-made from gold and silver and set with precious and local gemstones.

Open Wed–Sun 10–4.30. Also open BHs **C R W E D** 🚲

IAN LAVAL – CABINET MAKER

Meadow Bank Farm, Curthwaite, nr Wigton, ¾ m from Thursby off A595 ✆ *(0228) 710409*

Well-made furniture distinguished by the extensive use of inlays and highly-figured veneers which have been sawn in the workshop. Both contemporary and traditional designs, using hardwoods, which the cabinet-maker has felled himself, feature in the range.

Open Mon–Fri 9–5 & usually at wknds **C D** *credit cards* ⓐ ⓥ 🚲

Thurston

Suffolk   **Map 5 TL96**

MUDLEN END STUDIO LTD

(James and Bryn Hart) Unit 7, Thurston Granary, nr Bury St Edmunds (next to station) ✆ *(0359) 32082*

Hand-painted ceramic cottages and other buildings representing a range of English vernacular architectural styles, e.g. a labourer's cottage, a Victorian village school, a Georgian town house, as well as a collection inspired by Flora Thompson's book *Lark Rise to Candleford*.

Open Mon–Fri 9–5 **W E D** *& Mail Order* 🚲 *by appt.*

Tintagel

Cornwall   **Map 2 SX08**

CORNISH RUSTICS

(D I Dunbavin) Bossiney Rd ✆ *(0840) 770787 (home)*

Unusual ornaments, suitable for indoor or outdoor use, hand-crafted from North Cornish slate. The models – about 6–12 ins high – include a rustic bridge, a wishing-well and an open-roofed roundhouse. Nesting boxes, bird tables and souvenirs also available.

Open Mon–Sat 9–5.30 in summer only, but can open any other time by appt. **C W E D** 🚲 *by appt.*

THE GLASS STUDIO, TREVILLICK CRAFT WORKSHOP

(Dr B P and Mrs M Saville) Pendragon House, Trevillick, nr Tintagel

A selection of hand-engraved crystal, hand-blown glassware and various items of leatherwork.

Open daily 10–5. Other times by written appt. Closed Xmas & Etr **C W E D** *credit cards* ⓐ ⓥ ⓧ ⓓ 🚲

Tisbury

Wiltshire   **Map 3 ST92**

COMPTON MARBLING

(Solveig Stone and Caroline Mann) village is 16 m W of Salisbury ✆ *(0747) 870691/870894*

Manufacturers of hand-marbled paper, available in a variety of patterns and colours. Products include lamp-shades, albums, envelopes, notepads, file boxes and gift tags. Catalogue and sample book available.

Open by appt. only **C W E D** 🚲 *by appt.*

PAMELA CURRIE KNITWEAR

Rose Cottage, High St, village is 16 m W of Salisbury ✆ *(0747) 870306*

Made-to-measure couture knitwear available in exclusive designs and spectacular colours.

Open any time, by appt. **C E D** *credit cards* ⓐ 🚲

Tiverton

Devon   **Map 3 SS91**

TIVERTON CRAFT CENTRE

(S M and V A Chamberlin) 1 Bridge St ✆ *(0884) 258430*

A very large range of locally-made crafts can be seen in the showrooms here. Stock includes canework, jewellery, house signs, leatherwork, glassware, slatework, soft toys, woodcraft, fabrics, woollens and original paintings. Pottery and ceramic-decoration studios are on the premises.

Open Mon–Sat 9–5.30 **C R W E D** 🚲

Torpoint
Cornwall **Map 2 SX45**

KINGSAND POTTERY
(Hugh M Perry) Fore St, Kingsand, nr Torpoint
✆ *(0752) 822833*

Traditional English slipware pots for oven and table use, various lamps and a collection of vases and plant pots are all made on the premises. Silverware, jewellery, knitware and paintings of local scenes for sale as well.

Open Mon–Sat 10–6. Also open Sun Jul–Oct. Closed for lunch & Xmas **C W D** *credit cards* ⓐ Ⓥ ⇻

Totnes
Devon **Map 3 SX86**

ASHRIDGE WORKSHOPS
(Christopher Faulkner) Ashridge Barn, Tigley, nr Dartington (3 m W of Totnes off A385) ✆ *(0803) 862861*

Working with two or three full-time students, Christopher Faulkner produces a wide range of traditional and modern furniture to individual designs. He uses home-grown and exotic hardwoods – both solid and as veneers. A permanent exhibition of work is on view at the workshop. Member of the Devon Guild of Craftsmen.

Open Mon–Fri 9–5, by appt. Closed for lunch & Xmas, Etr & for Aug **C D** ⇻

BROOK HOUSE JOINERS
(Paul Terrell, Mike Vickery, Mike Johnston and Shirley Martin). Leave Totnes on Higher Plymouth Rd, then turn r to Dartington. Brook House is ¼ m on l ✆ *(0803) 865961*

Makers of all sorts of woodwork in hard and softwoods from joinery to conga drums, chessboards and screens. Specialities are turned bowls, plates, goblets and other small items, including geodesic domes, and painted furniture. Work mostly made to commission.

Open Mon–Fri 9–5. Also wknds by appt. Closed for lunch & Xmas & Etr **C R E D** ⇻

COUNTRY SCENE
(Mrs J Hockings) Langford Farm, Harberton, nr Totnes ✆ *(0803) 862836*

An attractive selection of greetings cards, writing paper, calendars, bookmarks, gift tags and so on, all decorated with flowers grown and pressed on the farm.

Visitors (trade) by appt. only. **C** ⇻

RENDLE CRANG (WOODCRAFT)
20 Burke Rd ✆ *(0803) 865447*

Wood-turner specialising in making wooden bowls from a variety of English and foreign hardwoods. A range of stools, lamps and kitchenware is also available. Newel posts and bannisters made to customers' requirements.

Open Mon–Fri 9–5. Also wknds, by appt. Closed Xmas, Etr & annual holiday **C R W E D** ⇻

LION BREWERY
(Colin Kellam) South St ✆ *(0803) 863158*

Domestic stoneware: lamp-bases, large plates, garden and indoor planters, all hand-made and hand-decorated – mostly with floral designs. Only seconds are available here.

Open Mon–Fri 9–5. Closed for lunch & Xmas & Etr **W** *(***D** *seconds only)* ⇻

LOTUS POTTERY
(Michael Charles Skipwith) Old Stoke Farm, Stoke Gabriel, nr Totnes ✆ *(080428) 303*

Michael Skipwith specialises in making planters and vases in stoneware and porcelain for both the house and the garden; most of his work is wood-fired. A wide range of clays, glaze materials, small tools and equipment is available.

Open Mon–Fri 9–5.30, Sat 9–1. Closed for lunch & Xmas & Etr **W D** ⇻ *by appt.*

Trent
Dorset **Map 3 ST51**

TRENT SMITHY & STUDIO OF CONTEMPORARY FORGED IRONWORK
(Michael Malleson) 42 Rigg La, nr Sherborne ✆ *(0935) 850957*

All types of forged ironwork for gardens, homes, hotels, restaurants, churches etc, designed and produced to a high standard. Any style undertaken, but there is an emphasis on original designs for contemporary settings.

Open Mon–Fri 9–5, but advisable to telephone. Other times by appt. Closed for lunch & Xmas & Etr **C R E D** ⇻

Trerulefoot
Cornwall **Map 2 SX35**

CHILDSPLAY – WOODEN TOYS & PLAY EQUIPMENT
(John Ward) Bethany, nr Saltash ✆ *(075538) 636*

Robust, safe, imaginative toys and play equipment designed to stimulate creative play and/or physical activity. Lots to choose from: pull-alongs, swings, games, farms, houses etc etc. Catalogue available.

Open Mon–Fri 8.30–6, Sat 8.30–5.30. Closed Xmas **C W E D** *credit cards* (a) 🚐 *by appt.*

Truro

Cornwall   **Map 2 SW84**

GUILD OF TEN
19 Old Bridge St ✆ *(0872) 74681*

A retail shop co-operatively owned and staffed by craftsmen working in Cornwall. Their work includes textiles, toys, knitwear, ceramics, jewellery, leatherwork, furniture, metalwork, turned and carved wooden items and dress-making.

Open Mon–Sat 9.30–5.30. Closed for lunch & Xmas & Etr & BHs **C R W E D** *credit cards* (a) (v)

NEW MILLS POTTERY
(John Davidson) New Mills, Ladock, 8 m E of Truro on A39 ✆ *(0726) 882209*

A wide range of functional and decorative hand-made stoneware and porcelain. John Davidson is a member of the Guild of Ten (see above).

Open Mon–Fri 9.30–6, Sat 9.30–1 **C D**

Tutbury

Staffordshire   **Map 8 SK22**

TUTBURY CRYSTAL GLASS LTD
Tutbury Glassworks, Burton St, 1 m from Burton-on-Trent ✆ *(0283) 813281*

Hand-made, hand-cut full lead crystal glassware of exceptional quality. A complete range of table glasses, plus many lines in fancy pieces such as bowls and vases, are all available in a variety of beautiful designs.

Open Mon–Sat 9–5, by appt. Closed Xmas **C R D** *credit cards* (a) (v) 🚐 *by appt.*

Uckfield

East Sussex   **Map 5 TQ42**

JOANNE HILL CHATTAWAY – POTTER
High Cross Farm, Eastbourne Rd, Little Horsted, 2½ m S of Uckfield on A22 ✆ *(082582) 678 (evngs)*

A large selection of hand-made domestic stoneware – ovenware, jugs, bowls, mugs etc – most of which is slip-and/or sgraffito-decorated.

Garden pots of all sizes are also made.

Open Mon–Fri 9–5, & at wknds, by appt. Closed for lunch & Xmas **C W E D** 🚐

Uffculme

Devon   **Map 3 ST01**

COLDHARBOUR POTTERY
(A Townsend) Coldharbour Mill ✆ *(0884) 40960*

Hand-thrown and mould-made pottery, slip and cast ware, mould-making and screen-printing all undertaken. The Mill has been restored as a working wool museum.

Open daily 2.30–6. Closed Xmas **C R W D** 🚐

Ulverston

Cumbria   **Map 7 SD27**

FURNESS GALLERIES
(Anthony and Julie Irving) Theatre St ✆ *(0229) 57657*

Wooden dolls' houses and furniture to scale are made by hand on the premises where visitors can watch: many styles available. The showroom has an extensive collection of high-quality Cumbrian art and craftwork and there is an exhibition gallery. Refreshments available.

Open Mon–Fri 9.30–5.30, Sat 9–5.30. Closed Wed Jan–Jun & Xmas & Etr **C R D** *credit cards* (a) (v) 🚐

Shaping wrought-iron on the anvil

GREENSIDE WOODCRAFT
(John and Wendy Gott) Greenside House, Duke St, Askam-in-Furness, nr Ulverston ✆ (0229) 63716

Wood-turning and carving, cabinet-making, antique restoration and traditional upholstery all undertaken. Furniture, made to traditional designs in many types of wood is available.

Open Mon–Fri 10–4.30, & wknds by appt. **C R W E D** 🚐 *by appt.*

Upavon
Wiltshire   **Map 4 SU15**

BRAYBROOKE POTTERY
(Sally Lewis) 17 Andover Rd ✆ (0980) 630466

Commemorative, decorative and domestic earthenware and stoneware individually decorated with a range of patterns and specially developed glazes. The items produced range from egg cups to fountains, including some wall-mounted plant-pot holders with elm-ash glaze which gives a granite-like texture.

Open most days but advisable to telephone. Closed Xmas & Etr **C D** 🚐

Uppingham
Leicestershire   **Map 4 SP89**

J F SPENCE & SON
(Derek C Spence) The New Forge, Station Rd ✆ (0572) 822758

Ornamental ironwork, including hand-forged items, of all descriptions: fire-baskets and furnishings; gates; rose arches; garden furniture; hanging-basket brackets; boot-scrapers etc.

Open Mon–Fri 8–5, Sat 9.30–12.30. Closed for lunch & Xmas, Etr, BHs and last 2 wks in Jul **C R W D** 🚐

Uxbridge
Middlesex   **Map 4 TQ08**

JOHN H MAW
141 Tilehouse Way, Denham, nr Uxbridge ✆ (0895) 833206

Maker of fine bows for the violin, viola and 'cello.

Open any time, by appt. **C W E D** 🚐

Verwood
Dorset   **Map 4 SU00**

SAXON FORGE
(Mr R D Haigh) Silver Snaffles, Verwood Rd, Three Legged Cross, nr Wimborne ✆ (0202) 826375

Ornamental ironworkers, making lanterns, door-furniture, mangers, companion sets, fire canopies, gates and wall screens, plus many other items. Traditional sheet-metal work on jugs, skillets etc undertaken.

Open Mon–Sat 8–6. Closed Xmas **C W E D** 🚐

Wallingford
Oxfordshire   **Map 4 SU68**

BLENHEIM POTS & TILES
(Lucienne de Mauny & Anthony Fletcher) Blenheim Farm, Benson, nr Wallingford ✆ (0491) 39707

A small production pottery manufacturing a wide range of hand-thrown slip-decorated earthenware for the dining room and kitchen, together with a variety of pots for plants. There are smaller runs of more specialised items such as bonsai pots and paté dishes. Hand-made, slip-decorated 4 in tiles, house nameplates and commemorative ware made to order.

Open Tue–Sat 10–5.30, Sun 12–5.30 and other times, by appt. **C W D** 🚐 *by appt.*

MICHAEL BRACKEN
(David Moren-Brown) The Green South, Warborough, nr Wallingford ✆ (086732) 8354

David Moren-Brown designs and makes furniture to suit both modern and traditional needs, using the finest English and foreign hardwoods, and also restores antiques. Michael Bracken concentrates on upholstery and curtaining; he has a vast range of fabrics which are made up and installed to order.

Open Tue–Fri 9–5.30, Sat 10–5. Closed Xmas, Etr & BHs **C R** *(some* **W E)** **D** 🚐

ALISTAIR FRAYLING-CORK
2 Mill Lane

Antique-furniture restoration, French-polishing and wax-finishing undertaken; also special commissions. A selection of small wood-turned items is always available.

Open Mon–Fri 10–5.30. Closed for lunch & Xmas, Etr & BHs **C R D** 🚐

WALLINGFORD TEA & COFFEE CO
(Richard and Leonorah Luff) 4/5 St Peter's St ✆ (0491) 36263

Specialist suppliers and blenders of quality teas and coffees. Coffee is freshly roasted on the premises. Richard Luff is a tea-taster.

Open Mon–Sat 9–5 (closed Mon & Wed pm). Closed for lunch & Xmas & Etr **C W E D** 🚐

Wantage

Oxfordshire   Map 4 SU48

DAVID F BUZZARD LTD
*(Charles Escritt) Home Farm, Ardington, nr
Wantage ☎ (0235) 833677*

A picture-framing workshop and art gallery are
run here side by side. Special skills offered
include the use of oval and multiple-opening
mounts, wash and line work, the stretching
and framing of textiles and box-framing.
Ardington Gallery's principal aim is to promote
the work of local artists.

*Open Tue–Sat 9–5.30. Also open May–Sep Sun
2.30–5.30. Closed Xmas & BHs* **C R D** 🚗

**NICHOLAS DYSON – FURNITURE
DESIGNER & MAKER**
*Unit 2, Home Farm, Ardington, nr Wantage
☎ (0235) 834311*

Free-standing and fitted furniture individually
designed and made to an exceptionally high
standard of craftsmanship. Both solid timber
and veneers are employed.

*Open Mon–Fri 9–5.30, Sat 9.30–12, or by appt.
Closed Xmas & Etr* **C W E D** 🚗

Waresley

Cambridgeshire   Map 4 TL25

THANE STUDIOS
*(Laurence Broderick) Vicarage Rd, nr Sandy, 17 m
from Cambridge on B1040 ☎ (0767) 50444*

Sculptor Laurence Broderick works in bronze
and various kinds of stone, including marble,
granite and serpentine. Movement and simpli-
city characterise all his studies which en-
compass wildlife (particularly otters) the
female nude and ecclesiastical themes. He also
undertakes portraits – cast in bronze.

Open any time, by appt. only **C E D** 🚗

Warwick

Warwickshire   Map 4 SP26

WARWICK GALLERY & CRAFT SHOP
(Una Forde) 12–14 Smith St ☎ (0296) 495880

High-quality work from a number of British
artists and craftsmen can be found here. All
made by hand, the goods include many different styles of pottery, etchings and silk-screen
prints, silver jewellery, engraved glass and
batik. Also picture framing and restoring.

Open Mon–Sat 10–5 (closed Thu) **E D** *credit cards*
ⓐ ⓥ ⓧ ⓓ 🚗

**HATTON CRAFT CENTRE (see also
pp 11–12)**
*(A J Arkwright) George's Farm, Hatton, 3 m N of
Warwick off the A41 ☎ (092684) 2096*

Winner of the AA/COSIRA Craft Centre of the
Year Award, these workshops, which occupy
converted 19th-century farm buildings, welcome visitors and display a very extensive
range of specialist, high-quality work. This
includes, among many other things, batik,
wooden tiles, saddlery, patchwork, armour,
needlecraft, stained glass, statuettes and folk
clothes. Not all the craftsmen are there every
day, but there are always some workshops
open. Refreshments available (not Mondays).

*Open daily. The 1st wknd in each month from Mar–
Dec has special opening times for the workshops.
Closed Xmas* **C R D** 🚗 *by appt.*

Watlington

Oxfordshire   Map 4 SU79

OLD CARPENTER'S SHOP
*(Ken Hulse) Watcombe Manor, on B480 Oxford–
Henley rd ☎ home (049161) 3210*

Old timbers used to make up to order English
country furniture, mostly in pine, to own or
customer's designs. Mainly commissioned
work, but a few sample pieces kept in stock.
Fitted kitchens and some antique restoration
also undertaken.

*Open Mon–Fri 9–6, wknds by appt. Closed for
lunch & Xmas & Etr* **C R W E D** 🚗

Wells

Somerset   Map 3 ST54

WOOTTON VINEYARD
*(Colin and Susan Gillespie) North Wootton, 3½ m
SE of Wells ☎ (074989) 359*

The vineyards, which cover six acres, are best
seen between June and October when the
vines are in leaf. The wine is made during
October and November and bottled in April
and May: there is no activity in the winery in
summer. Visitors are always welcome and
wine is sold on the premises.

*Open Mon–Sat 10–5. Closed for lunch & Xmas &
Etr* **W E D** 🚗 *by appt.*

Wells-next-the-Sea

Norfolk   Map 9 TF94

BURNHAM POTTERY
*(Thom and Jan Borthwick) Old Station, Maryland
☎ (0328) 710847*

Domestic, gift and garden pottery, including tableware in a variety of colours, novelty mugs, amusing ceramic cats, ornamental pieces (boxed) and terracotta planters.

Open Mon–Fri 9–5, wknds 10–6. Closed Xmas **C W E D** 🚐 *by appt.*

Welton
North Humberside   **Map 8 SE92**
JACQUELINE STIEGER
Welton Garth ✆ *(0482) 668323*

Jacqueline Stieger has an international reputation as a sculptor and jeweller and has exhibited widely. She works in various materials, particularly bronze, and casts all pieces by the lost-wax method in her own foundry.

Open by appt. only **C D** 🚐

Westbury
Wiltshire   **Map 3 ST85**
STYLEWHIRL LTD
(Bill and Fiona Davis) Unit 26, The Craft Centre, West Wilts Trading Estate ✆ *(02214) 4767*

Furniture-makers and repairers specialising in producing dining-room suites and occasional furniture in Regency and Victorian styles.

Open Fri 2–7, Sat 9–4. Other times by appt. Closed Xmas **C R D** 🚐

WHITE HORSE POTTERY
(Stephen & Alice Humm) Newtown, nr Westbury ✆ *(0373) 864772*

Pottery for practical use in homes, restaurants or pubs is made in the workshop where visitors are welcome to watch. Many different plant-pot containers and pots of all sizes in glazed and unglazed terracotta are available as well; commissions are welcome.

Open Tue–Sat 10–5, Sun 12–5. Also open BHs. Closed Xmas–New Year **C W D** 🚐

West Hallam
Derbyshire   **Map 8 SK44**
BOTTLE KILN POTTERY & GALLERY
(Charles and Celia Stone) High Lane West (8 m from Derby on A609) ✆ *(0602) 329442*

Unusual and distinctive salt-glazed ceramic sculpture based on fantasy and poetic themes. There is also a fine-art gallery, a café and a conifer-tree nursery on the premises.

Open Tue–Sun 10–5. Closed Xmas **D** 🚐 *by appt.*

Wetwang
North Humberside   **Map 8 SE95**
NORTH WOLD ENTERPRISES
(Douglas and Shirley Page) The Old Granary, Main St, 6 m from Driffield on A166

Wrought-ironwork, furniture and jewellery, plus paintings in oils, pastels and water-colours, are produced in the workshop and studio. Ceramics made by a local potter and a selection of hand-made fancy goods, e.g. leatherwork, glassware and wooden items, are sold here as well.

C R E D *credit cards* ⓐ ⓥ ⓧ ⓓ 🚐 *by appt.*

Weymouth
Dorset   **Map 3 SY67**
JON ROBBINS
The Orchard, Nottington (on edge of Weymouth, towards Dorchester) ✆ *(030581) 2639*

Fine porcelain distinguished by a subtle use of colours derived from local clays, and individual ash glazes. Jon Robbins' work includes a range of bowls and a series of hand-built studies of characters past and present. Also sculpture in ceramics and other materials. Courses in photography, ceramics and other arts.

Open by appt. only **C W E D** 🚐

Whaddon
Buckinghamshire   **Map 4 SP83**
SNAP DRAGON
(D G and M K Stewart) The Glebe, Nash Rd, nr Milton Keynes ✆ *(0908) 501928*

High-quality, distinctive children's clothing, ladies' dresses and knitwear made in 100 per cent cotton to original designs by Maggie Petch. Reversible frocks and smocks a speciality. Everything is hand-finished and features unusual binding details.

Open Mon–Fri 10–3. Also wknds by appt. Closed Xmas & Etr **W E D** *credit cards* ⓐ ⓥ 🚐 *by appt.*

Whichford
Warwickshire   **Map 4 SP33**
WHICHFORD POTTERY
(Jim Keeling) nr Shipston-on-Stour (off A34, SP from Long Compton) ✆ *(060884) 416*

Frost-proof terracotta flowerpots and horti-cultural ware of every possible size and shape, decorated or plain, from wall pots and hanging baskets to 'Ali-Baba' jars. Very large pots a speciality. Visitors are welcome to watch the pottery's specialist throwers at work.

Open Mon–Sat 10–4. Closed 25 & 26 Dec & Etr Sun **C W E D** 🚗 *by appt.*

Whittlesey

Cambridgeshire Map 4 TL29

THE CRAFT SHOP/WHITTLESEY MINIATURES

(Lisa Linton and Keith Over) 6 St Mary's St, nr Peterborough ✆ (0733) 203620

Specialists in the making of miniature figurines – particularly military subjects – using the centrifugal process to cast batches in white metal. Also clocks, musical boxes, jewellery caskets and ornaments made out of, or set into, real egg shells.

Open Mon–Sat 9–5.30 (closed Thu pm). Closed for lunch & Xmas **C R W E D** 🚗

Wicklewood

Norfolk Map 5 TG00

LOCALITY ARTS LTD

(Nigel Gwyn Jones) Coign House, Hackford Rd, nr Wymondham ✆ (0953) 602186

Manufacturers of gifts – such as melamine trays, cheese-boards and table-mats – which feature local views, plus a range of framed pictures depicting similar scenes. All kinds of picture-framing equipment is made here, and a full picture-framing service is available. Demonstrations can be arranged. Member of the Fine Arts Trade Guild.

Open Mon–Fri 9–6 (closed Thu), Sat 9–5. Closed for lunch & Xmas & Etr **C W E D** 🚗

Widecombe-in-the-Moor

Devon Map 3 SX77

MOORLAND CRAFTS CENTRE

(B P and R B D Hutchins) Moorlands, Haytor Rd, 10m NW of Newton Abbot, between Bovey Tracey & Widecombe-in-the-Moor ✆ (03646) 479

The many craft goods on display are supplied by both resident and part-time craftsmen and artists, as well as local people who work from home. Crafts include reed and rattan basketry, pottery, woodwork, pokerwork, needlecraft, leathercraft, corn-dolly making, glass and slate engraving and knitwear.

Open daily 9–6 in summer & 11–dusk in winter. Closed Xmas Day **C R W E D** *credit cards* ⓐ Ⓥ 🚗

Acanthus-leaf decoration carved in wood

Wiggenhall St Germans

Norfolk Map 9 TF51

JEAN ROWDEN – RIVERSIDE CRAFTS

Lynn Rd, 4½ m SW of King's Lynn ✆ (055385) 424

Hand-painted china and porcelain items such as beakers, plates and bells; pokerwork decoration on boards, spoons, spatulas etc, turned wooden lamps, clocks, penholders and so on, all made on the premises. Many other locally-made craft goods also for sale.

Open Wed–Sat 10–5. Also open 2nd & 3rd Suns in the month & BH Mons. Closed for lunch **C D** *credit cards* ⓐ 🚗 *by appt.*

Wigton

Cumbria Map 10 NY24

THE POTTERY

(Mike Dodd) Wellrash, Boltongate, nr Wigton ✆ (09657) 615

Hand-made stoneware and porcelain pottery for practical uses. The work is fired in a wood and oil kiln.

Open by appt. only **C W E D** 🚗

Wilby

Suffolk Map 5 TM27

CHURCH COTTAGE POTTERY

(Peter and Gillian Anderson) nr Eye, follow Wilby rd from Stradbroke village sign ✆ (037984) 253

Individually-made wood-carved sculptures and panels, as well as hand-thrown reduction-fired domestic stoneware and a small range of fine slip-cast porcelain.

Open daily 9–6, but advisable to telephone **C W D** 🚐 *(small numbers only) by appt.*

Wimborne Minster
Dorset   **Map 4 SZ09**
PATCHWORK SHOPPE
(V A Hanney and J Downs) The Old Mill, 13 Mill Lane ✆ *(0202) 881240*

Patchwork and quilting specialists. A selection of quilts, cushions, bags etc is for sale and all supplies, including books, fabrics, templates, embroidery silks, transfers and hoops, are sold here as well. Mail-order catalogue.

Open Mon–Sat 10–5. Mail Order & **C R D** *credit cards* ⓐ ⓥ 🚐

WALFORD MILL CRAFT CENTRE
(Dorset Craft Guild) Knobcrook Rd, ½m N of town centre, W of B3078 ✆ *(0202) 841400*

The shop stocks a representative range of work from members of the Dorset Guild of Craftsmen. Crafts include woodwork, textiles, ceramics, lace-making, calligraphy, stone-carving, bookbinding, embroidery, gilding, metalwork, spinning, knitting, musical-instrument making, cane- and rush-work, plus lots more. Regular exhibitions, demonstrations, lectures and courses. Refreshments available.

Open (from end April–Sep) daily normal shop hours; May–Oct closed wknds. Closed Xmas **C** *(contact craftsmen direct)* **R** *(of work by the Guild)* **D** *credit cards* ⓐ ⓥ 🚐

Winchcombe
Gloucestershire   **Map 4 SP02**
WINCHCOMBE POTTERY
(Mr and Mrs Ray Finch and Mike Finch) nr Cheltenham, 1 m N of Winchcombe off A46 towards Greet ✆ *(0242) 602462 (pottery only) or 603059*

Winchcombe Pottery was established in 1926 and the old bottle-kiln is still standing. Today, high quality hand-thrown domestic stoneware is produced, using a wood-fired kiln. Wood-turned items made by Stephen Marchant, jewellery and water-colour prints are also for sale in the showroom. Cabinet-maker William Hall and sculptor/metalworker Keith Jameson work (to commission only) on the premises. All are members of the Guild of Gloucestershire Craftsmen.

Open Mon–Fri 8–5, Sat 9–4. Closed Xmas **C** *(wood-turning & metalwork* **R***)* **W E D** 🚐 *by appt.*

Winchester
Hampshire   **Map 4 SU42**
JULIET VERNEY – ORIGINAL KNITTING
58 Chilbolton Ave ✆ *(0962) 51563*

A unique collection of sweaters knitted in pure Shetland wool to original designs in a variety of rich colours. They are hand-framed in limited numbers.

Open by appt. only **C W E D** 🚐 *by appt.*

Wing
Buckinghamshire   **Map 4 SP82**
JOHN GREENWELL
Old Airfield, Cublington Rd ✆ *(0296) 688905 (workshop) (0525) 372689 (home)*

Any wooden item for the home, farm or stable can be made to order. Work encompasses the

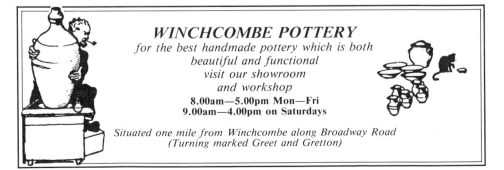

making of free-standing and fitted furniture, turnery, treen, sign painting and carving.

Open Mon–Fri 8–6 & wknds, by appt. Closed Xmas **C R W E D** ♿

Winton
Cumbria **Map 11 NY71**

LANGRIGG POTTERY
(Mrs J R Cookson) 1 m from Kirkby Stephen, just off A685 to Brough ✆ *(0930) 71542*

Pots for everyday practical use that are also attractive and pleasant to handle: tableware, plant pots, lamp bases etc. A small selection of purely ornamental plates is made here as well. Lettering and specific designs undertaken.

Open daily 9–5 from Etr–mid Oct, Tue–Sat 9–5 in winter. Closed Xmas **C D** ♿ *by appt. (max 20)*

Witney
Oxfordshire **Map 4 SP30**

RICHARD ANDREWS RESTORATIONS
The Gardens Workshop, Eynsham Hall, nr Witney, opp. North Leigh turning on A4095 to Bladon ✆ *(0993) 882495*

Full restoration of all kinds of antique furniture undertaken: specialist in giltwork. Locks can be repaired and keys can be cut.

Open Mon–Fri 9–5, Sat 9–1, by appt. **R D** ♿

SIGN STUDIO
(Rosalind F Hughes) Eynsham Park Sawmill, Cuckoo La, North Leigh. Cuckoo Lane is 1st r after leaving Witney on A4095 to Woodstock ✆ *(0993) 881999*

All types of lettering work undertaken, using traditional methods to achieve a high standard of craftsmanship. General signwriting; commercial vehicle writing; shop signs; pictorial and heraldic signs; poster writing; specialist gilding; glass etching; narrowboat and fairground art; graining; marbling; murals.

Open Tue–Fri 8–5, Mon & Sat 8–12, but advisable to telephone. Closed Xmas **C R D** ♿

THE STABLE
(Jane and Stephen Baughan) Kingsway Farm, Aston, nr Witney ✆ *(0993) 850431*

High-quality ceramic plates for people who enjoy presenting food attractively. The range consists of octagonal, hexagonal and rectangular dinner and serving plates, some plain, or decorated with pineapples, crabs, lobsters or

fish cast in relief on the surface. Hand-printed tablecloths and napkins with matching designs available.

Open daily 9–6 **C W E D** *credit cards* ⓐ ⓥ ♿ *by appt.*

Wolseley Bridge
Staffordshire **Map 7 SK01**

MIDLAND CRAFTS
(G J Foulkes and D W Fecher) Cromwell House, nr Stafford, 2 m from Rugeley on A51 to Lichfield ✆ *(0889) 882544*

Manufacturers of onyx and alabaster goods for the home; tables, lamps, clocks etc. A good selection of mineral specimens, gemstones and gemset jewellery also available. Everything for sale at wholesale prices. Demonstrations for parties by appt.

Open Mon–Fri 10–5, wknds 1.30–6. Closed Xmas **C R W E D** *credit cards* ⓐ ♿ *by appt.*

Woodbridge
Suffolk **Map 5 TM24**

BERNARD ROOKE GALLERY
(Bernard and Susan Rooke) No. 1 Market Hill ✆ *(03943) 6570*

Studio-pottery designed and made by Bernard Rooke whose work has been widely exhibited. The spacious showrooms display a selection of lamps with rushcloth or cotton shades, pierced lamps, vases, clocks, animal sculptures and decorative dishes, plus original paintings and drawings.

Open Mon–Fri 11–5.15 (closed Wed) Sat 10–5. Closed for lunch on Sat, & May BHs (some **C**) **W D** *credit cards* ⓥ ♿

Woodhall Spa
Lincolnshire **Map 8 TF16**

EDMUND CZAJKOWSKI & SON
(Michael Czajkowski) 96 Tor-o-Moor Rd ✆ *(0526) 52895*

Cabinet-makers and specialists in the restoration of antique furniture, clocks and barometers. Skills include French-polishing, carving, gilding, marquetry, boule work and upholstery. Reproduction or modern furniture designed and made to order – all bearing the carved oak-leaf trademark. Barometers in stock.

Open Mon–Sat 9–6. Other times by appt. Closed Xmas & Etr **C R W D** ♿ *by appt.*

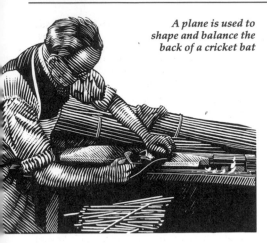

A plane is used to shape and balance the back of a cricket bat

Woodstock
Oxfordshire　　　　　　　Map 4 SP41
MANOR CRAFT
(Andrew C Tilley and Christopher S Smith) The Workshop, Ball La, Tackley, nr Woodstock (turn r off A423 opp. Sturdy's Castle (signposted Tackley) ✆ (086983) 611

Andrew Tilley and Christopher Smith are designer-craftsmen working in wood. They specialise in furniture-making and treen, using a variety of home-grown, tropical and exotic timbers. A representative selection of products can always be seen in the showroom, and they also work to commission.

Open Mon–Fri 9.30–5.30. Also Sat by appt. Closed Xmas & Etr **C R W D** 🚐 *by appt.*

Wooler
Northumberland　　　　Map 11 NT92
THE POTTERY
(Vanessa Taylor) High Humbleton House, High Humbleton, take Burnhouse Rd in Wooler, then 1st l ✆ (0668) 81623

Vanessa Taylor specialises in Mocha-ware, a form of decoration first introduced into this country in the 1780s in the Potteries area. It is so-called because the moss-like character of the pattern resembles a moss-agate stone. The unique effect results from the reaction of an acidic solution on the slip which produces an infinite variety of patterns formed by capillary action.

Open Mon–Fri 10–5, Sat 10–4. Closed at Xmas **C W** *(some* **E***)* **D** 🚐

Wootton Courtenay
Somerset　　　　　　　Map 3 SS94
MILL POTTERY
(Michael Gaitskell) nr Minehead, off A396 or A39 ✆ (064384) 297

A good choice of finely-thrown attractive pottery for everyday use; jugs, mugs, bowls, casseroles etc, and more ornamental items such as vases and lamp bases. A display workshop for the information of visitors is under construction, it will be powered by a waterwheel.

Open daily 9–6. Closed Suns Nov–May, for lunch & Xmas **C D** 🚐

Worthing
West Sussex　　　　　　Map 4 TQ10
SMUGGLERS ANNEX (CROMETY ROSS WORKSHOP)
(Miss P M Ross) 3a Ferring St, Ferring (5 m W of Worthing) ✆ (0903) 49854

Herb sachets, neck cushions and pot pourri, a range of cotton mob and shower hats, plus a 'country' hat available in tweed, cord etc, are all made for Cromety Ross on the premises. These and other British-made craft goods are for sale in the Smugglers Annex.

Open mid Jul–mid Sep & during Dec; Tue–Sat 9.45–5; in other months Tue, Fri & Sat only 9.45–5. Closed for lunch & Xmas & Etr **C R W E D** *credit cards* ⓐ 🚐 *by appt.*

Wrangle
Lincolnshire　　　　　　Map 9 TF45
WRANGLE POTTERY
(Steven and Julie Saxton) Main Rd, nr Boston ✆ (0205) 870013

A new workshop where visitors are welcome to watch hand-made pottery in production. The range of stoneware, porcelain and terracotta extends from garden pots to highly-decorated teapots, dishes and boxes. Other craftwork, plants and cards for sale. Refreshments available.

Open Mon–Fri 9–5.30, wknds 9–6. Closed Xmas **W D** 🚐 *by appt.*

Wrotham
Kent　　　　　　　　　　Map 5 TQ65
TROSLEY CRAFTSMEN (ODIN)
Gore Cottage, Green La, Trottiscliffe, Nr Wrotham ✆ (0732) 822217

Deep-cut engraving undertaken to commission only. High-quality full lead crystal chalices, wine glasses, tumblers and decanters available. Design specialities are animals, initials in medieval script and landscapes.

Open Fri–Mon 10–10, by appt. **C E D** ♿

Wroxham

Norfolk — **Map 9 TG31**

WROXHAM BARNS (see also p 13)
(Rupert Latham and Ian Russell) Tunstead Rd, Hoveton, 1½ m N of Wroxham ✆ *(06053) 3762*

An extensive centre for rural crafts with several studio workshops and a large gallery. Among the resident craftsmen are a cabinet-maker, a potter, a glass engraver, a lacemaker, a spinster, a printer and a boat-builder. The gallery has a very wide selection of additional crafts and gifts. Refreshments available.

Open daily 10–6 (tea room 11–5). Closed Xmas **C R D** *credit cards* ⓐ ⓥ ⓧ ⓓ ♿ *preferably by appt.*

Wykeham

North Yorkshire — **Map 8 SE98**

ANKARET CRESSWELL
(Justin P Terry) nr Scarborough ✆ *(0723) 864406*

Handweavers producing exclusive fabrics in wool, silk, mohair and other luxury fibres, with the emphasis on originality of design. Short lengths are supplied to garment makers.

Open Mon–Fri 9–5. Closed for lunch & Xmas & Etr **C W E D** ♿

Yarpole

Hereford & Worcester — **Map 7 SO46**

ART WOODCRAFT DESIGN
(John and Carol Morris) Byecroft Stables, Bircher, nr Yarpole ✆ *(056885) 530*

All types of furniture designed and hand-made to the customer's requirements, using home-grown hardwoods such as elm, oak, beech and fruitwoods. A limited display of the Morris' work can be seen in their home. Joinery and ecclesiastical work undertaken.

Open Mon–Sat 8.30–5.30, by appt. Closed Xmas **C D** ♿

Yelvertoft

Northamptonshire — **Map 4 SP57**

NIGEL OWEN
(Nigel and Michael Owen) 42 High St (2 m from M1, junct 18) ✆ *(0788) 822281*

Alabaster and marble workers making table lamps, clocks, barometers and various other small items in English alabaster, and marble hearths, chess tables, shelves, bases etc to order.

Open Mon–Fri 9–5.30, Sat 9–5. Closed for lunch & Xmas, Etr & BHs **C R E D** ♿

York

North Yorkshire — **Map 8 SE65**

RUTH KING
Fulford House, 45 Main St, Fulford, nr York ✆ *(0904) 33331*

A good range of individual, hand-built stoneware pottery.

Open by appt. only **C W E D** ♿

D F B PALFRAMAN & CO
Cockhill Farm, Moor Monkton, 5 m W of York off A59 ✆ *(09083) 343*

Traditional English furniture and a selection of turned items all made in English hardwood.

Open Mon–Fri 9–7, Sat 9–6. Closed for lunch & at Xmas **C W E D** ♿

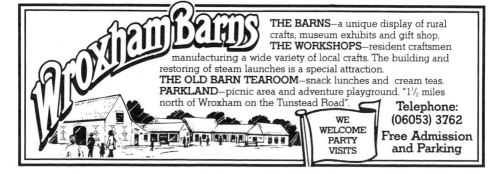

THE CRAFTS COUNCIL

The Crafts Council exists to promote contemporary crafts, encourage high standards of craft work and increase public awareness of the crafts. It receives an annual grant from the Office of Arts and Libraries, which is partially passed on to clients as grant aid and support, and also used through activities directly run by the Council – including a national exhibitions service, publications, professional advice to makers, educational activities, CRAFTS magazines and a public enquiry service.

The Crafts Council has something to offer, not only to practising craftspeople but to anyone interested in crafts and keen to find out more. Whatever your particular interest, perhaps as an amateur who sees crafts as a relaxing and fulfilling pastime, or as a buyer, collector or patron of the crafts, or even as a manufacturer with a keen eye for design, a visit to the Council at Waterloo Place, two minutes from Piccadilly Circus, is to be strongly recommended.

There you will find the gallery, (there is a programme of regularly changing exhibitions, some of which tour nationally and even internationally), a bookshop (with a good selection of books, including the Council's own publications) and, upstairs, the information centre and coffee bar.

A unique feature of the Crafts Council, among national bodies, is the way in which the public can obtain information directly, by letter, telephone or by visiting the centre. An increasing number of people are making use of the information facilities. Many come to view or borrow slides from the library of 25,000 colour slides, covering work by makers on the selected Index, makers in receipt of Crafts Council grants, slides of the Crafts Council Collection and work exhibited in the Council's galleries. Others visit the Council to obtain advice on courses, both full and part-time, or workshops in subjects ranging from musical instrument making to patchwork quilting. Still more visit the Council to find out about craft exhibitions in a given area, or museums with special craft holdings, or future trade fairs.

Craftspeople may wish to advertise themselves, at no cost, on the non-selective register, thereby attracting possible clients. They are coded by name and by craft medium, subdivided into counties, and those based outside London are automatically registered at their local Regional Arts Association as well.

If you are interested in buying or commissioning a craft item, perhaps as a special present or as a commemorative gift, the Crafts Council's resources and experienced staff will help point you in the right direction. With its unrivalled knowledge and extensive records and slides, the Crafts Council can identify makers of exceptional quality countrywide.

Although the Crafts Council cannot guarantee to solve your Christmas shopping problems, it can provide advice on the best place in a particular region to buy works of fine craftsmanship. All the shops and galleries at the end of this section have been selected by the Crafts Council for the quality of work stocked, the standard of presentation and the knowledge of contemporary work displayed. The Crafts Council produces a free leaflet, called the Crafts Map, which shows major roads and details of the location of each shop. This and other information leaflets are available free from the Crafts Council Information Section.

A survey, recently commissioned by the Crafts Council, showed that the average craftsperson works a 60-hour week for a mere £3,500 a year in return. To help them enjoy a reasonable standard of living, the Crafts Council devotes considerable effort towards improving their promotional skills and business methods through publications such as "Running a Workshop", and business forums held around the country on subjects such as accountancy, marketing and law. It also offers financial assistance in the form of setting-up grants, loans, workshop assistant schemes, advance training as well as biennial bursaries and special project grants. Craftspeople interested in any of the above should apply to: the Grants and Services Dept. of the Crafts Council.

The Crafts Council believes that the key to helping craftspeople lies in the stimulation of public interest in the crafts. Exhibitions created by the Crafts Council are now touring nationally to an increasing extent, making more craft work accessible to the public, and the Crafts Council works closely with the Regional Arts Associations in England and Wales.

If you have any queries, or would like more information on the Crafts Council, contact the Information Section, Crafts Council, 12 Waterloo Place, London SW1Y 4AU. Tel: 01-930 4811

CANDOVER GALLERY
22 West St, Alresford, Hants
✆ (096273) 3200

BEAUX ARTS CERAMICS
York St, Bath, Avon
✆ (0225) 64850

ST JAMES'S GALLERY
9 Margarets Bldngs, nr Royal Cres, Bath, Avon
✆ (0225) 319197

COPERNICAN CONNECTION
Lock Hse, Waterside Rd, Beverley, N Humberside
✆ (0482) 882309

FENNY LODGE GALLERY
Simpson Rd, Bletchley, Milton Keynes, Bucks
✆ (0908) 642207

CHESTNUT GALLERY
High St, Bourton-on-the-Water, Gloucs
✆ (0451) 20017

LAURIMORE GALLERY
Swan St, Boxford, Suffolk
✆ (0787) 210138

HUGO BARCLAY
7 East St, Brighton, E Sussex
✆ (0273) 21694

PRIMAVERA
10 Kings Pde, Cambridge, Cambs
✆ (0223) 357708

CIRENCESTER WORKSHOPS
Brewery Ct, Cirencester, Gloucs
✆ (0285) 61566

CIDER PRESS CENTRE
Shinners Bridge, Dartington, nr Totnes, Devon
✆ (0803) 864171

HIGHER STREET GALLERY
1 Higher St, Dartmouth, Devon
✆ (08043) 3157

SIMON DREW GALLERY
13 Foss St, Dartmouth, Devon
✆ (08043) 2832

YEW TREE GALLERY
The Square, Ellastone, nr Ashbourne, Derbys
✆ (033524) 341

NEW ASHGATE GALLERY
Wagon Yd, Farnham, Surrey
✆ (0252) 713208

CONTINUUM
38 Castle St, Guildford, Surrey
✆ (0483) 66436

SOUTH MANCHESTER GALLERY
Ashley Rd, Hale, nr Altrincham, Cheshire
✆ 061-941 6244

GODFREY & TWATT
7 Westminster Arcade, Parliament St, Harrogate, N Yorks
✆ (0423) 525300

LOWEN GALLERY
Hartshill Rd, Hartshill, Stoke-on-Trent, Staffs
✆ (0782) 623762

ABBOT HALL CRAFT SHOP
Kirkland, Kendal, Cumbria
✆ (0539) 22464

FIRE & IRON GALLERY
Rowhurst Forge, Oxshott Rd, Leatherhead, Surrey
✆ (0372) 375148

COLLECTION
131 The Southend, Ledbury, Heref & Worcs
✆ (0531) 3581

CRAFT & DESIGN SHOP
City Art Gallery, The Headrow, Leeds, W. Yorks
✆ (0532) 462485

Continued on p 176

INDEX OF CRAFTS

LOCATION ATLAS

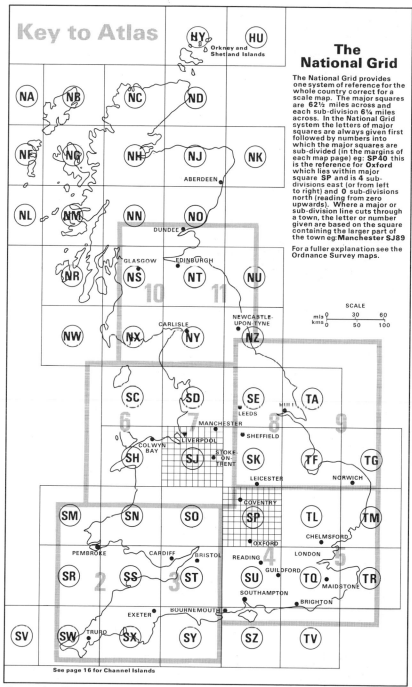

Key to Atlas

The National Grid

The National Grid provides one system of reference for the whole country correct for a scale map. The major squares are 62½ miles across and each sub-division 6¼ miles across. In the National Grid system the letters of major squares are always given first followed by numbers into which the major squares are sub-divided (in the margins of each map page) eg: **SP40** this is the reference for **Oxford** which lies within major square **SP** and is **4** sub-divisions east (or from left to right) and **0** sub-divisions north (reading from zero upwards). Where a major or sub-division line cuts through a town, the letter or number given are based on the square containing the larger part of the town eg: **Manchester SJ89**

For a fuller explanation see the Ordnance Survey maps.

SCALE

mls 0   30   60
kms 0   50   100

Orkney and Shetland Islands

See page 16 for Channel Islands

Maps produced by

The AA Cartographic Department (Publications Division), Fanum House, Basingstoke, Hampshire RG21 2EA

This atlas is for location purposes only: see Members' Handbook for current road and AA road services information.

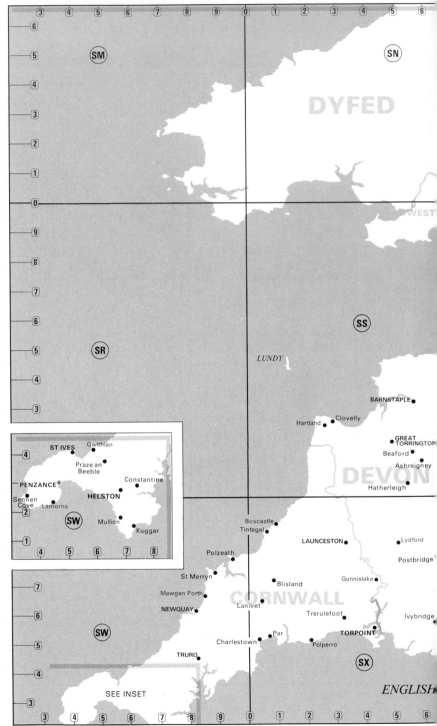

2

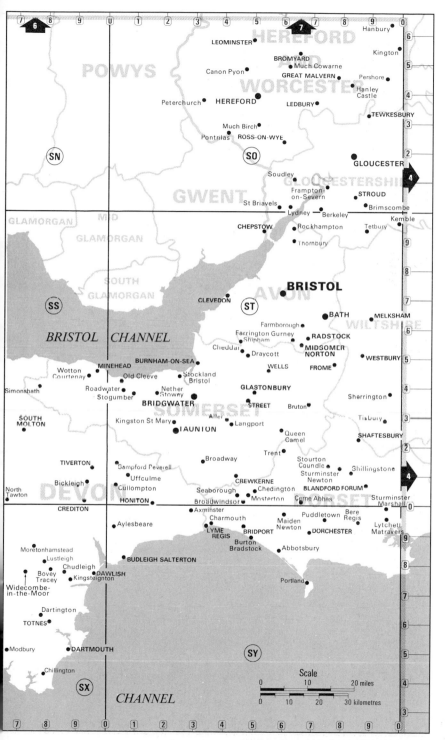

Regions/Counties: POWYS, HEREFORD AND WORCESTER, GWENT, GLOUCESTERSHIRE, GLAMORGAN, MID GLAMORGAN, SOUTH GLAMORGAN, AVON, WILTSHIRE, SOMERSET, DORSET, DEVON

Grid references: SN, SO, SS, ST, SY, SX

Bristol Channel / Channel

Places labelled (north to south, selection):

Hanbury, LEOMINSTER, Kington, BROMYARD, Much Cowarne, Canon Pyon, GREAT MALVERN, Pershore, Hanley Castle, Peterchurch, HEREFORD, LEDBURY, TEWKESBURY, Much Birch, Pontrilas, ROSS-ON-WYE, GLOUCESTER, Soudley, Frampton-on-Severn, STROUD, St Briavels, Brimscombe, Lydney, Berkeley, Kemble, CHEPSTOW, Rockhampton, Tetbury, Thornbury, BRISTOL, CLEVEDON, BATH, MELKSHAM, Farmborough, Farrington Gurney, RADSTOCK, Shipham, MIDSOMER NORTON, Cheddar, Draycott, WESTBURY, MINEHEAD, BURNHAM-ON-SEA, WELLS, FROME, Wotton Courtenay, Old Cleeve, Stockland Bristol, Simonsbath, Roadwater, Nether Stowey, GLASTONBURY, Sherrington, Stogumber, BRIDGWATER, STREET, Bruton, SOUTH MOLTON, Kingston St Mary, Aller, Langport, Tisbury, TAUNTON, Queen Camel, SHAFTESBURY, Trent, Stourton Caundle, Shillingstone, TIVERTON, Sampford Peverell, Broadway, Sturminster Newton, Bickleigh, Uffculme, CREWKERNE, Chedington, BLANDFORD FORUM, North Tawton, Cullompton, Seaborough, Mosterton, Cerne Abbas, Sturminster Marshall, HONITON, Broadwindsor, CREDITON, Axminster, Charmouth, Maiden Newton, Puddletown, Bere Regis, Lytchett Matravers, Aylesbeare, LYME REGIS, BRIDPORT, DORCHESTER, Burton Bradstock, Abbotsbury, Moretonhamstead, Lustleigh, Chudleigh, BUDLEIGH SALTERTON, Bovey Tracey, DAWLISH, Kingsteignton, Widecombe-in-the-Moor, Portland, Dartington, TOTNES, Modbury, DARTMOUTH, Chillington

Scale

0 — 10 — 20 miles

0 — 10 — 20 — 30 kilometres

3

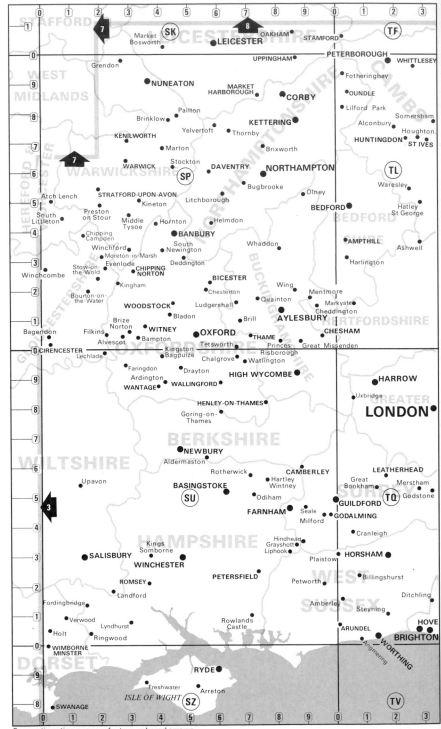

4

For continuation pages refer to numbered arrows

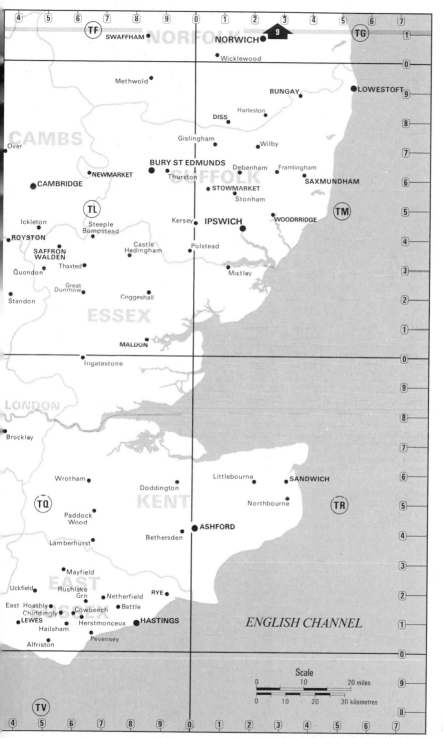

Scale

0   10   20 miles

0   10   20   30 kilometres

5

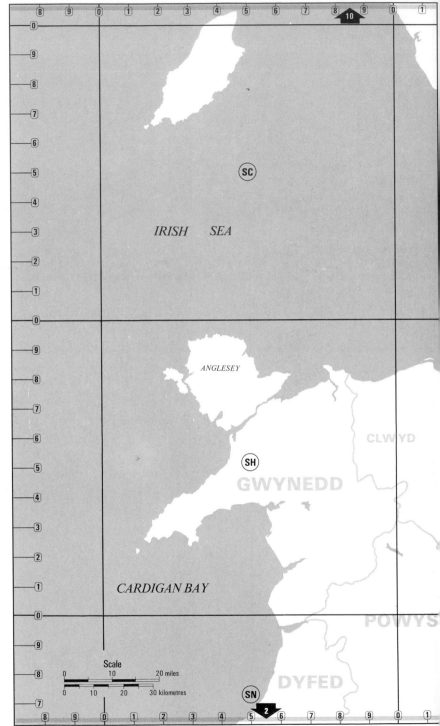

IRISH   SEA

ANGLESEY

CARDIGAN BAY

CLWYD

GWYNEDD

POWYS

DYFED

SC

SH

SN

10

2

Scale

0   10   20 miles

0   10   20   30 kilometres

6

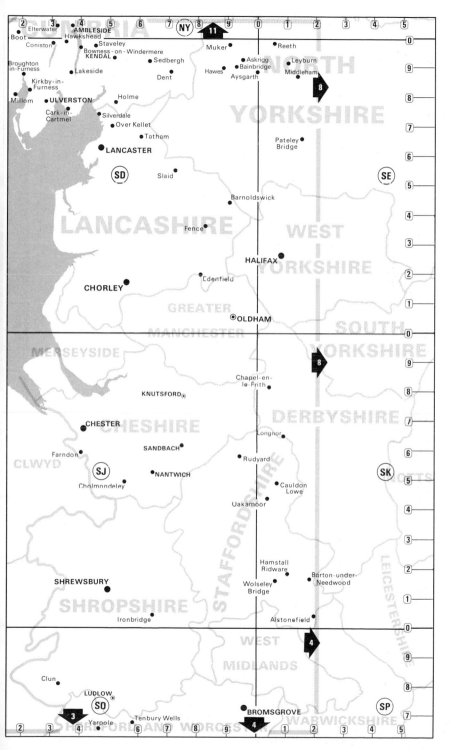

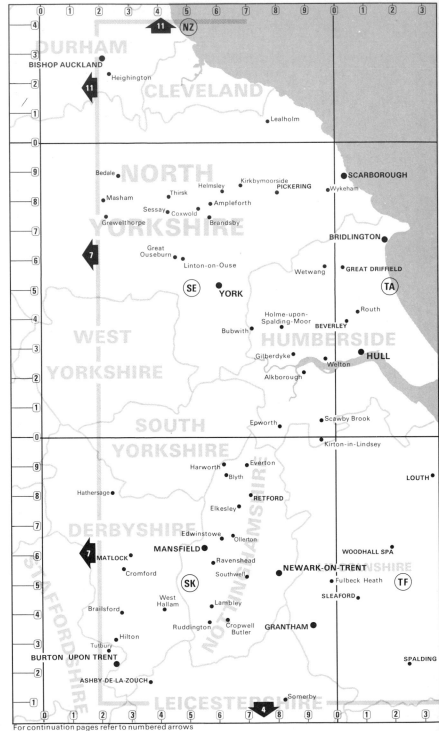

8

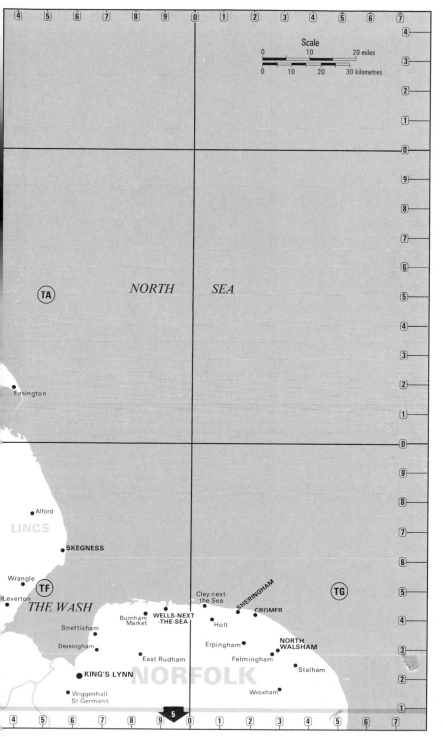

Scale

NORTH   SEA

TA

Easington

LINCS

Alford

SKEGNESS

Wrangle

TF

Leverton

THE WASH

Snettisham

Dersingham

KING'S LYNN

Wiggenhall
St Germans

Burnham
Market

WELLS-NEXT
-THE-SEA

East Rudham

NORFOLK

Cley next
the Sea

Holt

Erpingham

Felmingham

Wroxham

SHERINGHAM

CROMER

NORTH
WALSHAM

Stalham

TG

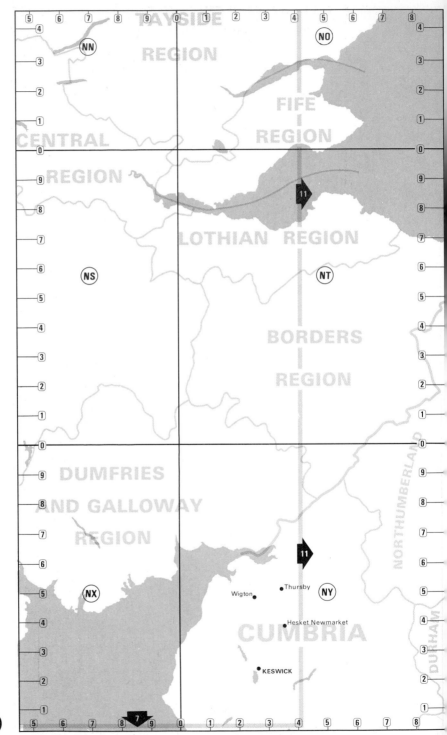

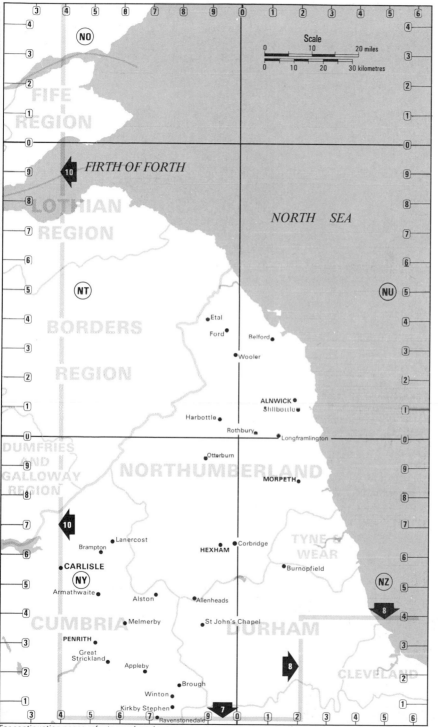

Scale

| 0 | 10 | 20 miles |
| 0 | 10 | 20 | 30 kilometres |

NO

FIRTH OF FORTH

NORTH SEA

FIFE REGION

LOTHIAN REGION

NT

BORDERS REGION

NU

DUMFRIES AND GALLOWAY REGION

Etal
Ford
Belford
Wooler
ALNWICK
Shilbottle
Harbottle
Rothbury
Longframlington

NORTHUMBERLAND

Otterburn
MORPETH

Lanercost
Brampton
CARLISLE
NY
Armathwaite
Alston
Melmerby
PENRITH
Great Strickland
Appleby
Brough
Winton
Kirkby Stephen
Ravenstonedale

Corbridge
HEXHAM
Burnopfield
Allenheads
St John's Chapel

TYNE & WEAR

NZ

DURHAM

CLEVELAND

CUMBRIA

11

BLUECOAT DISPLAY CENTRE
Bluecoat Chambers, School La, Liverpool,
Merseyside
℘ 051-709 4014

London
AMALGAM
3 Barnes High St, SW13
℘ 01-878 1279

ANATOL ORIENT
28 Shelton St, WC2
℘ 01-836 1977

ARGENTA
82 Fulham Rd, SW3
℘ 01-584 3119

ASPECTS
3–5 Whitfield St, W1
℘ 01-580 7563

BRITISH CRAFTS CENTRE
43 Earlham St, WC2
℘ 01-836 6993

CASSON GALLERY
73 Marylebone High St, W1
℘ 01-487 5080

COLERIDGE
192 Piccadilly, W1
℘ 01-437 0106

CECILIA COLMAN GALLERY
67 St John's Wood High St, NW8
℘ 01-722 0686

CONTEMPORARY TEXTILE GALLERY
10 Golden Sq, W1
℘ 01-439 9070

CRAFTS COUNCIL SHOP
Victoria & Albert Museum, SW7
℘ 01-589 5070

CRAFTSMEN POTTERS SHOP
William Blake Hse, 7 Marshall St, W1
℘ 01-437 7605

LESLEY CRAZE SILVERSMITH
5 Essex Rd, N1
℘ 01-226 3200

ELECTRUM
21 South Molton St, W1
℘ 01-629 6325

THE GLASSHOUSE
65 Long Acre, WC2
℘ 01-836 9785

JK HILL
151 Fulham Rd, SW3
℘ 01-584 7529

LEIGH GALLERY
17 Leigh St, WC1
℘ 01-242 5177

DAVID MELLOR
26 James St, WC2
℘ 01-379 6947 &
4 Sloane Sq, SW1
℘ 01-730 4259

CRAFT CENTRE
Royal Exchange, St Ann's Sq, Manchester
℘ 061-833 9333

GOLDSMITH'S GALLERY
27 Market Pl, Olney, Bucks
℘ (0234) 713046

OXFORD GALLERY
23 High St, Oxford, Oxon
℘ (0865) 242731

ARTIZANA
The Village, Prestbury, Cheshire
℘ (0625) 827582

NEW CRAFTSMAN
24 Fore St, St Ives, Cornwall
℘ (0736) 795652

COURCOUX & COURCOUX
90–92 Crane St, Salisbury, Wilts
℘ (0722) 333471

TIDES
6 Claremont Rd, Seaford, E Sussex
℘ (0323) 896623

STAFFORD ART GALLERY
The Green, Stafford, Staffs
℘ (0785) 57303

PETER DINGLEY
8 Chapel St, Stratford-upon-Avon, Warwicks
℘ (0789) 205001

LONG STREET GALLERY
Tetbury, Gloucs
℘ (0666) 53722

HOLLY HOUSE GALLERY
14 Front St, Tynemouth, Tyne & Wear
℘ (0632) 592753

MARIE JORDAN GALLERY
659 Barnsley Rd, Wakefield, W Yorks
℘ (0924) 255419

TERRACE GALLERY
7 Liverpool Ter, Worthing, W Sussex
℘ (0903) 212926